First published 2021 by Playdead Press

© Kerry Ellis 2021

Kerry Ellis has asserted her rights under the Copyright, Design and Patents Act, 1988, to be identified as the author of this work.

A CIP catalogue record for this book is available from the British Library.

ISBN 978-1-910067-90-1

Playdead Press
www.playdeadpress.com

I would like to thank…

All my friends and family that have loved, supported and given me the courage to be me.

To all my fans who constantly bring me joy, I'm grateful to each and everyone of you that allow me to keep doing the shows and albums that I love.

It is not easy to share your life and story with the world but I wanted to write them all down while I can still remember the details.

FOREWORD

Kerry Ellis as I see her

I could probably write the definitive book on Kerry Ellis. But happily she has done it herself – it's right here – and I have only to add a few words.

I first glimpsed her on stage in a production of My Fair Lady. In the starring role? No – just in the chorus, dancing and singing amongst a small mob. But, even given such a small scope, she managed to stand out and somehow command attention. Sometime later she was to create the role of the rebel *Meat* in the maiden production of our Queen Rock Theatrical – *We Will Rock You*. When we filmed the final rehearsal, I remarked that, frozen in every possible still frame, Kerry looked like a sculpture – she has a natural physical flow which applies as much to her elegant Instagram workouts as her work on stage.

But above all else, of course, it's that Ellis voice which sets Kerry head and shoulders above all others. Then as now, she was evidently blessed with a beautiful instrument, equally at home crooning soft and low as tearing it up on a climaxing 'money note'. And I couldn't hear the join!

When we encounter musical theatre performers in auditions, they have been generally encouraged to sing "in their head voice" for the high notes – which we would call 'falsetto', and there is often a sharp and uncomfortable dividing line between lows and highs – the 'break point'. Kerry is one of the very few singers from this world who can kill throughout her range - it's a smooth and flexible vehicle for a huge range of emotions.

And the final element of the Ellis magic? She is utterly and completely dedicated to using that beautiful instrument every day of her life. Dedicated to learning, improving and just 'doing it' constantly, because she loves it. The combination of this tenacity and the abilities she was born with is devastating.

Many years ago I watched a young Freddie listen to his voice being played back in the studio, and saw his dissatisfaction, which drove him to create himself in the mould he visualised. In a similar way, I watched Kerry's first steps in the studio, and saw her joyfully seize every opportunity to raise her game, find new places to go, and build each new experience into her armoury of skills.

In a live situation, too, I've seen Kerry make her first shy attempts at linking songs as a self-professed 'girl of a few words' – and then as time passed, developing into the relaxed and confident entertainer she is now. She has an irresistible way of being able to move effortlessly from the immersive drama of a song to a moment of shared humour in an 'audience moment' – and then back again. It's a wonderful talent; for such a performer there are no 'mistakes' – only more opportunities to be 'live' – in the moment, and just have more fun.

I've been lucky enough to have some great moments in my musical life – not least of which was standing on that roof of Buckingham Palace, live and living on the edge, but one of my proudest moments ever was playing the Festival of Remembrance at the Royal Albert Hall, with Kerry, performing the spine-chilling 'Anthem' from *Chess*... I'd arranged it especially for Kerry to triumph in – backed up by my own guitar. And triumph she did. And we did! So many other proud moments come to mind, from Verona to touring in Eastern Europe, to Paris, to the Montreux Festival, to our own Royal Albert Hall show ... and though Kerry has since then veered much more back to her musical theatre roots, she still has that power in her - the ability to be that vision of a shining figurehead on a sailing ship, a Rock Star carved out of pure gold.

First Half? Yes, Kerry has achieved more in half a life than most people manage in a whole life. She sings, she speaks, she entertains, she is a role model to thousands of aspiring girl performers, and she always has time to talk to them. She runs a young household and is an incredible Mum to two small boys. And every day of her life she generates warmth and smiles to all around.

And she still has so far to go. I hope I'm around to witness it. See you in Carnegie Hall, Kerry!

Brian May

BUMPKIN TO BROADWAY

PROLOGUE

As I stood waiting to go on stage, I felt a crazy sense of calm come over me which was kind of weird considering I was about to do the biggest gig of my career to date. The show was being televised live across the whole of Italy and I knew there were so many things to potentially go wrong, but for me that was the beauty of it. The thought of what would I do if something went wrong and how would I respond and react, is what I absolutely thrive on. It's strange really, as all through my life it's felt like stuff has happened to me at the time it should, and this was no exception so yes, I was excited and nervous but calm at the same time. I had never been more ready for anything in my life. I was also about four months pregnant with my second son!

By now I'd been working and touring with Brian May for years, but this concert was on another level. Brian was equally excited but had already made his way to a different entrance as he was on stage before me, and as he and the orchestra played the intro of 'Who Wants To Live Forever', I stepped out through a brightly lit stone archway and the sight that met me literally took my breath away. It was one of those moments I will never forget. Thank god it was a long intro because it took me all that time to walk down to my spot and gather my composure. I remember that walk so vividly, just looking around taking everything in, seeing all these singers and musicians whilst thinking....

"I will remember this moment for the rest of my life".

It was magical, and of course I was performing with Brian which topped it all off. I think being there with him also gave me added confidence. I slowly made my way down to the front to sing before the 12,000-strong audience plus the rest of Italy. I was so ready and this was everything I wanted it to be.

> *There's no time for us*
> *There's no place for us*
> *What is this thing that builds our dreams*
> *Yet slips away from us...*

As I sat alone in that same arena five years later, now empty and silent, apart from a few tourists, the memories came flooding back. I could almost hear the echoes of my own voice from that night back in June 2015 and see myself once more on that stage performing in what is undoubtedly up there as one of the incredible highlights of my career. I got goosebumps just remembering it, and as I looked around still trying to take in the enormity of the occasion I thought, not for the first time, "Why me?"

It was the end of February 2020 and I had been booked by the Italian concert promoter Francesco Sanavio to do a corporate gig in Verona, which in itself was a huge and quite prestigious occasion and one of many I'd done for him over the years since he'd booked us for that night in 2015. As it was just the one concert and such a short trip I had decided to go alone without the family. Although I've been to Italy many times over the years I'd never had the chance to revisit the arena and as I had a few hours to spare this was the ideal opportunity.

The Verona Arena is an ancient Roman amphitheatre, which I believe was also originally used for gladiator games and could hold more than 30,000 people in ancient times. Now each summer they hold a massive Festival of Opera there, celebrating all the great and important operas. Italians have always been massive Queen fans and by this time Brian and I had also built up a little bit of a relationship with Italy during a recent tour and as a result Francesco had invited us to perform at a special evening to be held just ahead of the 2015 festival.

Throughout my entire career I've always made sure that I've done all the ground work leading up to my next challenge whether big or small, so that when it arrives I feel totally ready for it, and it was the same on this occasion. The scale of the evening was mind-blowing. It was easily a hundred-piece orchestra including three harps, and what seemed like a thousand-strong choir on either side of us, with another gospel choir in front of them. We also had a band and Brian and I were in the middle of all this crazy madness. There were so many incredible singers and musicians with us on stage during our thirty-minute set, including the Italian operatic tenor Vittorio Grigolo.

In Brian's words "it was a stupendously beautiful arena with stupendously beautiful singers, a stupendously brilliant orchestra and a stupendously beautiful audience". The spectacle, the scale, the number of people out there and the flying cameras all around me was breathtaking and I genuinely thought that if I never did anything again I would be ok with that. This for me is what it was all about. Even now looking back at the video of it I can't quite take it in.

> *A hand above the water*
> *An angel reaching for the sky*
> *Is it raining in heaven*
> *Do you want us to cry...*

Singing 'No One But You' with Brian that night was so memorable and poignant for both of us and the whole occasion was a real turning point in our journey. It felt like all the hard work and grafting around, doing our tours in small venues and building up what we were doing, had finally paid off and we had arrived. Whenever I watch it back I still critique it and certain things or notes annoy me but at the same time I can step back and be objective, realise that it was a real moment, and appreciate the 'liveness' of it. Having all those people, choirs, orchestra and band all performing live just doesn't happen that much these days as so much stuff is recorded, and I am forever grateful that I was given the opportunity to be part of that concert.

Backstage, if you can call it that, is just literally one big round corridor circling the arena with a number of stone archways and stone steps and just a few tiny little 'rooms' off it. During my return visit I managed to sneak another look and it was just how I remembered it. Although I don't recall much about the actual show itself, I think there were about 500 Italian and international artists taking part and seem to remember there were various huge pieces of what looked like Egyptian sets randomly lying around behind the scenes with bizarre people frantically running past in elaborate costumes from all different operas. I'd never seen anything like it before or since. As we were due to close the show Brian and I just sat there very calmly in our dressing room amidst all this chaos, taking it all in and patiently waiting for our time to go on.

11

My husband James had come out with my eldest son Alfie to see me in the show. My Dad was also there. I hadn't known he was coming, he just randomly booked a ticket and surprised me on the day and then sent me a photo from one of the restaurants outside the building of him having a lasagne and a strawberry milk shake, which was so lovely and made it even more special. James and Alfie were able to watch the sound check but sadly they couldn't watch the show. Kids weren't allowed which I think was something to do with the seating.

Looking round again brought back so many things I'd forgotten and I started thinking how lucky I've been to do all the things that I have. As a result, some of my career, especially latterly, just blurs and merges into one which got me thinking, what if I didn't remember much of it in another twenty or thirty years? I vowed then to one day write part one of my autobiography when I had the time. Little did I know that we were just about to go into lockdown due to a global pandemic and I would have plenty of time, and that the corporate gig I had just done would be my last one for several months.

CHAPTER 1

I was always the favourite child. A blonde-haired blue eyed little girl who could do no wrong in her supportive parents' eyes, and who they gladly ferried around to a different hobby every evening. Well, that's what my brother always jokingly says. We still giggle about it to this day but it's all light-hearted fun. The truth is Andrew and I are just very different. Apart from a bit of football after school and swimming lessons which he did with me, his main hobby was fishing from a very early age and as he got older he would happily disappear to the nearby river for hours on end, whilst I was being taken here and there by my parents. Of course they would have done the same for him if he'd needed it.

In the theatre industry the press and media are always looking for that broken childhood or dark family secret but I can honestly say I had a really secure and happy, almost idyllic, childhood. Don't get me wrong, we didn't have loads of things and Mum and Dad were proper working parents but we had a really stable life. Andrew and I were, and still are, very close.

My parents Terry Ellis and Sandra Wynne had both grown up in London and went to school together. Funnily enough they met in Sydenham near where, years later, I bought my first flat, in Brockley, in the borough of Lewisham. They got married in church in 1974, as most people did then. Neither of them were religious, in fact my Dad was, and still is, an atheist and although Mum has found religion a bit more just recently, but I wouldn't say she is devout and only goes to church occasionally. She certainly had no interest back then. It wasn't a particularly big wedding as they didn't have lots of money. They were quite young, both in their early twenties which again was common at that time, and to many it seemed they were childhood sweethearts.

Once married my parents were keen to buy a house but it was way too expensive in London. Dad worked for a telephone company at the time and managed to get a transfer to the area and it wasn't long before they had happily settled into their new home in the sleepy country village of Haughley in Suffolk. Not long after the move they had my brother Andrew and three years later I was born in May 1979. If it had been left to my Dad, I would have been Chloe Jane Ellis but they compromised and settled on Kerry.

My childhood home was a detached chalet bungalow in a row of about ten houses. There was nothing particularly special about it apart from the fact that we were surrounded by a massive amount of amazing open space. There were probably only about twenty houses in the entire village and our nearest town was Stowmarket, which was approximately three miles away.

Andrew and I had a bedroom each and mine was at the back of the house. Our garden backed onto a huge expanse of fields and I remember once listening to my Dad striking a deal with the farmer who owned the land, and buying a tiny corner plot of his field, so we ended up with this long thin strip of garden which seemed huge to me at the time but was probably just over a hundred metres.

Being a country girl, insects and creepy crawlies didn't bother me at all. We had bats in our loft, hedgehogs outside the door and foxes, pheasants, mice and rabbits regularly on the lawn. We saw everything and it became the norm. My dad would always call us over to have a look at whatever creature was paying us a visit and we would just pick them up without a second thought. For me though the pipistrelle bats were my favourites. They were only tiny little things and occasionally when they were there, one would drop through into my brother's room and we would get so excited. Of course they are protected so we couldn't do anything to harm them but we just loved them. Nowadays I'm always the one who gets the spiders out of the house as my husband James really can't stand them!

We were lucky in as much as Dad was really handy and was able to make the most of all the space in the house. He built a shower room and airing cupboard in the loft space and little playrooms come storage rooms for us at the side of our bedrooms in the eaves. I loved my bedroom and if I wasn't playing make believe games outside that's where I'd be found. It was where I dreamed my biggest dreams. Over the years I would climb up onto my bunk bed gazing out at the ever-changing landscape, watching the beautiful golden sunsets whilst imagining a life faraway in the future. A life on some of the biggest stages in the world. There wasn't a flicker of doubt in my mind it was where I was heading. I knew it would happen but at that point I just didn't know how.

CHAPTER 2

Whether it was moving to Suffolk or the fact he was now a family man with responsibilities I'm not sure, but soon after Dad began to re-evaluate his life and came to the conclusion that if he stayed in his current job he would have no real future prospects and more importantly no pension. He made the decision he would either become a fireman or a policeman and promptly sent the application off to both. He heard back from the police force first and was eventually offered the job, which he accepted when I was about two years old.

Subsequently Dad worked for the Suffolk Police in Ipswich until he took early retirement, when he was about fifty, and his patch covered all our local area including Stowmarket where I went to school. As the local bobby Dad got to know everyone in the surrounding villages as well as the local market traders and businesses in Stowmarket, and we probably got to know what was going on in the village more than we should, although to be honest it wasn't that much and it was quite boring in that respect. We didn't have any scandal, affairs or village gossip going on, as Haughley was too small for that. In fact, there was nothing at all where we lived apart from houses. The neighbouring village, Onehouse, wasn't much bigger but at least had a little village hall where I attended playschool and dance classes. I think it might even have had a sweet shop and newsagent but that was it.

Having a Dad who was the local bobby was fine initially and didn't really impact on me. Later on, when I was a teenager, things became more interesting though when on a couple of occasions my friends and I were trying to get into the pubs in Stowmarket. He didn't really get involved as such, but we knew he was around keeping an eye on us. He was great though and very fair even when I was throwing up from drinking vodka and orange squash. Everybody knew him and he would look out for all of my friends.

There were some perks too and occasionally, as a treat, he would take Andrew and I to see the working police dogs, mostly German Shepherds and black Labradors, in their kennels outside the station, which as a massive dog lover I absolutely adored. Very occasionally one would be brought home to visit which was such a joy.

Dad has a tiny little scar on his forehead and when I was really small my imagination would run riot and make up all kinds of stories as to how he got it. I was very proud of him and I thought maybe he'd been attacked whilst bravely trying to arrest a burglar. As it turned out he'd been hit by a bubble car as a young boy. I was intrigued by this story and my brother and I would giggle hysterically wondering what on earth a bubble car was. When Dad described it to us I still found it really funny and obviously failed to see how potentially serious the whole incident might have been. It's strange what sticks in your memory!

Mum had a successful career in Social Services and did this for pretty much her whole working life, eventually working her way up to becoming the manager of a care home in Ipswich. She worked part time after having us, and my Dad worked shifts, so they juggled everything between them. Mum was a very strong and independent woman, and really confident throughout our childhood. I really looked up to her, she had a good job, two children and was running a marriage and home but I often wonder now if she was just project-managing her life. In her older years I think she's allowed herself to step back a bit and as a result she seems to have lost that confidence.

I attended playschool in Onehouse Village Hall. My Mum says I would scream and cry trying to stop her taking me in but I don't remember that at all, and wonder if that's the first example of me blocking out negative experiences. It's something I have tended to do throughout my life even if not always intentionally. If something doesn't serve me in a positive way or make me feel good I get rid of it from my mind and focus instead on the positive aspect. My glass is always half full and that attitude has helped me so much over the years. With that in mind I prefer to think I was a happy, all singing and dancing sociable little toddler, running into playschool!

I have really good memories of the hall itself which I can vividly picture to this day and can still visualise my own little peg where we would hang our coats and bags. We used to have orange juice and a biscuit every morning. One of my favourite games was the chocolate game. We would all sit around in a circle and in the centre of the circle were a pair of mittens, a hat, scarf, knife, fork and a ball. We would take it in turns to sit in the middle and the aim was to pass the ball round a bit like like pass the parcel, while whoever was in the middle had to put on the gloves and hat and scarf then break off a piece of dairy milk chocolate with the knife and fork before the ball had completed its full circle. Trying to get some chocolate wasn't as easy as it sounds but it was a good incentive! I don't suppose kids can play that now as they wouldn't be allowed the chocolate let alone the knife and fork, but it was great fun.

CHAPTER 3

My parents encouraged me to try lots of different hobbies, which being a parent myself now I can totally understand and I've done exactly the same with my kids. I think when your children are little it's all about finding an activity for them that they enjoy and gives them a different social network, allowing them interaction with other kids whilst developing new skills. At one point I tried sending my eldest son Alfie to a weekly musical theatre and dance class but he just did not gel with it. He is constantly active and sporty and loves football and cricket and swimming. He uses the house as his own jungle gym and when we do go out to a park he is on the monkey bars all the time. On the other hand, Fred, my youngest, is a little bit more on the back foot and has actually shown a bit of interest in musical theatre. He goes to the same weekly dance and drama club we tried Alfie with, and seems to have really taken to it. He was immediately focused and I really think he'll run with it now, which is more or less what happened with me although I tried many other hobbies before I got to that point! Basically, if there was anything physical or active on offer, I tried it. I wasn't frightened of any physical challenge.

I started trampolining at around three years old, roughly the same time I started dancing. These were regular classes held at the local sports centre in one of the large, echoey halls. I was one of many kids and there were quite a few coaches so I didn't necessarily have the same one each time. I was also able to practice at home as I had a small, blue square trampoline in the house, which I absolutely loved. I can see myself now as a little tot in my red pyjamas happily bouncing away on it for hours. I think I must have had a bit of natural flair for it as it came quite quickly and easily to me. So much so, that later that year, I got on the trampoline at the summer village fete and was showing off all the little tricks I had learned and caused a bit of a stir. News got round to the local newspaper reporter in attendance and he seemed very impressed with my skills and I subsequently found my photo doing a split jump in next day's paper. Maybe it was because I was so little but hey I got my first publicity shot!

Trampolines back then were very different from how they are now and the bounce mat was made out of a kind of thick net. Whatever it was I remember it being quite hard on my feet. I used to have to get a bunk up onto the trampoline as I was so little and couldn't get up there on my own. The teacher would then tie a jumper round my waist to teach me how to do somersaults. I can remember the smell of those big blue crash mats to this day! They were so hard. It was a lot more dangerous back then but I survived any injuries!

Whenever we went away to the holiday parks I would always beg to go on the horses. I went on to have weekly lessons after school when I was about ten, from a girl called Paula who was the daughter of one of my Dad's colleagues. She had a beautiful black pony and lived near Bacton going towards my Nan's so it was a perfect arrangement and meant we could combine it with a visit to my grandparents. It was tough but I loved it and ended up riding for a few years until I was thirteen or fourteen. Again, luckily, I never sustained any serious injuries, although the horse did run with me a few times and threw me off on a couple of occasions but I was pretty resilient as always!

I also belonged to the swimming club at the same sports centre where I was trampolining in Stowmarket. My brother and I both had lessons and my Dad helped out with coaching a bit. I think he got roped into it as a parent helper which he was happy to do. It's what parents do I have since discovered. Alfie now goes to football each Sunday and James wants to eventually try and get involved helping in some way. We entered all the swimming competitions although my brother was really good and a much better swimmer than I was but I enjoyed taking part.

He was also far cleverer than me, always has been and always will be. Things would come to him naturally so he didn't have to try as hard. I was definitely more of a trier and would work harder to achieve what I did. Growing up in the country it's hardly surprising that Andrew is now doing really well as a freshwater fish consultant. He doesn't like towns or cities or lots of people or crowds, and is a bit of a lone soldier, just happy to be out there doing his thing in the middle of the Cotswolds. As I said before, we couldn't be more different and now lead completely different lives.

As kids we had no friends nearby that we could just call on and knock about with in the village, and we relied on each other a lot so it was a good job we got on really well. We obviously had school friends but they weren't close by and if we wanted to get anywhere as we got older we had to rely on a lift from our parents, ride our bikes or get the bus. We didn't even have a shop nearby let alone a pub, although I seem to remember a tiny post office on the side of somebody's house.

We rarely watched television as we were too busy with our hobbies or playing. There were only three channels to watch back then but we enjoyed a bit of Thundercats and Power Rangers. I did enjoy films though and a big favourite was Labyrinth which I watched constantly on repeat. I also loved Never Ending Story and the Wizard of Oz, which was probably my favourite musical. It's kind of stayed with me as I went on to perform in it when I was ten as part of the kids' ensemble, at what was then the Wolsey Theatre, and then of course I came full circle by being in *Wicked* in later years. It's always been quite a special and significant musical for me.

As a family now we watch loads of films, in fact we have seen so many that we find it difficult to find one on Netflix that we haven't seen. I love all genres, you name it, thrillers, action, and of course musicals. The Shawshank Redemption is one of those films I never tire of and can watch any time, and Grease is another big favourite along with anything heavy and deep that I can sob to.

My absolute favourite musical at the time of writing has to be Dear Evan Hansen, which I saw on Broadway with Ben Platt a few years ago. I was there on my own and got a last minute ticket in one of the balconies and I just fell in love with it.

Notes from...

What can I say about my daughter? Proud doesn't come close. Considering all the amazing shows she has been involved with, and the number of famous people she has met and performed with, she has always remained totally grounded. I personally haven't found anyone who's ever met her or worked with her that hasn't liked her. I still get as much pleasure watching her perform all over the world as I did when she was a child performing at local festivals and shows. She's a good wife to my great son in law James, an amazing mother to Alfie and Freddie, and the best and loveliest daughter a dad could wish for. I love her to bits

Terry Ellis

CHAPTER 4

Andrew and I would spend endless hours playing in the garden, either on our rickety old swing, or in our paddling pool. We were proper rough and tumble kids or country bumpkins as my husband now calls me, getting our hands and knees dirty and leaves and twigs in our hair, making mud pies, climbing the trees at the end of the garden and building our own little tree house where we could hide away from the world. We had a little fence which split our garden where we would play tennis using the fence as a net. We'd spend hours just making up our own games. It seemed like I was forever outside in our own make believe world.

I guess being so active as a child kept me healthy, and our outdoor games in all the mud and dirt allowed me to build up an immunity, and I consider myself to have been kind of lucky throughout my life health-wise. Of course I had all the usual childhood illnesses, and I'm sure I remember being sent to a chicken pox party once. The worst illness I remember though was whooping cough where I was off school for about two weeks and they had to send work home for me. I was really poorly.

The flip side of being so active meant I had my fair share of accidents but luckily nothing serious or life threatening. Ironically most of our accidents seemed to happen indoors. We had a wooden staircase and I lost count of the number of times I fell down them, probably in my rush to get outside. I think my shins were permanently bruised. One particularly rainy day we were playing inside letting off a bit of steam and I think Andrew must have been throwing stones or something at me, as brothers do. I ran to hide in our glass conservatory just as he was taking aim, however in the excitement his aim was way off and this stone hit the top of the roof with full force and with that the whole conservatory shattered all around us. It all seemed to happen in slow motion and I just froze as the noise of the breaking glass seemed to go on forever. It was so loud and I didn't know what was happening. I'll never forget my brother's face which was a mixture of shock and fear, and then the muffled sound of my Dad's shouting getting louder as he came to investigate. Thinking about it, he was probably terrified as it must have sounded like a bomb exploding and we must have looked a sorry sight. Incredibly we escaped without so much as a tiny cut but I think we were probably grounded for a year following that!

In quieter moments we'd play with our pets. We'd always wanted a dog but my parents refused at first so we made do with hamsters, gerbils and cats, my brother even had a stick insect at one point. We had the lot, but all we wanted was a dog, nothing else would do. Eventually my parents gave in to our constant pleading and one day my dad came home with this little fluffy bundle and I completely fell in love. My dad had got him from one of the farmers down the road and he became our much loved family pet until his death when I was seventeen. He was officially named JR because my mum was a huge Dallas fan, even though most people assumed it was because he was a Jack Russell. Somehow he got nicknamed JJ and then just shortened to J. We were inseparable, I would dress him up and put him in my dolls pram and he stood for it all. He was so docile and soppy. As we got older he would join in all our games or patiently curl up for hours, with one eye on me, listening to me singing, although to be fair he was a proper family dog and had no favourites, sharing his time equally between us all. As anyone with a dog will know he became another family member and was my best friend and playmate rolled into one. He came on endless long walks with us and had a wonderful and happy life.

Being the older one Andrew would usually drag me into all his favourite games which didn't bother me at all, I loved them and I was happy to go along with it. He had quite a good collection of Star Wars figures and we'd play with them along with his Scalextric and cars. I wasn't a one for dolls so my own toys consisted of a collection of teddies and a few My Little Ponies. We also had a joint Sega Mega Drive, but other than that we were just too busy being outdoors and constantly on the go, which was our favourite thing to do.

I didn't have a bike of my own until I was about sixteen and got a brand new mountain bike. Prior to that I always had Andrew's hand me downs which again didn't bother me. We had a green striker and a red BMX which was a favourite. Society is so different now and things are readily available to youngsters, whereas we had to save up for everything, which gave it more value.

We would get lots of presents at Christmas. Of course I believed in Father Christmas but having an older sibling the truth was always coming my way and I probably found out earlier than I should have done, although

I don't remember an exact moment and it was probably drip fed for a few years. I certainly don't remember being traumatised and the main thing was it didn't stop us getting our stockings. Our traditions were much the same as everyone else's. I loved opening my advent calendar in the lead up to the big day, then getting up super-early and finding stockings and pillow cases stuffed full of presents at the end of the bed, looking for tree presents later in the day, then having a couple of extra surprise presents in the afternoon which was probably planned just to space things out a bit and give my parents a break. These are all things I try and do with my kids now.

There was just one toy shop in Stowmarket called Simpsons which was run by the same family for six generations. Whenever we had birthday or Christmas money that is where we would go to spend it and it was a really special occasion. I was so sad when it closed down quite a few years ago after one hundred years of trading. Nowadays, everything is so accessible to kids which actually annoys me. They have the likes of Amazon and even all the supermarkets sell toys. I try and restrict what I give Alfie and Fred, as I want them to appreciate the value of what they have, whereas James tends to give in a bit more, which I think is for his benefit as much as theirs! I guess we strike a good balance!

Our parents just didn't have those kind of worries with us and our childhood was so simple in comparison. We were trusted to cycle off on our own to explore the woods at the top of the road. There was a little circuit we would do and my parents allowed us to go as they knew it took about twenty minutes round trip. We were given quite a free rein probably because there was literally nothing there, we could virtually go anywhere because there was a three-mile radius before you hit a town. It was just fields and was completely safe. As I got older I would walk our elderly neighbours' dogs for them on my own. I remember once needing sponsorship for something I was doing and Mum and Dad had no qualms at all about me going round the neighbourhood alone knocking on people's doors at a very young age, much younger than I would ever let my kids. Everyone knew each other in the village, and we all looked out for one another. The only rule Mum and Dad insisted on was when we did go out to play and explore we had to tell them what time we would be back.

Whenever I think back on my childhood I remember those long, hot carefree summer days with clear blue skies and the smell of freshly cut grass. It's funny though, in all my time spent outside and playing in those fields I never once suffered with hay fever but now I get it chronically. I know now how lucky I was to have such a simple childhood with memories to treasure always. Even then, something inside was telling me that there was a different life altogether waiting for me. As it turned out my upbringing grounded me and enabled me to cope with the not so secure career path I embarked on.

CHAPTER 5

I quite enjoyed all my hobbies but nothing compared to performing. Once I discovered that it became my life 24/7 and I loved it with a passion. If I could have given up everything else in return for singing, dancing and acting all day for the rest of my life then I would have done so with no question. I immediately had a very clear vision of what I wanted to do.

I started dance school in the local village hall when I was three or four and took part in all the local shows. Whatever school production was staged I was in it. I have no idea where my natural talent or ambition came from. Neither of my parents sang and I certainly wasn't one of those kids growing up surrounded by instruments or lots of drama and singing in the house.

James is uber confident socially, and I am uber confident creatively and professionally, so it was inevitable our boys would be confident. Additionally, they are surrounded by such stability in terms of family and have travelled the world touring with me, and stayed in numerous hotels. They have got used to being around lots of people which in turn has also given them social confidence.

Despite that my boys are very different in respect of their personality and interests, although essentially they have had the same upbringing. The only thing different is one of them is the older sibling and one of them is the younger, which I do think makes a slight difference but not to that extent. They've had the same experiences in terms of people, surroundings and everything else.

As a child I would never just turn the radio on and listen to pop music of the day, although I did like a bit of Whitney and Cher occasionally. My Dad enjoyed listening to music though and a lot of my early influences came from him. He would always play music such as Meatloaf, Status Quo, and the Beatles when we were in the car, so I think that's massively where my love of rock started. Ironically, years later Meatloaf was playing at the O2. Brian knows him and knowing that I had grown up listening to Meat's music, suggested we go along to watch the concert and meet up with him after. I guess things really came full circle for me that night and getting to meet him was joyous. He was amazing to watch and I really had to pinch myself. I mean it's not every day you get to meet one of your childhood idols. Bless him though, years of performing had taken a bit of a toll on his voice and I know he'd been quite poorly, but he still had that power and presence. Meat's drummer John Miceli, who is now a good friend and played on lots of our music, was also playing that night, and seeing him in action was so powerful. He had an amazing energy and it was such a special and memorable occasion.

I remember wearing out a cassette of Magic of the Musicals with Mark Rattray and Marti Webb which had all the well-known musical hits on of that time, and the next minute I'd be rocking along to Meatloaf, Bonnie Tyler, or Queen. I constantly had these two different styles which I loved meshing together. Nothing else mattered or entered my mind at the time as I just wanted to be a performer. I didn't really think beyond that or quite know how it would develop but I would visualise myself on that stage knowing it would happen.

One of my earliest appearances on stage was at the Regal Theatre, Stowmarket when I must have been about four years old, in the local am-dram pantomime production of *Aladdin*. I was one of the babes alongside Dad who starred as Widow Twankey, which was the nearest he ever got to performing. It was such good fun and great for everyone in the community to see their local village bobby up on stage making them laugh.

Mrs Thomas was my very first dance teacher and I went to her for a couple of years until I was five years old. We would go to Onehouse Village Hall for ballet, tap and modern lessons but also to another hall in Stowmarket which I remember vividly. My Mum tells me that the children would all disappear into this hall and we'd be gone for an hour or so. She remembers peering through this tiny window along with the other mums desperate to see what we were doing. I totally get that because I do the same where Fred goes now although the windows are bigger and I get a better view! I remember the excitement of putting on my little ballet shoes and then dancing on the dusty floors to the music from the old cassette player. I idolised Mrs Thomas, she was lovely, with big curly early eighties hair and would often wear an amazing cat suit or leg warmers and short ballet skirt. She really was your typical eighties dance teacher but brilliant and I loved her. There were only about five of us in the class and I was hooked from the moment I started. Out of all my hobbies this was the one I had that strong sense of commitment and passion for and I couldn't get enough of it.

I would practice my tap dancing on the laminate floor in the kitchen at home and remember taking big chunks out of it in my enthusiasm. My Dad would go berserk, but it was the best place as we didn't have tiles or hard flooring anywhere else, and this was way too tempting. Adam Garcia was one of my guests in Season One of my podcast and he mentioned a tap mat he practises on. I don't think there was any such thing when I was a kid but that would have been the perfect solution!

At this time I became friends with Bobbie Wignall, now my oldest long term friend, and her sister Michelle. Bobbie and I were the same age so inevitably we were closer as kids whereas Michelle was two years older and in the dance class above us. The Wignalls lived in the next village and Bobbie would often come and stay over and vice versa. We were inseparable and even ended up going to Laine Theatre Arts together. She teaches dance now at a school in Suffolk and has two girls and we remain incredibly close.

Once Mrs Thomas retired, the three of us moved on to Sandra Bromley's dance school in Bury St Edmunds and continued the ballet, tap and modern with her for a further couple of years following the ISTD (Imperial Society of Teachers of Dancing) syllabus. She's retired these days but we are regularly in touch so if I do a show close by, she always comes to support me, which is really lovely.

I left Sandra's class to move on to Ann Holland's Dance School which was altogether a bigger concern and by that time I was beginning to take dance a bit more seriously. Ann had classes all over the area including Onehouse Village Hall which is where I returned to and continued with all three dance disciplines. I think I reached intermediate in ballet and advanced level in tap and modern. It was only when I got to college that it all hit home where I stood in terms of standard. The people I left college with were unbelievable dancers, some ending up in the Royal Ballet, some in contemporary companies. I'm not approached for dancing roles now, however I love it when I do get the opportunity to do more dancing which is why I loved doing *Cats* so much in later years. I only really dance now if a show brings it to me. I certainly don't consider myself good enough to be cast as a principal dancer, nor would I want to.

During our time with Mrs Thomas our chances to perform for the public extended to the local rec or in the field at the local village fete opposite the hall where the classes were held. Nothing glamorous. We would just do one routine, end up with muddy feet and that was it. No-one would really watch apart from the doting parents but we enjoyed it and it was something a bit different and exciting. However, things became a bit more serious at Sandra Bromley's and we were given the chance to enter various dance festivals. The school would seek out these competitions to put on a showcase of their students performing and the standard they had achieved that year. We would dance whatever our dance teacher decided we would do, and it was their interpretation of the piece and whatever they came up with.

We lived for those festivals, which were held in such places as Sudbury, Braintree and Bury. They would usually go on for a week throughout the summer in venues that could accommodate the event. Sudbury festival was held in a school that had a studio theatre, which was perfect as they were always in school holidays. It was flat floor staging with a raised seating area. Every year we would travel there each day and stay for our numbers, sometimes for the entire day before going back home, only to return the following day. It was so exciting and I competed until I was fifteen. Sometimes if we were really tired or it had been a long day, we might get a McDonalds on the way home as a real treat.

I won my fair share of trophies and medals both as part of a group and for my solo performances, especially at Sudbury festival where I won the Song and Dance Cup a lot. So much so that some years after I'd left I donated a special cup. It was my Dad's suggestion, as he thought it would be a nice thing to do. All these years later I can now go back and present the newly engraved Kerry Ellis Song and Dance Cup to the winners which is just so lovely. Now it's grown to become an even bigger event whereas at the time it was fairly small. Even though I entered relatively locally, festivals such as these were held all around the country. All-England was like a massive hub which where all the regional winners would come together for one big national competition. The adjudicators at each of the regional festivals would submit a certain amount of winners depending

30

on marks, to then be entered into the All-England finals. I got to that level one particular year when I was fourteen with my song and dance performance and it felt professional and exciting and really organised. It was held in a proper theatre and felt like the next step up for me. However, although I got a placement I sadly didn't win.

Notes from...

Kerry joined my Stage School at the age of eight. I remember a fresh-faced happy little girl with a cheeky grin, and a wicked laugh that still exists today. She enjoyed her lessons, loved a challenge and always tried hard to please. It wasn't always easy for Kerry but with her willingness to work, and the ever-important parental support, she would practice endlessly to achieve her goals. She was a popular member of the school and a source of encouragement to all. She was a willing pupil and we had fun but we worked hard too. A pleasure to teach! Kerry loved performing and still has that passion to this day, which shows in all her work, and gives me pride every time I watch her perform. I consider our continued friendship a privilege.

Sandra Bromley (Miss Sandra)

CHAPTER 6

My Mum is an only child and as the only grandchildren we were super close to my Nan and Grandad, Doreen and Dennis Wynne. They originally lived in Bromley and whenever we visited the journey seemed to go on forever. I was always relieved when I saw the iconic fibreglass Catford Cat as I knew we were close. They moved to Bacton, Suffolk when I was about six, which was great because now they were only ten minutes away by car and we would regularly visit, sometimes stopping to feed the ducks on the way. Occasionally Andrew and I would bike it but that was quite a journey, even for us adventurers. Playing in their garden was like walking into a scene from Hogwarts, full of adventure and creatures to play with. My grandparents were keen gardeners and it was filled with a variety of plants, flowers, and shrubs. It was a really long garden with a curvy winding path all the way down to a greenhouse growing cucumbers, tomatoes and peppers and surrounded by huge bushes and trees towering over us. Andrew and I would run up and down the winding path making lots of mud pies and playing with insects as standard. It was probably just an ordinary garden but that's how I saw it from my child's perspective with a vivid imagination.

Once they'd moved Nan and Grandad were always on hand to help look after us and would come on holiday with us occasionally. Mum and Dad would also go away every year on their own for a couple of weeks and they would move in to look after us. Mum and Dad were really sociable and I remember them going to lots of parties so if my grandparents couldn't babysit we had a couple of regular babysitters they called upon who lived close by. Emma Taylor and Jackie were daughters of my Dad's colleagues in the police force and we loved them. Emma would sometimes stay over and just occasionally let us stay up a little bit to watch television. She was like a big sister to us and I really looked up to her.

It seemed like my grandparents were always around and spent so much quality time with us. Nan taught me how to knit and Grandad was really handy around the house. He would decorate brilliantly and I wish so much that I'd paid attention to what he was doing. Whenever we decorate now or have any DIY problems I often regret not watching and learning things from my Grandad. When we were older and both driving Andrew and I continued visiting them as often as we could to have a cup of tea and chat with them and remained incredibly close. They were a huge part of my life and we just adored them. When Nan died recently at the end of 2019, it broke my heart. It was tragic and I miss her so much.

We didn't see as much of Dad's parents, Mary and John, as they were so busy. As well as my Dad they'd also had twins Peter and Pam. Dad often says my youngest son Fred is so like his brother Peter, in that everybody runs round doing everything for him! Pam also had two children my cousins Kevin and Nicola, so my grandparents would divide what little time they had between us all. We'd often go and stay with my Auntie Pam and the kids in Romford. We are all still in touch even though we are busy with our different lives. As well as travelling a lot which they loved doing, Dad's parents also ran a busy pub, the William 1V on Shepherdess Walk, London N1 near Old Street Station. It was a proper old fashioned London pub, selling jellied eels and the lot. We didn't go there that much but I remember the trip to London being quite an adventure. Once there the grown-ups would enjoy a drink and chat while my brother and I would play in the flat upstairs with their dog, Princess, as we were too young to be allowed in the bar area itself. Even in the flat the air smelt musty of beer and stale smoke but it all seemed very grown up and sophisticated to us. Funnily enough they also moved to Bacton, Suffolk once they'd sold their pub, about a year after my other grandparents.

CHAPTER 7

Mum is very headstrong and tough and can be quite distant at times. She can also be extremely stubborn, which I get from her! She was constantly running around between us and her job, all of which kept her fit and trim. She was quite athletic looking actually and when I look at photos of her back then we are identical and have the same body shape whereas my brother and Dad are very alike in both character and looks.

Both of them were very hands on parents and would always help me with my homework although my Dad could only do so when he wasn't on shift which was a lot of the time. We didn't see him much and it was Mum who was ever present and there for me constantly, supporting me in whatever way I needed. I never wanted for anything and I will always be grateful for what she did. She was so good at needlework and would make all my costumes for the festivals and shows. Thankfully she still is and repairs my concert dresses even now. She was, and is, such a brilliant Mum and I adore her.

She would ferry me around everywhere but would often split the driving with Bobbie's mum Jane. They became close friends and are still best mates now. Jane is like a second mum to me, I could and can go to her with anything. We all grew up together and we are like one big extended family. We also went on quite a few holidays together, sometimes camping but mainly caravanning. We didn't go too far, a favourite holiday spot was Kessingland Beach and another was Great Yarmouth, or the Norfolk Broads. I remember they were tiny little caravans and I have no idea how we all fitted in them but we loved it.

In the early evening the gas fires would come out and we would all sit round for a barbecue. The parents would play loads of silly games with water pistols, behaving like carefree kids themselves. As well as the Wignalls, the Muskitt family would sometimes join us with their two boys, Emlyn and Nathan, and a friend of my Dad's in the police, Gary Pooley and his wife Shirley, who were lovely.

Sleeping in the caravans was so exciting. I always had the top bunk which was really fragile and just felt like a bit of net. My Dad would take me to the toilet in the middle of the night, about a ten-minute walk away and it felt like a scary adventure but at the same time I knew I was safe on my Dad's broad shoulders.

The entertainment was dated but we loved all of that stuff. Although all us kids spent a lot of time in the swimming pools it was the discos, talent shows and kids club and all the simplicity that came with it were what the holiday was all about as far as I was concerned.

Having said that I had a weird phobia of those talent shows on holiday and entered them very reluctantly. Dad would have to quite literally pay me to do them which surprisingly seemed to help me conquer my fear! We laugh about the fact he bribed me to sing now. My go to performance pieces were 'One Moment in Time', 'Tomorrow', 'Memory' and 'I Dreamed a Dream'. Big songs for a little girl but these were songs I had rehearsed many a time in my bedroom. I have no idea why I was so shy and nervous of the talent shows as I wasn't by nature a shy child and loved to perform but I think putting myself in that unfamiliar situation worried me even though I won loads of times. '

In the evenings we would always go and watch whatever show or cabaret was on although I was more interested in the dance floor and the dancing. They were simple holidays but they were the best holidays ever and I hold them as such special memories.

We did go on a couple of European holidays to Ibiza and Tenerife and Mum and Dad also took us on a magical trip to Disney World, Florida when I was ten. I seem to remember it was the last time we could benefit from a particular discount or I could get a child's price. I love Disney but wasn't exactly crazed by it and I certainly wasn't a Disney Princess type of girl. We were allowed one souvenir each in the gift shop and I chose this big purple dragon called Figment which I've since found out is meant to be the literal embodiment of the phrase "figment of the imagination" and a mascot of the Imagination pavilion so was quite fitting for me. Figment was special to me because of the trip but let's face it, I'd have got Mickey Mouse if I'd loved Disney that much!

We loved the rides though and were proper adrenalin junkies. We'd always loved theme parks and we'd often go to Pleasurewood Hills or Chessington World of Adventures. I'd also been to Blackpool Pleasure Beach but everything seemed so rickety there and I always wondered if it was safe. It didn't stop me though and the bigger and scarier the ride, the better, even from early on.

We had family in the Everglades so managed to combine the week in Disney staying in a hotel with driving to the Everglades and staying with Dad's Auntie Jean, my Nan's sister, who had a farm out there, for another week. My Nan and Grandad had been out to see them on a few occasions, but I'd never met them before and it was so strange as Auntie Jean was exactly the same as my Nan. I remember being fascinated by this and thinking she was absolutely beautiful with this long blonde hair which she tied up in a bun. They had these two houses set apart from each other and a huge crystal clear sparkling lake in the middle, which I was told had a crocodile, and was set amidst acres of land. She lived with her husband John in one house, and their daughter, Hazel and husband Lindsey with their daughter Charlene lived in the other house which looked like a tepee. Lindsey had Indian heritage and we just loved him. They had cows and dogs and we even saw a calf being born whilst we were there. I was in my element. After the frantic excitement of Disney we just absolutely loved it as we could play freely outside again. I only ever saw them a couple of times after that when they visited the UK.

My boys have been so lucky and had travelled all over the world on tour with me before they'd even started school, as well as coming with us on lovely holidays. However, we have to kind of check ourselves sometimes and we've both said we need to take them on those special memory holidays that we were given. I mean, when your four year old says to you "Mummy I want to go to Abu Dhabi again," I start thinking to myself no, this is not good! As a result we have now been camping three times in lockdown, and I've been so proud of the kids jumping in wholeheartedly and getting stuck into the experience, as they do everything. They have loved it.

CHAPTER 8

As we lived out of town we had school transport and every day we would get on the school bus which collected us just outside our house, to Abbot's Hall Primary in Stowmarket. Bobbie and I didn't go to school together until middle school, but I think if we had done we would have been joined at the hip. Being separated from her forced me to make new friends and one in particular, Katie Gooding. We quickly became good buddies and went through the rest of our school days together.

Mrs Tweddle was our Headmistress and was quite cuddly in the nicest possible way. She usually wore brown tweed dresses and brogues; combined with a name like that and curly hair like just like Supergran, she could easily have stepped straight out of a children's book. She would come into our classroom at random times and stand on the tables dropping sweets or pieces of paper and you would suddenly have a little competition on the go. She was quite forward thinking for her time, quite strict and I suppose a little eccentric, but brilliant. She would always think out of the box.

There was one class in each year group so it was quite a small school with one long corridor and all the classes leading off it, then the hall at the far end which also doubled as the dinner hall. We would line up with our different coloured little plastic trays for such delights as burger and chips on a Friday and my favourite chocolate crunch and pink custard. I've always had a sweet tooth!

As kids we were brought up to eat what we were given but I always quite enjoyed whatever was served at school anyway. Although my Mum would cook she wasn't the best, so school dinners seemed okay and I was alright with them. I hate cooking now, but my husband enjoys it and is good at it thank God! I am a foodie though and genuinely enjoy all kinds of food. We always love eating out and my absolute favourites are Thai, Japanese or Indian and basically anything with strong flavours. I am a vegetarian now and have been for about four years. Brian is vegetarian and together we have done a lot of work for the Born Free Foundation with Virginia McKenna, an international charity that campaigns to 'Keep Wildlife in the Wild' whilst protecting them in their natural habitat. I've always been surrounded by vegetarians and, I think if I was going to do it for ethical reasons, I would have done it a long time ago. So although I obviously supported the charity I was still eating meat. It was one Christmas when James and I ate so much food we had really overdone it and we were still feeling the effects on Boxing Day. I had to leave early for a concert in Liverpool that evening and James came with me. On the way and still suffering he announced that he was going to go vegetarian just for that day to give his stomach a rest. I joined him thinking why not, it's just for a day. From then on I carried on making choices regarding the food I was eating and I continued with not eating meat for a couple of weeks. After two weeks I started to feel such a change in my body and how I processed food and because I felt so much better I kept going, and after three months I didn't even think about meat at all and basically haven't eaten it since. It wasn't a conscious decision but because of the obvious health benefits I'm happy to keep going. James doesn't eat much red meat now either, although he will have a bit and he too feels much healthier.

CHAPTER 9

I moved up to Stowmarket Middle School when I was nine along with most of the friends I had made. It wasn't really far in terms of distance but was a world away in other respects. It was there I made a new friend, Alison Pettitt, and Katie, Ali and I became really close mates.

Ironically I was terrified of reading aloud at school which is ridiculous really considering the industry I eventually went into and what I was doing at the time, but I was petrified about getting something wrong in front of people. My brother was very academic and extremely clever whereas I had to really work at it. It didn't come easy for me although I was ok with English Language, probably because of my love of performance. I made up stories and used vocabulary quite well. Reading however was a big problem for me though, and kind of always was until I went to college really. I was quite frightened of it. I've often wondered if I was possibly slightly dyslexic but I don't think so, I just found it really difficult. I remember in class random people would be picked to read a certain section of text in whatever book we were studying at the time. It was horrifying. I would walk into my English class filled with dread thinking...

"Oh my God I can't do this."

It was a deep fear within me of getting something wrong or starting to stutter which in hindsight I think was probably something to do with the performance value of it. I didn't want to be rubbish or make a fool of myself. It got me in such a panic and it must have been obvious because I remember my Mum saying...

"Just go and speak to your teacher about it," which I eventually did. I have to say my English teacher was really understanding.

"Ok we can get round this" she said., *"If you come to me at the end of class the day before I will let you know exactly what you are going to read next time."*

And that is what we did, which meant I could go home and rehearse it almost like learning lines. It was fine from then on. Having that time to rehearse a little bit made a massive difference. I think most people find it difficult to be handed something and just go with it but I've got so much better with age. The more I do the easier it gets really. I do a lot of voice overs now and have to read there and then on the spot which has given me so much more confidence.

I wasn't a great reader as I found it hard, although I did enjoy The Lion the Witch and the Wardrobe. Thinking about it, all my favourite stories were fantasy based. I was slow at reading as it took me time to work stuff out and I would get frustrated quite quickly. Nowadays I quite enjoy it although I don't get the time. Just recently I did a programme for Radio 4 called *A Good Read* where I had to read three books and review them. One of the books was *100 Years of Solitude* and it was like going back to school for me and brought all those memories flooding back, but this time I actually, really enjoyed the struggle of it. Another one was *I Owe You One* by Sophie Kinsella which was much more of an easy read. Sometimes certain songs and music resonate with you because of the particular time in your life and the same can be said for books because of where you are when you read them and where you're at. Personally, I love *The Beach* which I read at a good time in my life when I was looking for escapism, and the story stayed with me. Sometime later I was lucky enough to go to Thailand and got to see Hat Maya, the main beach of Phi Phi Leh Island near Phuket where they actually filmed it. If I'm being honest though I just don't pick books up these days, yet I should because I love them and ironically here I am writing one which I really hope people will want to pick up!

We had a visiting professional theatre group on this one occasion and we all sat around them as they performed in the middle of us. Even being so young I thought it was great that were no wings and they weren't up at the front. Their performance was based around kids being evacuated in wartime and it really stuck with me, maybe because they were professional or perhaps because it was happening right there in front of me and seemed so real. I was mesmerised.

Mr Arbon the Headmaster, was very musical and would strongly encourage music or musical talent whenever he saw it. He understood what it took. His assemblies were always full of different styles of music and he always encouraged me. In fact about four years ago I was invited back to sing at Stowmarket Church at Christmas and took Alfie with me. Mr Arbon was there and played the piano for me as I sang a carol, which was so lovely for us both. Mrs Durrant was our Head of Year and sports teacher which I enjoyed. I am still in touch with her. She used to come to all my musicals and if I do anything in Suffolk she always comes along and says hello. I think all drama teachers have to be a little bit crazy and Mrs Shaw was no exception. As well as regular lessons I also attended a Saturday club that she ran and of course took part in the shows she produced, including *Bugsy Malone* and *The Matchgirls*.

It got to a point where I had to choose which hobby to concentrate on as there just weren't enough nights in the week. The dancing was quite prominent and took over fairly quickly but I wanted to do it all and by now I desperately wanted piano lessons.

"It's not that we're saying you can't Kerry, you just haven't got enough time. You can't do them all and you are going to have to choose which one is most important to you?" was my Mum's response. So dancing it was. I would still love to learn the piano to this day and I think it would be so beneficial for me for me to do it now.

Having made my choice, when I was ten, I auditioned for the *Wizard of Oz* to be staged at the Wolsey Theatre, my first 'proper' job as such. The Wolsey Theatre is a playhouse in Ipswich which was then operated by the Wolsey Theatre Company, a regional repertory company. It's now the New Wolsey Theatre I believe. They put tons of shows on and they were holding open auditions nearby for local children to play the munchkins and jitterbugs and make up three teams of ensemble kids. Mr Arbon who was so supportive of me allowed me to take time out of school for the audition which to me felt so professional and I was so excited to get through. Bobbie also got through the audition but was in a different team from me. It didn't matter though as we all got on so well with a shared sense of excitement and purpose and we had the time of our lives.

If we weren't on stage we were hanging out in the dressing room chattering excitedly as we changed into our amazing costumes. Our families came along to watch and support us. This was all so new to me but I knew I wanted more of it and for it to be my life. For the first time I experienced that strange sense of loss and purpose artists experience when a show or project you have given your whole being to comes to an end. I was devastated after the *Wizard of Oz* and sobbed my heart out.

Your fellow cast members become like family and then they're gone. I used to even experience it when my Nan would leave after staying with us for a while and get on the train back to London. It's what my podcast series is based on and I talk about it with Brian all the time. The bigger the experience the harder the loss and separation. If you are in a big company or you go on tour and have a special experience with that group of people it is like mourning the loss of them.

I've been back to the New Wolsey Theatre since with my own show and the backstage area seemed so small, god knows how we all fitted in. It was so strange to be there again and brought back so many memories. I was immediately transported back to that magical time when the ten-year-old me would study the principal cast at every opportunity, in complete awe, imagining that one day it would be me up there as Dorothy and JJ could be my Toto.

It was about this time that I was finding ballet really difficult. Mainly because of my body shape. I just wasn't built to be a ballerina, even though I tried very hard. I struggled with everything from the turnout to pointe work and I remember when I was about ten or eleven going to my Mum in tears, telling her I didn't want to go any more. Mum basically sat me down and calmly explained:

"Kerry, I think you have to keep going because ballet is a strong discipline, and, if you carry on, it will help you so much with everything else. Just do your best, give it a bit more time and if you still don't like it then we will reassess it," she promised. Of course, I did keep going with it, right up to college, where I attended lessons at eight o'clock every morning for three years.

They were such wise words, and I thank God to this day that Mum encouraged me because she was right, and, although I have never gone on to become a professional ballet dancer, if I hadn't kept to that strict discipline and pushed through that little boundary at ten years old, who knows, the rest of it might well have fallen apart.

Nothing worth doing is easy and I would say that anyone having a moment of self-doubt but particularly children, might just need a bit of encouragement and support to keep going, and to give it a try, and the outcome might just be worth the effort.

I was no trouble to my parents, my brother was more of a problem really as he was a bit of a tearaway. He will tell you that I was the good little girl and he was branded the naughty one. I think it's always the way, and I see it with my own kids, that you let the second child get away with so much more than you ever did the first, and you are so much quicker to place your trust in them as the eldest one has been through it already, or rather you as a parent have. I think I gave the impression to my parents that they could trust me, which doesn't mean to say I didn't get up to all sorts of harmless mischief but I think they just thought I wasn't, and I wasn't going to put them right!

I wasn't really much of a daredevil though. The craziest thing I remember was skiving in middle school when I was about eleven with Alison Pettit. We bunked off French but didn't even go out of the school grounds and just sat in the hallway. I guess because I was usually quite a good girl at school it got reported that we hadn't turned up for this French lesson and the school called the police which of course instantly got to my Dad and then my Mum. I was mortified but I guess I wasn't that kind of kid and it was so out of character for me so everyone was worried about me.

Andrew just pushed the limits and the boundaries a bit more. He and his big group of friends were your typical teenage boys and because I was so busy and therefore not getting into trouble I think it was more apparent that he was!   His first car was a little red Ford Fiesta and he would tear around Stowmarket in it.   He smashed a church window once and I think he also spent a night in a cell but I can't remember if it was legit or if my Dad was trying to teach him a lesson. I'm a bit soft with my own boys. Back then parenting was so different, we knew the boundaries very quickly as you'd get a smacked bum quite early on and you knew what the limits were. My kids really push their boundaries, I think that's what boys do and times are very different now.

Despite getting into a few scrapes Andrew would always look out for me as we got older. We were strong allies and in turn were massively supported by our parents.   We were a really tight knit family group.   It was such a pure upbringing and I am forever grateful for it.

TOP TIPS FOR PARENTS

- Try to support your children and be there for them without being forceful or overpowering. I was so fortunate to have that from my parents and I'm now trying to do the same for my boys and aim to be as supportive and encouraging as I can be.

- Expose your children to a variety of different hobbies and activities. Provide those opportunities, even if its not something you would necessarily have thought of yourself. DO help them find their passion. Finding something they enjoy, that is fun and makes them smile is key and it's massive. People can be quick to dismiss fun things as a career, believing it should be all very serious. That's not always the case and there are lots of opportunities out there that don't have to cost a fortune. Most children don't know what they like or don't like, so give them the chance to find out for themselves. It certainly helped me figure out what I liked, and I'm doing the same for my boys.

- Try not to be too pushy. I think forcing a child in a certain direction if they have shown no interest can be dangerous and could have the opposite effect, as they might rebel. There's no need to push kids, they will find their own way eventually if you just provide those opportunities. I try not to force my own ambitions on my boys or influence them with what I want.

- Take time to find the right stage school. Your child may be desperate to dance and sing but that doesn't necessarily mean that any stage school is the right one. There are so many opportunities out there now and it's important to find the right school or class where they are happy. One size definitely does not fit all.

- Encourage commitment. If your child tries something and likes it, make sure they stick at it for at least a term. Kids are so quick to say they've gone off something or don't want to go again, because they'd rather play with their friends, but don't let them give up too easily. They may have had a bad day but they might really enjoy it next time. Teach them the skills to get through those tough times as they will need them in this business. Encourage them to try their hardest, not to give up and most importantly HAVE FUN – this is what we always say to our boys.

45

CHAPTER 10

After playing in our paddling pool, I would always hang my swimming costumes up outside the conservatory to dry. All of a sudden they started going missing and my parents blamed me, thinking I had lost them at school, or carelessly put them somewhere else. I could be a bit forgetful now and then, but I knew it wasn't me, and I hadn't mislaid them. Underwear was also going missing from my drawers, and over quite a long period of time other stuff went missing but not quite enough for us to realise it. It wasn't until a couple of my swimming costumes eventually turned up in pieces down the road that we realised something more sinister might be going on.

It wasn't until there was a big sweep one night, when a machete went missing from the shed, along with a little bit of money that had been left on the side and I think one of my Mum's underwear drawers had been ransacked as well as mine, that my parents reported it and the police investigated. As a lot of people did back then, we always kept a spare key outside in a safe place and the police asked if anyone else knew where our key was. We could name a few people but it was only when my brother and I were questioned further about our friends and who would come round to the house that this boy's name cropped up. We hadn't really thought of him, as he lived ten doors down from us, and would occasionally ride his bike with Andrew. Soon after, the police spoke to him, searched his house and found all the evidence they needed. It was all a bit dark and the police cautioned him.

As a parent now I don't know how my Mum and Dad restrained themselves, I'm not sure I could. How they didn't react is beyond me although my dad was a policeman and couldn't. I dread to think what happened to him in later life and to be honest I don't even want to think about it.

Thankfully I haven't experienced anything like that since or had anyone stalking me physically or online. I've had brilliant fans who have supported me right from the start. One in particular, Janet, has been following me since *We Will Rock You*, so for nearly twenty years, and she literally comes to everything I do and is at every stage door before me. I can't remember the last show that she missed.

I don't consider myself a role model although I get a lot of drama school students who say they want the career I've had, and to do what I've done, which I think is mainly down to the fact I have appeared consecutively in big, high-profile shows that everyone knows. However, when I was in *Wicked* I would get so many letters, cards, gifts and messages on social media. Elphaba is a troubled young soul, and all these young people, both girls and boys, who didn't fit in or felt different in some way, were identifying with her character and would share it with me as they thought I would understand. I had a lot of young girls writing to me and talking about their mental health and I know a couple of them were self-harmers. I found that tricky. I felt as if I had a bit of a duty then to do the right thing and to set a good example, but I didn't want to get involved mainly because I didn't feel like I could do anything. I had my own issues in doing the show, and I just didn't have the energy or emotional resources to give, plus, I wasn't a professional in that field. I do feel a bit of a responsibility to behave in a certain way publicly, but that is just decency and how I am. I still occasionally receive cries for help but I just say I hope you're ok and that is it. It's not that I don't care, I just don't think I could help and would hate to make things worse.

I think it's rubbish when young impressionable fans follow hugely celebrated people who behave ridiculously. I don't think it's smart, and it's not ok for those kids because in a way they are looking to you for answers. It's quite a loaded responsibility.

CHAPTER 11

I don't remember a specific moment or turning point when I realised I could sing and people enjoyed listening to me. I always did well in the song and dance competitions at the festivals so it was probably more a gradual realisation stemming from that. I didn't win to begin with but I would always be placed or mentioned and as I got older I did generally win. Whenever we did a big ensemble piece Bobbie and I would be picked to split the main part. The adjudicators would make some comment about me having a future career in the business, and that I would go far. To me it was always a case of, I want to do this, I'm not sure if I'm good enough but I want to do it and I will.

I would never sing in front of my family, or at any family gatherings, as I was too shy. I was quite happy for them to hear me from my bedroom though and so I would save the singing for there, or a performance such as the festivals. To this day I am horrifically nervous if any of my family are in the audience. I've relaxed with it a little bit as time has gone on but I am still acutely aware whenever they are in. They look at you differently and they know you differently, it's weird.

When I was twelve, my parents found out from my dance teacher Ann Holland that The National Youth Music Theatre were looking for teams of kids for a production of Aesop's Fables and they took me to London to attend an open audition. I was asked back for a second audition where I had to recite a monologue, which I had rehearsed with Mrs Shaw, my drama teacher at middle school. I'd never really had to learn a monologue before and had to take two to this audition, I think one was Shakespeare and I also had to sing a song from music they had given us to learn.   I was delighted to get through as this was a big deal and yet again the next step up. We rehearsed in London first, then did a performance in Blackheath in South East London, near Greenwich, before being taken up by bus to the Edinburgh Festival. There were about twenty of us and accompanying adults and this was my first time away from home without my parents, even Bobbie wasn't with me, but I was so ready for it and just threw myself into the experience.

Considering my relatively sheltered upbringing compared to most of the other kids, where London and big shopping centres weren't accessible to me, it just didn't faze me at all and was all the more exciting. I suppose I felt so supported and grounded that I didn't question anything. I had such a strong sense of security that negative thoughts just didn't cross my mind. We had chaperones to keep an eye on us and transport us everywhere. Our makeshift dormitories were in a University campus and it was like like a scene from Annie with loads of beds lined up in each room. Cue for a song!

To me the Edinburgh Festival is such a grown-up thing and I was just too young to have any appreciation or sense any of the excitement or buzz of it. Not that we got to see anything else. The truth is I was more excited about the show we were doing and the people that I was working with. I've been back since as an adult and loved it but as a kid, I don't think I had an awareness of the scale of it. There I was aged twelve performing at the Edinburgh festival for a week with this massive, prestigious company and taking it all in my stride.

Although neither of them were musical themselves my Mum and Dad always enjoyed going to shows and concerts and on my thirteenth birthday they took me to London as a special treat to see *Les Mis*. I will never forget that day. First we went shopping to TopShop, which as a now teenager, made me happy enough, but then we went for dinner followed by the show. I'd been to lots of shows before that, such as pantomimes with the school and local productions at the Wolsey Theatre with my parents but *Les Mis* was the first biggy and made me realise the power of live theatre. We were sat right at the back but that didn't matter; I was totally involved and it made me cry. I really think that was the moment that solidified it and confirmed I wanted to make a career out of it. By the end of the evening I was completely blown away and had fallen in love with the show.

My parents knew how important dancing was to me and supported my dream of being on the stage, but insisted I do well at school or at least as well as I could do. They wanted me to get the right amount of GCSE's to get into college, so as a result school became a hurdle for me to get through in order to be a performer.

Young people nowadays are told to have a back-up plan just in case it doesn't work out for them, but I just didn't see that as an option and certainly didn't have one. I eventually took the traditional way into the business via college and then auditioning for parts in musicals, gaining experience along the way. Now, there are so many colleges, writing schools, specific drama schools and how to be a pop star schools, you name it there are just so many options out there. I think there were only six big theatre colleges at the time I was applying and that was it.

I talk about my route and experience of the business a lot, especially when I do workshops with young musical theatre students who are constantly asking me how I did it. I can look at a room full of those students and pick out those who are likely to go on and have a career in the industry. It's not necessarily to do with their level of talent but more about their level of doubt. The doubt in their own heads holding them back saying, "*Ooh well if it doesn't work out I will perhaps do this or maybe that.*" My view is if you are thinking that now before you've even started your career, there is no way you are going to make it, let alone sustain a career. I've always had that positive approach. My glass is half full and will get fuller. I always try and put it out there in the ether in some way. I will throw something out there, an idea maybe, in an email, or make a suggestion to someone, or perhaps give a certain answer in an interview somewhere, and if it happens then great, and if it doesn't that is fine as well, but I strongly believe you have to instigate things. It's not that I am following any particular spiritual path; it is just the way I naturally am and it works for me. I ask students now if they could be or do anything in their life what would it be and some of them just look at me blankly because they don't know. This is an alien concept for me. How can they not know? I don't understand it. At the same time I realise I'm not necessarily the norm and understand how lucky I am. My husband works in football and we share that common passion. He works with young people who have this deep yearning and need to play football so he understands that. Regardless of the hobby or interest, the passion for it can be the same. Without it, you won't get through the dark times. When you are in your deepest darkest hour doing some shitty little show getting paid nothing, it's the passion that keeps you going.

I found life at Stowmarket High School hard. Again, we'd all moved up together but suddenly education got a lot more serious and I had to really work at it. It wasn't just English and reading, I didn't find any of the academic subjects easy and getting up for school every day was just a chore. I enjoyed the social element of it, and I continued to love Drama and P.E. but as I've said before, if I could have given it up for dancing full time I would have done so in a heartbeat. It was a means to an end to me and something I had to get through.

At that time my life consisted of dancing, boys and school in that order. I would go out with friends if I didn't have any other commitments, and that really is the story of my life. If it was a Saturday night and I wasn't doing anything dance-related; then yes, I would go to that party or cinema or whatever was arranged and really enjoy it, but I would never sacrifice my dancing to go out, never. It was so important to me and made me happy. I liked the discipline, the structure, the physicality and the routine of it. It's what made me tick. Now as an adult in this profession, I know I'm almost too blinkered sometimes and I've had to learn to make time for my husband, kids and family. I've had to force myself to allow more time for my emotions and mental well-being. It's so easy to become too wrapped up in your career, too focused and conditioned, and to be forever planning for what's next. People are constantly asking me to do things and of course I want to do everything and grab every opportunity. It doesn't occur to me I could put it off for next week, next month or even next year.

I was never bullied at school, although I was always going to be picked out, because I was a bit different and was off doing showbiz things, and I was confident and secure within myself. I occasionally got picked on but it was just a bit of name calling by some of the bigger girls and nothing I couldn't handle, plus I had an older brother in the school which really helped.

I do remember getting caught at the school gates once and being surrounded by some girls from another school who were being really intimidating. My reaction was to give no reaction at all and to just walk away, which seemed to work. Emotionally I was quite developed and mature, partly because I was very clear in what I wanted to do and I knew my path, which in turn gives you an inner confidence. I was also interacting with a lot of people outside of the school environment and I think that builds up a certain maturity. Physically I was just your average girl but with a not so average talent. In some way I probably put myself up for it as Bobbie and I would often do dance routines in assembly so I obviously wasn't afraid to put myself out there to be hammered! As a teenager it was social suicide really to do that, at least it was at the time, but I could handle it and it didn't stop me being passionate about my craft. I was proud of what I did and no one was going to make me feel ashamed.

So, although I had a glimpse of bullying, it was nothing like a lot of kids have. Bullying these days can be brutal. If I ever found out my boys were being bullied I would be frightened of my response and that's the truth. I would be that lioness. I am very fortunate because they are tough boys. Alfie in particular has a beautiful heart and soul but he is boisterous and very physical and I like to think no one would pick on him but you just don't know. They are confident and self-assured and I can only hope it never happens to them.

CHAPTER 12

I knew I wanted to go to drama college quite early on, but we didn't know much about how it all worked or what I was supposed to do, as of course my parents weren't theatrical, so had no experience of these things. All we knew was what Ann Holland told us, as she'd attended Laine Theatre Arts College in Epsom Surrey, predominantly a dance college. She also told us about Doreen Bird College, and I auditioned for them both when I was fifteen. They were my preferred two but we looked at a few others as well. I didn't get into Bird but luckily was offered a provisional place at Laine, dependant on me getting the right amount of GCSE's. Barely had the excitement of this worn off when we quickly realised we then had the problem of getting some sort of funding or grant to cover the fees, otherwise that would have been the end of my career before it had begun, as there was no way my parents could afford to send me. Luckily we got a grant from the council and also some sort of bursary, but my parents still had to find a fair amount towards my fees out of their own pockets.

The college arranged digs close by for the first year students, and I went to live with a family with two other students, Faye Pearce and Kelly Mills, all of us strangers and suddenly living in this house together. I shared a room with Faye who was a beautiful ballet dancer. We couldn't have been more different, like chalk and cheese, but quickly became best buddies. She is now a yoga teacher in Austria and we are still good mates.

Being away from home didn't bother me in the slightest. I was a bit of an old hand at it by now having been to Edinburgh with the NYMT, plus I had done a week's work experience at Potters Leisure Resort on the East coast between Great Yarmouth and Lowestoft, right next to Gorleston in a place called Hopton-On-Sea, as one of the holiday entertainers which I suppose was a bit like being a Pontins Bluecoat or Butlins Redcoat. It is now Starmakers Entertainment but back then we were just the entertainments team.

Prior to that I'd spent a week at a dance school working in the reception which I absolutely hated. If ever I had been in any doubt about my career choice I knew then that photocopying and making tea was not going to be my chosen path and I couldn't get out of there quick enough. My second week at Potters was a different story altogether and I couldn't believe my luck. We'd been on holiday there as a family the year before which I loved and whilst there we spoke to them about the possibility of me doing work experience and if it would be an option. Sometime later I wrote to them and was accepted. I was involved in all aspects of the entertainments programme, trying my hand at everything including card games and bingo calling, all of which was invaluable experience. That one week led to me going back regularly to work at weekends and summer throughout college and a lifelong affinity with the place. In fact, over the years I have made a point of going back to Potters at various times to visit. Recently they put on a special evening that I think was to celebrate a special anniversary or birthday to which they'd invited various musical stars to appear and I did a fifteen minute set for them. It was amazing, yet so strange to be back there performing in that exact same spot after all that time, and really did feel special. It brought it home to me a bit how far I had come in my career and how grateful I was to them for all they had done for me. They were like my family at one point and I am still very close to them. I just hope and pray the place survives the pandemic and continues on, as I think it has been hit quite badly.

I don't remember my first days or even that period of time starting out at college as such, apart from feeling excited, nervous and slightly overwhelmed. Luckily I had an ally in Bobbie who was also starting, which really helped, even though we weren't living together. I had also previously attended summer school at Laine when I was fourteen, which was a week of workshops and classes and was basically a way you can try it out first to see if you like it. I think my parents must have seen it advertised when I was looking for colleges. We used to get *The Stage* newspaper each week which was one of the only ways to find out about auditions and theatre schools or anything showbiz and entertainment related back then before we had the internet. I had met a few other students from that week of workshops who also started at the same time I did so I already had a few contacts and was familiar with some of the teachers including of course the Principal and founder Betty Laine who developed the school into a full time dance and musical theatre college which is now recognised as one of the leading performing arts institutions in the UK.

Louise Dearman was one of those summer school students who of course went on to become hugely successful in the industry. Lou, Bobbie and I had stayed in a house together with a family who, each summer, housed the wannabees from summer school as well as the full time students all year round!

Starting college though was like entering another world, from the moment I stepped into one of the two main dance studios for the first time and met Miss Laine properly. As we were brand new first years they played us an inspiring video which gave us a tantalising insight of what was to come and was super-exciting, followed by our timetables which was equally exciting but daunting. This was going to be tough, but at last I would spend my days living my passion which is all I had wanted since I was three years old going to my first dance class. I was also for the first time surrounded by people with the same outlook and dedication that I had for the industry. We were all supporting each other. I felt like we were real-life kids from Fame!

I knew that it wasn't going to be an easy ride, as on average I was down for three or four dance classes a day, plus the musical theatre element of the course and however much I loved it, it was going to be quite full-on, and a test of my commitment. I was right, it was mentally, physically and emotionally tough and tiring. The day would start at 8.30 am with registration, then a ballet class at 9.00 am, followed by jazz or tap at 10.00 am. After lunch we would have a musical theatre class, a contemporary dance class and the day would finish with a vocal class or maybe even another dance class. On top of all that there were after hours extra classes, such as choir, show class and audition class.

As a year group we all bonded quickly, probably because we were all experiencing this difficult ride together whilst supporting each other through it. We became so close, and I made lifelong friends, one of whom was Steven Paling who has been a huge part of my life ever since. I really felt that I was part of a good club and like I'd arrived, and we certainly all made the most of living in London. We would often go and get last-minute theatre tickets for a fiver and go see as many of the big musicals as we could, *Starlight Express* being a particular favourite.

This was also when I met Caroline Deverill for the first time; she was a year below me and we were both very similar inasmuch as we were big belty singers. During college we went on an unforgettable girls' holiday together, with two others, to Tenerife which was absolute carnage. I'm sure I absolutely pickled my liver on that holiday. I still can't quite get my head round how much cheap, nasty, alcohol young people can consume. If we weren't pickled we were sick, and spent the whole time in one state or the other. We would dance on the bars dressed up like, and thinking we were, the Spice Girls. We went on a booze cruise and again we were all completely drunk and sick. We did karaoke in some absolutely horrible place at 4 am one morning. I must have been so drunk as I don't like karaoke and never have done. I get so embarrassed by it. I always end up thinking *'this is eggy'* (a word I used to use a lot meaning, egg on your face – cringey), so don't often put myself in that situation. That whole holiday was one of those experiences that you have to do and get it out of your system, and because I did it early enough with them, I've never felt the need to do it again. Caroline was and is a great friend though and we've since done pantos together, shared accommodation, and she rented a room in my flat when she first left college. I was also Maid of Honour at her wedding which is how I met James, my husband. It's funny really how thinking back on my life and career, and digging deep into my memory for this book has forced me to remember a lot about people I have met along the way and how they have weaved in and out of my life. Whilst I know a great many people I would say I have only a handful of very close friends.

There were three year groups at Laine and generally there was a big divide between the years, probably because the level of talent and development from a first year to a third year is quite significant, which is testament to the training there. Us sixteen-year-old first-years were like fresh-faced blank canvasses and we would look up to those third-year students, the finished creations, in the hope we would one day be like that.

Ruthie Henshall in particular was a bit of an idol at the college and her name lived on as one of the students that everyone looked up to. She went on to become a big success story and I actually know her quite well now as we've done bits of work together. I think I identified with Ruthie because she was an actual story that I saw happen which was achievable. She was only a couple of years ahead of me and I could relate to her.

As ex- 'Lainies' will know, Miss Laine was renowned for having her favourites, and it was usually geared towards the dancers, the beautiful tall slim gorgeous people, which wasn't me at all. However, in fairness, she did like me and has been supportive since I left.

Being in this industry the pressure is on to be slimmer and look better which I think is a condition of the business, and I was no different. I am constantly trying to look my best as part of the job. During my whole time there, issues with food and weight were really heavy. There were girls with bulimia, girls with anorexia, probably a couple of boys as well; in fact there were so many people with eating disorders at college. We were all aware of it, but it was never really spoken about, as it is now. At college you're in a leotard and tights for eight hours a day, every day for three years, stood in a ballet class next to all shapes and sizes and you can't help but become very aware of everyone's body type, which naturally is going to play on your brain. I was very aware of it but I don't think I particularly had an issue.

Now I work in companies with young, incredibly fit, beautiful dancers and I'm a forty-something mum of two who tries hard to keep physically fit, but at the same time I am realistic with who and what I am, when I look in the mirror every day. I definitely still try and aspire to be slimmer but I think that is normal and a high percentage of women in general are a little bit body obsessed. I do have my insecurities, which are heightened through being looked at and photographed all the time. For example, if I've been photographed at a concert from an unflattering angle, in a particular outfit, then that's it, I won't wear it again. I also cover my arms now for that same reason! I've been on constant diets over the years just like many other women but not in an obsessive way. I would say I'm aware of my body and weight but I'm not poorly with it and it won't stop me drinking a couple of glasses of wine and having a bar of chocolate or chunk of bread.

My friend Rhiannon, who I've known about a year now, had an eating disorder throughout her time at theatre college. She went on to train as a nutritionist and now has a completely different relationship with food. I originally contacted her to talk about my diet. She delved right back into the history of my relationship with food, and told me that I didn't have an unhealthy relationship with it but my brain just needed to be reset because I was eating the wrong things. I used to think that I didn't want to eat loads, so it was a good idea to just snack on something silly, and then not eat a proper dinner. I knew all this was wrong deep down but needed someone to point it out.

My eating routine is still constantly messed up which is usually down to circumstance. The kids eat at 5pm then James doesn't usually get in till half nine when we will snack, and then if I'm doing a show I probably won't eat beforehand so end up eating quite late in the evening. Being in lockdown my diet is healthier than its ever been and we've been able to sit and have lunch and dinner together as a family, which just doesn't happen in a normal day.

When I was a student at Laine I think there were only about thirty or forty in each year. Class sizes would vary and could range from a tap class of four or five in one of the smaller studios upstairs, to perhaps twenty in one of the jazz classes in a bigger studio. I hadn't had a pianist in any of my dance classes until I went to college and remember thinking at the time *"Ooh, we've got a pianist in our ballet class, this is very posh"*.

In the first year everybody basically had to do the same course and study all the disciplines but by the second year it was a bit more tailored to suit individual talents or interests, although everyone had to keep up an element of dance throughout the entire time. I ended up doing a combination of dance and musical theatre although some people specialised in one or the other. Even at that stage, dancing was still kind of my thing.

We all flourished under the keen eye of Barbara Evans, the excellent jazz teacher, although if I'm being honest I was a little bit frightened of her, probably because she was so brilliant and I was definitely not one of the best dancers at college by a long way. Her classes were tough and the combinations were difficult and challenging, which I thrived on. Jerry Zookarello, affectionately known as Jerry Jazz, was equally brilliant, although his classes were a little bit more commercial and again I wasn't one of the best but I enjoyed every second. Maureen and Gwyn Hughes ran the musical theatre course and I spent a lot of time with them, becoming very close as a result. This was where I began to feel most comfortable as it came naturally to me and this time I was one of the better ones in the class.

Of course a massive part of being in college involved putting on and appearing in musicals and I was in my element. We had to audition for each show, and would be involved in all aspects of the production. They were staged in the musical theatre studio and we would do a run of about four or five shows with costumes we had either made ourselves, or from the costume department, and with an accompanying pianist, so nothing too grand but invaluable experience, and a great insight into the amount of work that went into putting on a musical.

Metropolis was our first-year production where I was part of the ensemble. We also did *Little Shop of Horrors* which lends itself perfectly to musical theatre students and where Lou (Dearman) got the lead part of Audrey and Steven (Paling) played Seymour. I was Ronnette, one of the three backing singers. I eventually got to play a lead role when I was cast as Mary Flynn in *Merrily We Roll Along*. Yes!! To this day, Lou and I are still up for the same parts. The big one for me in college though was *Evita*, in which I got to play Eva Peron, and to this day is the only time I have played that part. I would kill for it, as, for some reason I have always felt it was going to be my role. Of course Elaine Paige really set the benchmark for the show but even so, I felt I could really nail it, and do justice to it, and I would absolutely love to do it before I get too old. Her story and her journey is incredible and to play that would be a dream come true.

I enjoyed those musicals more than the annual summer show, which the entire college was involved in, and in which I would get to do a song or two if I was lucky. They were usually dance-heavy although they made sure everyone featured in something.

When I first started, Laine had its own agency which was very small and they didn't really do much with it. They had developed it a lot by the time I left. In my first year they sent about four or five of us girls who were singers along to audition for panto. I think I was the only first year student and I not only got a job in this big E & B panto in Basingstoke, I landed the leading role of Alice in *Dick Whittington*, which was a big deal. Suddenly here I was in 1996 aged sixteen starring alongside names

59

such as Maggie Moone and Hinge and Bracket. Everyone was lovely and being so young the entire company really looked after me. It was up to us to arrange our own digs during the run of the panto and luckily for me I was able to stay with an older couple who my Dad vaguely knew and had often stayed at Potters. It didn't dawn on me at the time but now I realise how calculating my parents were in terms of where I was scheduled to go and who I stayed with, especially before I was eighteen and whilst they were still helping me to fund college life. Everything seemed to just happen magically without me putting too much thought and effort into it and I was given a little bit more leeway each year as I moved into different accommodation and started driving. On reflection I realise how young and naive I was to suddenly be working in the industry professionally whilst living away from my family and all I had known. I think I only got home for Christmas Day then back again for the Boxing Day matinee. The next year 1997, saw me in *Aladdin* at the New Theatre Cardiff playing Princess Balroubador with Les Dennis as Wishee Washee, Tudor Davies, Kris Akabussi and my childhood hero the White Power Ranger! This time a lot of my college friends were also in the panto including my really good friend Caroline Deverill, affectionately known to me as Devers, playing the Genie of the Ring so it was a really nice social time for me. Being with your mates is a different ball game and we were able to share a flat together which was so much more fun and being in Cardiff was great over Christmas. We were in our own little bubble and stuck together really, blissfully unaware of anything else that was going on at the time. *Cinderella* at the Cliffs Pavilion Southend 1998, was also my final year at Laines, where again I was the lead and the wonderful Bobby Davro, still a dear friend today, was my Buttons. Alongside us were Bella Emberg and Sue Hodge as the Ugly Sisters, Bob Carolgees with Spit the Dog, and Ray Meagher from Home and Away. Bobby was a terrible prankster and we would often play tricks on one another which was kind of new for me. I had no idea that all this went on but Bobby educated me and I relished thinking up new jokes every night. One of my favourites was smearing vaseline all over the handles of the shopping trolley he had to bring on stage every night although he got me back so well and definitely won the overall challenge. There was a point in the show when Buttons had to bring Cinders a present which I had to pull out of a box. The normal gag was that it was a Teletubby, who of course were the big thing then, but ours was called Stinky Pinky which the kids thought was hilarious and it went down really well. On this one occasion Bobby put a wet fish in there which I could smell so strongly and of course I could feel the box was heavy.

"Come on Cinderella, open the box. I can't wait for you to see the lovely present I bought for you…"

Of course I pulled out this wet fish almost gagging at the smell whilst Buttons shouted, *"It's a Stinky Pinky Cinders, I got it especially for you…"*

Now I am the biggest corpser ever, in fact I'm worse now, but back then I was also still relatively inexperienced and I just completely dissolved into hysterical laughter. Apparently the audience were all in on the joke anyway so could laugh along with me.

I've never forgotten that and in fact I did a charity gig for him recently after not seeing each other for years and we spoke fondly about the wet fish! It was brilliant. He was warm and generous not only to me but the entire company and we used to talk for hours. He gave me loads of advice and talked a lot about the industry and was so supportive. I learned a lot about how to lead a company from Bobby. At the time I didn't really think about it and it was only later on in life that I understood how much I had taken on board from him. He took me under his wing and always kept in touch afterwards to check how I was getting on. If ever I drop him a line about anything he is always there for me. Given the direction of my career I haven't done panto since that time. I've had several offers over the past five or six years but haven't been able to commit. It is so time-consuming with often two or three shows a day over the festive period and I have to think of my boys, who are still very young.

In between everything else I also got a job working behind a bar. I'm not sure what led me to do this as I was working all the hours I could already, with weekends and summers at Potters, then Christmas spent in panto. I must have decided I needed more money and there was a pub called The Cricketers on the nearby park, advertising for bar staff, and I thought this would be an easy way to earn a few extra bob. As my previous work experience in the office at a dance school had taught me, this also proved that pulling pints was definitely not my forte. I absolutely hated it, and only lasted a couple of months.

I was desperate for my independence and started learning to drive properly as soon as I could. I had a few proper driving lessons, then Sean Hathoway, a guy at Potters, where by now I was working each weekend, also gave me lessons and took me out in his car. I was determined to drive as quickly as possible because I knew that once I got my licence it would open so many doors for me. My parents had previously driven me everywhere, and were still driving me to Potters every week, there and back. I remember when I was thirteen and my brother was just learning to drive, he and I 'stole' my parents' car from the driveway and Andrew drove it five minutes down the road to a dirt track where he let me drive. As soon as my Dad realised the car had gone he followed us and I can picture him now at the end of this track screaming and shouting as I was driving towards him.

Eventually I passed on the third attempt, and to suddenly have that independence was unbelievable. I was at college in London doing what I loved and I could drive anywhere. My dreams were starting to come true and there was no stopping me now.

My parents always kept me grounded and as a pair they've made me who I am. Although they were incredibly supportive they made me find my way on my own. I wasn't given loads of money or handed things on a plate, I had to earn it all on my own merit. Even when I wanted a car and they were getting rid of their clapped-out old Escort they said "*If you want this car you need to earn it and buy it,*" which I did for about five hundred quid. This was a lot of money then and took me forever to pay for it. They taught me very quickly to be self-sufficient. I knew they always had my back and would support me if I got into trouble but they taught me how to go it alone.

I'd finish college on a Friday night, jump in the car, then drive two or three hours to Potters, work the show for a couple of nights at the camp then drive back to Epsom in time for college on the Monday, all for about one hundred quid which barely covered the petrol. Potters would just fit me into whichever show they were putting on at the time. I would rehearse all the numbers and then just slot into them at the weekend, as the shows were on a rotation so me covering would basically give one of the team a night off, while I sang their track. I learned so much from Potters, it was kind of like additional training. I was with grown-ups, actually doing a job I was training to do. The staff really did feel like my family, as from the age of sixteen I was growing up in front of them.

Once I was on the road, you wouldn't believe the amount of times I broke down on the M25, which I think is one of the reasons I'm such a confident driver now. My car was so old it had a choke, and on one memorable journey the radiator burst, the bonnet blew up and water sprayed everywhere. I think I was on first name terms with the RAC at that period of time.

In our first year, evenings involved going back to the family we stayed with, who cooked us dinner, and we would spend the evenings chatting about our day, or watching television, but as we moved into the second and third years we had our own accommodation, and I shared a town house with Faye, Lindsay Platt, Tamlyn Platt, Louise Lenihan and Sebastian Harris. We were still within walking distance of college, and suddenly, with no one watching over our shoulder, we would virtually live in the local pubs and clubs in Epsom, drink too much, go to house parties, hang out with boys and all the usual teenage girls stuff. We certainly made the most of student life and did it all but I suppose it was nothing out of the ordinary. *Chicago's*, now long since closed, was a firm favourite, and was THE place to go for all the students. *Vaults* was another haunt in Kingston and once I'd passed my test I would happily drive us all there.

Notes from...

Well, where do I start? I've known Kerry for just over a quarter of a century!! Blimey, that long! We met at Potters resort when we were... well, babies really. Kerry had the most amazing voice, the most gorgeous long, flowing blonde hair and was just as stunning then as she is now... wow, was I envious!! I couldn't believe how shy she was; however, that was soon to change. As the youngest and most naive girls, we were inevitably always the first to be played tricks on. We now both thank our old pranksters for doing the things they did, for rounding our personalities and teaching us to not take ourselves so seriously! From birthday wake up calls in the form of egg and flour being tipped over us, to being told that Cameron Mackintosh was in the audience on the opening night of our Atlas Theatre and as a result us sweating in our pink satin dresses, which isn't a good look on satin. I think Kerry also went on stage in odd shoes on one occasion. We had so much fun, and whilst I can't write some of the stories, I'm certain if you ask Kerry nicely she'll recall some of them, although perhaps not all. Kerry is one of the loveliest people I have ever met and I am proud to call her my friend.

Rachel Badde

CHAPTER 13

It was during my second year at college that my secure, happy, stable life was rocked to its very core, and my parents split up. Maybe my brother saw it coming, as he was still living at home and possibly sensed it, I don't know, but I didn't have a clue. I'd seen it happen to other people but never thought it would happen to my parents. We were doing the prelims, which were basically competitions within the college where we would be competing against each other. I had got through to the song prelims and my parents had come up to see me. After the show I went with them to the car park, where they gave me a big round green ghetto blaster as a gift. I remember thinking it a bit strange but didn't think any more of it.

"*We have to talk to you Kerry...*" my Dad began shifting his glance downwards while my Mum remained silent.

"*What's happened?*" was my immediate response suddenly thinking one of them was poorly.

"*We'll discuss it tomorrow love,*" Mum continued, "*We'll both come round in the morning.*"

"*What's going on?*" I said in an almost jokey way. It still didn't connect then and really was the last thing I was expecting. I was more concerned that maybe one of them was sick.

The next day Mum wanted to be the one to break the news to me so my Dad left the room and only then did I begin to feel really uneasy.

"*I'm leaving your Dad, we are going to get divorced...*"

I never expected to hear those words from my parents EVER, never even given it any thought at all and hearing them quite literally took my breath away. I was totally gobsmacked. Dad came into the room and we all sobbed together. From that moment they went their separate ways. I'd never seen Dad cry before. He was my rock and my stability in life, as they both were, and now those rocks were wobbling and unstable, causing my world to suddenly shift. Yes, my support system was being swept out from underneath me, but I was more upset for my Dad. My reaction was to punish my Mum, by not speaking to her for two to three years, and Martin my now step dad for even longer. She would try and call me and I wouldn't answer. She would try and leave messages with my friends but I wouldn't return them. She would even come and see my shows but I wouldn't see her. As far as I was concerned she was totally to blame for everything and I cut her out of my life. She had left my Dad for another man and broken his heart. I couldn't see past that at the time. It was a dark and horrible time. Now of course as an adult and parent I can totally understand it and know that it was layered with lots of other things but as a vulnerable teenager I needed someone to blame and Mum was the easy target I guess. I never even gave her a chance to explain her side of the story. As a small child when parents divorce you almost don't have a choice of how you deal with it. You are told that you will see this parent on that day and that's it. The problem with being a slightly older teenager is that you do have an opinion, and you do have a voice, and a choice, and I'm not sure if that is a good or bad thing.

We have spoken a little bit about that time since, and I remember being home from college one time and thinking my Mum had got really thin. It must have been her birthday and I took her out for dinner to a Mongolian restaurant. Mum has since said that she was on the brink of telling me that evening, but she couldn't bring herself to do it. Her being so thin was perhaps the only clue I was given. I always lose weight when I'm stressed too but unfortunately it doesn't seem to happen often enough really!

It was my college friends who got me through that part of my life and why I got so close to Faye. Mum meanwhile to her credit, never gave up or stopped trying to rebuild our relationship and would always send me little presents, and try phoning, or coming to see me. I think eventually I just let her come to a show and gradually started to let her back into my life. I don't remember an exact moment when we began to talk as it was so gradual, and she had never given up, so although I wasn't speaking to her, she was still playing a part in my life. It must have been so difficult for her as she had it from both of us. I'm pretty headstrong but my brother is even worse. He is a closed book and not open at all. I would say there are only a few people in the world who probably know him really well as he doesn't let people get close. He was so scarred from the whole experience of my parents' divorce and won't let any woman get close to him as he is so terrified of being in the situation Dad was in. It breaks my heart because I think he'd be an amazing Dad and a great husband. He now runs his own successful business, and hopefully one day he will meet the right woman. Fingers crossed!

Since I've had the kids, things changed again and we've had a completely different relationship. Mum and Martin are brilliant with them and are totally supportive.

CHAPTER 14

I came out of college with my National Diploma in Musical Theatre. Whilst I don't think I could have gone into the business without having gone to college, I always think that bit of paper is not really what it's about. It's about the training and the whole experience and it wouldn't have worried me to walk out at the end of it without a diploma, because for me I'd done all the classes and got what I'd wanted from Laines and more besides.

At the time you had to get a certain amount of 'work points', and work a certain amount of hours, to obtain an Equity card, but you couldn't work in a show or get an agent until you had your equity card. It was mental and really difficult. Most people would go into summer season, which was the norm at that time, and I returned to do a summer season at Potters.

I always had the back up of Potters and whenever I wasn't working they told me that their doors were always open for me. This basically meant that when I left home at sixteen I never went back as during any down time I had that safety net of a place to stay where I could earn a bit of money. Mark Brewer was the Entertainments Manager in charge of all the shows and entertainment, and he basically kept me in work. Nigel Pattle was the Musical Director and taught me so much while I was there, in fact he was the one who encouraged me to get up and start singing the solos. He gave me so many tips on how to use a microphone and how to 'be on stage' but the main thing was he told me I was good and to stick with it. Rachel Badde had started there just before me and as she was only a couple of years older we'd often team up and sing duets such as 'I Know Him So Well'. Rachel still works there as one of the managers. As well as singing I had to oversee all the card games, the novelty sports competitions including the welly wanging, some of the kids' competitions and general entertainment. I was in my element.

At that time our accommodation was mainly in static caravans on the outskirts of the holiday centre, which thinking about it now were probably a massive fire hazard and would be classed as uninhabitable, but I loved them. To me, having my own little caravan represented my independence. It probably wasn't suitable for a paying guest but what did I care. If the worst happened and they were completely full I would just share with Rachel or Busby Allen who was another of the entertainments team. He'd been there when I was on holiday with my family and was the life and soul of the place. He was a big personality and had a huge impact on me.

There were lots of acts at the time that were doing the pubs and clubs circuit who would come in and do the odd Saturday night. It was a favourite for comedians of the day and they would all pop in, so there I was getting to meet all these seasoned professional acts from very early on, seeing first-hand how they were working. It was such an education, whilst at the same time providing me with the security of never really being out of work. Although Rachel, Nigel and Busby are all still there, the performers and casts have changed as young people come and go, but they still run it, which to me is amazing and speaks volumes. I was so lucky as they all took me under their wing and I still call them my second family.

Potters and the people in it play a very big part in my heart and although I do go back, it's not as often as I would like but always feels like going home. They still support. Since I was there many people have started their careers there, Lee Mead for one. I think I started a bit of a craze!

During that first summer after leaving college I had an audition with Mitch Sebastian, a Director and Choreographer, who was casting for a tour of *Magic of the Musicals* with Marti Webb and Dave Willetts. They already had four dancers and must have decided they needed an extra couple of swings as I seem to remember it being a last-minute audition. Steven Paling and I both went for it and to our delight both got the job. The plan was that in the bigger venues we were to go on as part of the show but for the smaller venues we'd be cut out completely. Because we were only add-ons, when we did go on, we didn't have microphones and so amused ourselves by making boom mics out of coat hangers covered in duct tape, which we found hysterical. If any of the four dancers went off sick we would also cover for them. It was a crazy length tour of about thirty dates up and down the country, sometimes on a tour bus, and sometimes we would drive depending on the schedule. There was no logic to our tour schedule, one minute we could be up in Glasgow, the next in Plymouth; we were at the mercy of the theatres and their availability.

Steven and I shared the driving when we had to, and shared a room. I'm not a smoker and never have been even at college, apart from during those three months on tour. We would smoke in the car on the journey between dates to relieve the boredom and try to suppress our hunger, so we could keep thin. I didn't really like it though and by the end of the tour, thought "What on earth am I doing? I don't need this in my life", so that was it and I didn't smoke ever again.

If we were on the tour bus it would pick us up at the venue after the show and we would sleep on the bus until we arrived at the hotel in the next town on the tour. If we had a day off however, to save on hotel costs the bus would drive the entire company back home to London after the gig, including the band and company manager but not Marti and Dave who had cars, and we would all be dropped off at Victoria Station at about 3.00 am in the morning, when of course there was nothing open. Steven lived in Southfields, just outside Wimbledon, as he had kept his house on after college, and as I didn't have my own place at the time I would stay with him so we would jump in a cab and split the cost. It was mental. Nowadays you'd at least be put up at a hotel. The whole tour was quite gruelling and, perhaps inevitably, Marti Webb was taken poorly on one occasion. There was no understudy in place as it was Dave and Marti's show, with their name above the title. The plan probably was, that if one of them were sick, they would just cancel the show. It just so happened that Mitch came in on that day with Marti having just been taken ill.

"Do you wanna sing a couple of the numbers tonight Kerry, so we can carry on the show as normal?" he asked casually.

I was grateful to Mitch. He must have had faith in me from the audition and naturally I wasn't about to turn down such a chance. I ended up singing quite a lot of the songs in numerous shows. It was tough because Marti was well known for certain numbers such as *Take That Look off Your Face* and *Tell Me On A Sunday*, and the audience had paid to see her singing those songs, but for me it was incredible. To suddenly be put in that position so soon, and fresh from college, was a unique opportunity. Perhaps I was concentrating on the job in hand and focusing on the positive, or maybe it was the arrogance of youth, but either way I was young enough to take it in my stride and aside from that nobody knew who I was, so it didn't matter and I had nothing to lose. *My Fair Lady*, a few years later, was by far tougher. I was so lucky as Potters had given me such confidence, and the tools to deal with most things that were thrown at me.   I had been allowed to make my mistakes there and grow from it, so by the time I was doing this show, I was ready.   I knew how to go on and I knew how to deliver a song.

Steven was also dance captain for the show and has since gone on to be a brilliant resident director and agent. Marti really liked him because he made her feel very comfortable. She liked me too as I was very respectful to her.   I was brought up to be respectful of those who were more senior, or who had more experience, and I think she appreciated that. It must have been difficult for her when I went on in her place, not because it was me but because of the situation.   At the time I didn't realise it but now looking back I know how stressful that must have been for her.   I have met her since on a cruise called *Stages*, which is a big musical theatre weekend cruise.   She was so warm and friendly and we had the loveliest catch up.

Notes from...

The moment I heard Kerry Ellis belt out the T'Pau classic '*China in Your Hands*', I knew she'd be a star. We were gathered in the studio at Laine Theatre Arts, green and nervous but that wasn't going to stop her. She had a natural gift.

We did one of our first jobs together, *Magic of the Musicals*, on the road, touring 90 venues in 3 months. What a mission, zig-zagging the country in my bashed up Peugeot, which had a nickname I can't share here. I also have no idea why we called her that! Many a room shared in a dodgy B & B in many a seaside town but what stays with me the most is the laughter. Twenty-five years later and we still laugh as much as we ever did.

I've had the privilege of working with Kerry a lot over the years, creating her first ever one-woman show. Looking back, we were naive, but I think that's why we pushed the boundaries so much. From the Royal Albert Hall and the London Palladium, to a very quick change side-stage at the BBC Proms that went totally wrong as neither of us thought it was worth rehearsing, to numerous gigs around the UK, one thing I can honestly say is that Kerry is a joy to work with and a true professional. Working with Kerry and my husband Craig, (her MD), has created some of the best moments in my career and all I can say is long may it continue.

Kerry is a star but more importantly she is my friend.

Steven Paling

CHAPTER 15

After returning to Potters for a while, the opportunity for a cruise came along. Faye and a couple of other college mates were auditioning as dancers for a few of the cruise liners and encouraged me to go for it too. I decided to go along just for the experience but to be honest I wasn't really that bothered about going on a cruise ship at that time. I was happy enough at Potters, pleased I'd done *Magic of the Musicals*, and was now really hoping for a theatre job to present itself. I went along to an open audition for this one particular cruise and ended up staying all day. It was one of those processes where certain people would get knocked out on each round and then go home. I made it to the end of that day and got called back for another day, with the end result that I was employed for nine months on the resident entertainments team, as lead vocalist on what at the time was a brand new liner, and the biggest ship in the world, The Voyager of the Seas. Faye got a job on one of the other liners so it was time to go our separate ways which was sad but exciting. I was about to set sail on my own!

Initially we were flown to Miami to rehearse, mainly as the offices were based there, but also because it was an international team including people from Japan, a guy from Sweden and a few from Miami itself, with only two of us from the UK. It was a real chore having to go all that way but I guess someone had to do it! Our home for the next six weeks was in an apartment block on South Beach, from where it was a twenty-minute walk to the rehearsal studios.

Part way through our time there, a tornado hit and we were given just a few hours to pack up our rooms ready to be evacuated to a Holiday Inn hotel inland, along with various other ships' crew and staff. It was all very dramatic. We weren't allowed to take everything and just had to pack a bag. If anything it was quite exciting, as there was no sense of panic so we just treated it like a little adventure.

I didn't feel particularly worried as those around us seemed in complete control of the situation. The locals were obviously used to this and all the hotels were prepared and had their shutters firmly down. The only thing I was anxious about was my family at home, hearing that I was in the midst of a tornado and fearing the worst. That worried me, but as far as

I was concerned it was all very well organised and we were told we were going to this hotel as a precaution, for our own safety, and we would come back once it was all over. It felt like a massive party as we were all on the same mission. We watched it reported on the news and saw it coming in but because we had been moved quite a way inland, apart from a slight change in weather we barely noticed it happening.

Apart from that the weather was gloriously hot and sunny. Starbucks was a massive thing to me then as they weren't around much in the UK at the time. I loved going in and grabbing an iced coffee, then walking along the beach on my way to work. The downside was I wasn't yet 21 so I couldn't go drinking with the rest of them when they were going to bars in the evening.

From Miami they flew us to Turku in Finland and we had a few rehearsals on board the ship, in dry dock. We were able to actually live on the ship which didn't set sail for another week. In fact we had to wear hard hats as it was still being built. We then set sail back to Miami and I didn't see dry land for two weeks. We had the entire ship to ourselves which gave us extra valuable time for teching in the theatre, and saved us having to do the run through when the ship arrived. We were ready for the passengers and nine months of Caribbean cruising!

Passengers boarded in Miami for their seven night Caribbean cruise and we would return the following week to start all over again with a different set of passengers. The team would do a couple of twenty-minute shows to welcome passengers on board, then two full shows, which we did twice within a week, and a short farewell show and that was it. I can't begin to describe how fantastic it was and I had the best time ever. I was young, I had my twenty first birthday on board, and I was with a bunch of other young like-minded people sailing round the Caribbean, singing in the evening. I mean, what was not to love? We weren't even really restricted on our time off. Because we were cast members, we had quite high 'status'; your role, dictated where you could go on board the ship. It's still the same now because I've been back since to do a guest spot on a show. We would also do the boat drills, demonstrating life jackets for the guests was so funny. I suppose it was because we had good English for starters, and we could connect with the passengers quite well.

I had a couple of boyfriends during this time, one of which was Steve-O, one of the resident clowns. He was exciting and charismatic and it was a whirlwind of fun.

He was totally bonkers and would do all these crazy tricks on and off stage, and he has gone on to be hugely famous in America as any fans of *Jackass* will know, getting himself into a few scrapes along the way. When his contract finished and he left the ship I was devastated. I did see him a couple of times after that when we docked in Miami but by then he was working elsewhere and it all fizzled out.

There was an ice rink on the ship and Matt Kessinger, a national and international competitor for the United States figure skating team, joined us soon after as part of the ice cast. He was from LA and it wasn't long before we got together and spent the remaining six months on board as an item. Time on board seemed so intense and a month seemed like a year so when we eventually left the ship I felt like we knew each other so well and I went with him to LA for three months on a bit of a whim. My visitor's visa still had three months left on it and I thought "Why not?" We were pretty close by then though, and he had become really important to me. Matt lived in Santa Monica, and had a condo in a little apartment block with a swimming pool which was almost an essential requirement there, as it was such a blistering heat. It sounds more glamorous than it actually was but I loved it. Matt went straight into a summer season at a huge theme park that was a bit like Alton Towers called Knott's Berry Farm, in Buena Park California, where he was appearing in an ice show. Weekends were when we would do our exploring. Matt showed me the sights of San Francisco and we'd drive down the freeway, or Route 101, the warm breeze through our hair, listening to the American radio stations as our soundtrack. We were both young and at the start of our careers with our lives stretching ahead of us and it all seemed so exciting. The world genuinely was at our fingertips.

It's funny when you look back at times in your life and the things that stick with you. One of those is American television with all the incessant adverts every five minutes, which really got on my nerves. I loved going to the shopping malls though, which were absolutely massive, and I would spend hours just wandering round feeling like I was in a film. We also spent a lot of our time on the beach. Not the commercial beaches which were always busy, but Matt knew some of the lesser-known ones which were far more peaceful and relaxing, surrounded by tall swaying palm trees. To me, because I hadn't grown up in this type of environment it was like *Baywatch*. The beaches were so long, stretching out for miles each way but then with a normal city or town behind them which seemed odd to me as I'd never seen anything like it on this scale before in my life. I met loads of Matt's friends, mostly skaters, who made me feel so welcome there. By this time I was 21 so I was able to make up for lost time and visit loads of bars and nightclubs in West Hollywood. Because Matt was working pretty much all the time I didn't get the chance to see any of the other shows apart from his, which I saw loads of times. I really regret that now but it didn't cross my mind at the time.

Everyone drives in LA and as a result there isn't really a heavy drinking culture. One night we'd been to a bar with friends and were driving back late at night. I don't know how it happened but all I remember is seeing bright blinding lights coming towards us. I since learned that this old guy had somehow literally pulled out in front of us, and we just smacked into him head-on. It's the only time I've ever been in a car accident. The noise was like nothing I've heard before or since, it was a dull sound unlike what is usually portrayed in films, with the screeching brakes and high-pitched smash. This was a dull, dark thud and then eerie silence. We spun around 360 degrees, and the air bags inflated in a flash. It's a feeling like no other as it's not something you normally experience and I must have immediately blacked out because the next thing I remember is Matt shouting…

"Get out of the car Kerry, get out of the car …"

We were in the middle of the road facing the wrong way and I had no shoes on, probably because I'd been wearing high heels all night that were too painful and I'd taken them off. I grabbed my shoes before getting out of the car and just stood dazed and confused in the middle of the intersection. The other driver had driven off and our car was totalled, but thankfully we were all right with no injuries, not even a bruise. I truly believe this was partly due to our age and how physically fit we both were, but mainly luck. I called my parents later that night to tell them, despite knowing how worried they would be. I was desperate to reassure them. *"Yeah I'm fine, I'm fine…"* I insisted brightly down the line.

The very next day my Dad flew out. He stayed for a few days just to keep an eye on me and check for himself.

Matt was fine about it and because I hadn't been driving it didn't affect me or put me off getting into a car again at all. It hadn't been our fault and we kind of saw it coming. It was almost slow motion. Perhaps if one of us had been hurt it might have been a different matter entirely, but we got back in the driving seat and cracked straight on again.

I even had a go at driving his car while I was there, which I don't remember being insured for but I'm sure he would have thought of that. I'm not sure I would do that now as I think I have become more cautious as I've got older. I soon got used to it and as I remember they didn't have many roundabouts; it was mainly intersections.

When we were still on the ship, Ben Vereen, the American actor, dancer and singer, had come on board and invited me up to his cabin to ask me to sing in his show one night, which I did. It sounds dodgy now but on a ship your cabin becomes your home, office and bedroom all rolled into one because you have nowhere else to go. As it happened there was a group of people already there including his MD but I hadn't known that and didn't really think of the potential risk.

Ben was pleased with my appearance in his show and I stayed in touch him for a while via email after getting off the ship. His MD had a studio in LA and Ben invited me along one day to do some recording even though he wasn't going to be there on that occasion.

It was about an hour drive to the studio from Matt's place and I drove myself in Matt's car without a second thought. I had just come off the freeway and was heading into the town so I was probably ten minutes away from the studio, when I got a flat tyre. I thank God to this day it didn't happen on the freeway as I would have just died, maybe literally, but definitely metaphorically. As luck would have it I had thankfully just passed a garage so I walked back to it, explained what had happened, and they sorted it out for me.

When I eventually arrived Ben wasn't there and it was his MD who greeted me. I immediately noticed this beautiful gleaming white grand piano in the middle of this quite dark navy blue room filled with books.

It was all set up to record, complete with microphone, and he played through a couple of songs which for the life of me I can't now remember, and I just sang along and recorded them. I only spent a couple of hours there, if that. It was quite random and there must have been some incentive for me to go, and I can only assume that it was with a view to working with Ben and touring round with him as one of his backing singers. Perhaps this was a chance for him to see what I sounded like.

It sounds so risky now and potentially dangerous for a young girl to be driving around America and meeting up with a man who was virtually a complete stranger. I didn't have a phone at the time and anything could have happened; I guess it was more by luck than judgement that it didn't.

I have certainly been lucky over the years and have never experienced the type of behaviour that you hear so much about nowadays with the #MeToo movement. If I was a household name, I think it might be different. Some people know me in my field, and others know me through Brian, so although I am recognised as such, I'm not on television all the time, and don't have that exposure which would increase the risk, and perhaps open me up to more of that kind of thing.

There was a nasty incident at Covent Garden tube station more recently where I was groped in the lift. Anyone who is familiar with the lift will know how crowded it can be. It was winter so I was wearing a skirt, tights and a jacket when all of a sudden I felt a hand right up under my skirt and grabbing a feel. It all happened so quickly and I reported it to the police immediately.

TOP TIPS FOR TRAINING

- Aim to put yourself in situations you find more challenging and come out of your comfort zone. At college I would attend the singing class or the musical theatre class because I was good at it and would shine, but as a professional going back I would put myself in those situations where I wasn't so strong to push myself and progress. I know it's difficult at sixteen because you're not really strong enough or experienced enough to make that decision, but try to learn as much as you can.

- Learn from others around you, older and younger. I'm still learning and will never stop. Look to people who you admire and who inspire you, and how they behave. Take in all the good bits from everybody and soak up all the information that you can. It will serve you well.

- Never take your health and physical fitness for granted and try to have a healthy diet, at least most of the time. I wish so much that I'd had a better diet and had looked after myself more at college. I was dancing all the time and active, which was great but I didn't do anything else like I do now. Exercise other parts of your mind and body for different reasons, such as meditation and yoga. I wish I'd known that in my teens.

- Try not to have singing lessons too early as I think it's important to find your natural style and ability. Before sixteen, you are too young and impressionable. However, I don't think there is any harm having the odd few lessons or going to workshops to learn different techniques and guidelines. The lessons I had were quite classical so it was almost like learning another skill. Remember your voice can still be trained later on.

- It's important not to get hung up on how you look. Easy to say I know. Back when I was training, there was a 'type' and you had to conform. If you were beautiful, tall, slim and talented you would do well. Now it's very different and I think there is a lot more being written and produced to give everyone an opportunity. We've moved away from the old traditional-style musicals. Colleges are

79

changing and there's room for everybody in the business, which is great. I did a workshop recently with people from all walks of life who were so interesting and brought their own unique talents. Anyone with a love and passion for the business will find their way whoever they are. If you are going to be different this is the industry to be different in, because we are so accepting of everyone.

CHAPTER 16

Once my visa ran out I had to return from my LA bubble back to the UK. Although we always knew we only had three months, leaving Matt and being separated from him was devastating, and we were constantly on the phone. We made plans for him to come over and visit a month later and I also made a couple of brief return visits. Even so it was tough, and I didn't deal with it very well. However, I was young and resilient, and as time went on we drifted apart and I met someone else.

So there I was, back in the UK with one show and one cruise under my belt. I was quite casual about it all then, and happy to see what came up next. The way I saw it, f nothing did, I would go back on another ship. Easy! As luck would have it, another tour of *Magic of the Musicals* presented itself. This time I didn't have to go through the audition process, they just called me up to tell me it was going out again, and would I like to do it. Apart from Dave and Marti, the entire company was different and I was the only original member. Mitch Sebastian was still the Director but this time Steven choreographed the whole thing and left when we took it on the road. We'd see him occasionally when he popped in but mainly he left us to it.

Steven has stayed in my life ever since college and we are really good mates, he was even Man of Honour at my wedding. Like me, he has remained in the industry and done so well, and we have worked together a lot over the years.

Upon my return from LA I had moved in with my Auntie Pam, in Romford, so when we were dropped off at Victoria I would go back to her. By then I was driving a lot more so it didn't happen quite as much thank god. I also stood in for Marti again on a couple of occasions but this time it was written into my contract as a back up. It certainly wasn't as dramatic.

After the tour finished, life continued relatively smoothly, and whenever I had any downtime, back to Potters I would go. As soon as I'd finished my time on the cruise ship when still in L.A, one of the first things I did was start looking around for an agent to represent me. I spent ages writing to a ton of agents, using the contacts we had been given in college. It was quite difficult to secure someone back then, but I was invited along to meet a few, one of whom was Jonathan Greatorex. He had a really fancy apartment in London and his office was basically his living room, with white leather sofas and shiny wooden floor. To me it felt like walking into a New York apartment with everything gleaming and in its place. I sat on the sofa, where we had an informal chat and just really hit it off. I explained what I done so far and I think because we got on so well he took me at face value. He said he'd be in touch, and just days later he took a punt on me and put me on his books. Not long after the second *Magic Of The Musicals* tour, Jonathan called me to tell me I had an audition for the forthcoming production of *My Fair Lady*. Excited, but with the confidence of youth, I went along to the National Theatre where the auditions were being held, clutching my audition pieces. I felt very well prepared as I'd had plenty of time to rehearse it. I also took in '*This is One of those Moments*' from Yentl and '*In His Eyes*' from Jekyll and Hyde to sing as, at that point, I was under the impression I was only being seen as a swing/ensemble cast member.

I had three auditions in total with Trevor Nunn, David White MD, Trevor Jackson the Casting Director and Matthew Bourne. I think Cameron Mackintosh was in the room at one point as well but I was so focussed on the job in hand that none of it really registered. In the second audition, I'd belted out my two songs after which they asked me if I had anything a bit more 'soprano-esque' prepared to sing. I didn't have anything with me but I knew a bit of *Pie Jesu* so the MD busked along with me to see if I could reach those soprano notes and I managed to get through it fairly well, although it was a bit rough round the edges. I then got another call back to meet Trevor Nunn and read a bit more of the script for him. I think it was Eliza's first scene that I read and I was so nervous, but he really put me at my ease and made me feel so welcome and comfortable. At this point I thought this was standard procedure and I was reading the script as part of the audition process.

It was only when later that day I got a call from Jonathan saying they wanted to offer me the swing role but also wanted me to be second cover for Eliza Doolittle, that I twigged I'd been seen for the part of Eliza without realizing it. It really took me by surprise and I was overjoyed. I honestly didn't think it would happen that quickly. After all, this was my first West End show and I thought I would have to go through working in ensembles and playing supporting roles and bit parts for quite a while yet. For it to be so big, and happen so fast was quite something. The show was going into the National Theatre, and rehearsals were due to start in a couple of weeks. It all tied in well, as by now I was sharing a flat in Morden with Faye from college, so I could commute in easily. It was actually a disgusting dingy little flat but gave me good incentive to keep working; unfortunately, we had a severe case of bed bugs and had to get the place fumigated which gives you an idea of my living standard at the time. We didn't stay there long though and moved further into London on the Northern line to Tooting Broadway.

For me, being so young and inexperienced, the rehearsal period was exciting enough, never mind the show itself. I was suddenly in the rehearsal studios at the National Theatre each day with the likes of Martine McCutcheon, Jonathan Pryce, Nicholas Le Prevost and Dennis Waterman, let alone Trevor Nunn himself. Even so, I don't think I quite grasped how big a deal it was and how respected these people were in the business. Of course I knew Trevor and Cameron were massive, but the rest of it I just took in my stride.

Trevor Nunn is known for workshopping everything very early on, which I didn't know at the time. We did a good few days if not more, of research, improvising and exercises, and I remember being freaked out that we were all doing this together. I was suddenly on this level playing ground and sat next to these incredible actors and we would all be doing these same silly games. Patsy Rowlands would sit on the floor with us all in the beginning and I just couldn't believe it. I was all the while thinking, *"God, she used to be in the Carry On Films and she's sat on the floor next to me!"* She'd be making jokes about being old and how she couldn't get up. It was so surreal.

Of course I realise now that everyone wanted to do *My Fair Lady* at the National with Trevor Nunn; I mean, who wouldn't, and consequently it was an incredibly experienced company who between them had achieved so much. It was just an honour to be amongst them all and surrounded by so much talent. I would sit and chat in the dressing room with various people on many occasions and I think just being around so much maturity, so early on, educated me and eventually further along into the run even spurred me on to take the big step of buying my first flat in Brockley. I shared a dressing room with Sarah Moyle who was in the process of buying her first flat too, so we were able to go through the highs and lows together.

I really wanted a bit of security, and thought it would be a good investment, especially as a performer in this business, with such an uncertain career. Owning my own home was probably going to be the most security I'd have which in turn would give me options. It was difficult though, as I didn't have any past accounts having been paid in cash on the ship so I only really had wage slips to show. Luckily my wages when I went on for Eliza were really good as I would receive a bonus payment for doing it which meant for a few months whilst applying for my mortgage, my wage slips were really healthy looking, enough for me to be accepted and able to buy my little flat, something I never thought I would be able to do, let alone so early and on my own. I think I paid roughly £96,000 for it and put down about £3000 deposit which I'd saved hard for whilst on the ship, plus Potters wages and the tour. From when I was really young my parents always said to me, if you want it, you work for it and you buy it yourself. Nothing was ever handed to me easily. That was ingrained in me from so early on and this was the next logical thing as I'd already bought my own car and was paying my own rent. Mum and Dad had helped me a bit during college, but once I could be self-sufficient I was.

I've always been surrounded by mature people, even when I was fifteen and working at Potters I was amongst adults and people who had lived a bit, so I was constantly being pushed into that kind of realm subconsciously, very early on, and I think business wise I was mature and a bit ahead of my time. Emotionally maybe not so. I am good with my money even to this day. Being so self-sufficient I've always made sure I can pay my mortgage and put petrol in the car. I've never been in debt, never had credit cards and always spent within my means. It helps that I've been fortunate to always be in employment.

Shows of the calibre of *My Fair Lady* just don't happen nowadays. Ensembles tend to be really young and you just don't have that scale of production or collective experience in one show. I do also think the work ethic in the business has changed over the years and nowadays the young generation coming through have such confidence and self-belief which is great and I wish I'd had that, but at the same time I think it's important to have respect for those who have been in the business for years.

There were six of us swings, three girls and three boys. A swing is basically an off-stage performer to cover the ensemble tracks. I learned a lot from the others and remember Margie in particular, a beautiful gorgeous dancer, a bit older than me and who really knew her stuff.   also became very close to another swing, Adam Jones, who had been around for years having done loads of shows.   He had about ten or twelve years on me, and he took me under his wing a little bit. We spent a lot of time rehearsing together, as, being swing, we had to learn more or less everything.   If I wasn't learning the ensemble choreography, I'd be with Matthew Bourne as I was covering the show.   I mean yes, *THE* Matthew Bourne for goodness sake!

It was quite a learning curve for me. I learned all about a swing bible, which I'd never heard of before, and put simply is basically as the name suggests, a big folder or file which is like a big diary of everybody's role or tracks as we call them, throughout the show and has each character's journey including their directions their harmonies, where they are on stage, their costumes, everything, with diagrams of the stage, plotting out where everybody is at every point in the show. So, say I had to go on for one of the ensemble who plays a tiny part, I'd have the whole track down in the book which I could reference quickly and then go on.

I'd never done a pas de deux before and I suddenly had to dance with other people. I had done a little bit in college but nothing like I had to do for the show. Adam really 'mothered' me through all of it, holding my hand through the whole process and we became great friends.

I had to sign in each time I walked in and we would do warm ups which again was totally new to me. I just didn't have a clue what was going to happen or what the routine would be, or the schedule, let alone what was expected of me. It was literally like being thrown in the deep end. Although I had done professional panto, this was a very different experience and suddenly felt very serious and professional with this huge cast and company. Everyone else seemed to know what they were doing and I felt like the only one who didn't. The costume fittings themselves were incredible and I remember saying as I was being measured up "*You mean I get my own costume and pair of shoes and wigs? Don't I have to wear someone else's?"* They must have thought me so naive, and I was.

Initially, for the first week or so, we had a rehearsal schedule pinned up on the notice board so we would know where we had to be, at what time, for what scene, but as time went on we just had a rough guide which could change daily.

As swings we had to learn a lot of scenes, so we were involved mainly in the workshops but also a bit in the main rehearsals where generally we would sit at the front watching and learning from these amazing professionals with years of experience between them. When the show was being placed, we would step in if someone was off for a costume fitting, which was really exciting for us. We would laugh and chat between ourselves in the breaks but mainly sit in complete awe watching these heavyweights of the industry perform their magic in front of us. One particular day, Jonathan Pryce had a bit of a tantrum and threw his pencil on the floor before storming out. This was a big thing, as there were about fifty people in the rehearsal room at the time and the whole room fell into a sort of uneasy silence. I can't even remember what it was about but Trevor had to run after him and obviously sorted it out quite quickly. This was dramatic stuff for a newbie in the business and I absolutely loved it. Martine McCutcheon was a joy to work with and she was so good in the role of Eliza. I only got to see her rehearse a scene once on her own when there wasn't anything going on ensemble-wise I remember her coming in on this one particular day after appearing on the front cover of the latest edition one of the big glossy magazines. This was a massive deal as we didn't have social media then and it was just super exciting to me as she was this big celebrity, and to suddenly be mixing with these household names who were stars blew my mind. I still to this day consider myself so lucky to have had these big experiences very early on in my career.

I was still with Matt during this time even though it was becoming increasingly difficult keeping a long-distance relationship alive, despite the odd visit. With no facetime or messaging we were reliant on telephone calls. We had a bit of time off at the end of rehearsals and Matt managed to fly back from LA to be with me for a few days. However, once he returned, and the show began we just kind of fizzled out, not helped by the fact that by now I had met Neil Johnson, an amazingly talented dancer in the show. I'd never seen a dancer like him, he was unbelievable, and was in fact the guy doing the high splits in the air on the iconic *Fame* poster. Neil had done a ton of West End musicals, so knew lots of places and people and we would go out a lot around London seeing them all. I was drawn to that level of maturity which is probably why we stayed together so long. Coincidentally, during *My Fair Lady* he literally lived round the corner from where I bought my flat in Brockley and we lived between the two flats. I was working hard but playing hard too and it was all fun and games.

Notes from…

We live in a random world and the history of theatre includes many chapters of accidents. When casting *My Fair Lady* (which, somewhat controversially, I directed at the National Theatre in my determination to widen the NT's demographic), I cast the show to include, in the ensemble, understudies and, for the main roles, second understudies. This is usual precautionary practice for big shows, even though it's understood that the second understudies rarely get on to play the role they're covering.

A chapter of accidents unfolded. A few weeks after we had opened, my Eliza fell ill, and had to be replaced by the understudy. A short time later, the understudy fell ill, and so that rare instruction went out, the second understudy has to go on. My second understudy was the young Kerry Ellis. I already knew I could be confident of her voice. At auditions, she had made it clear she had extraordinary range, power and technique. But as she hurriedly went into the role of Eliza, she revealed to me one further ability – the most important one of all.

Kerry can make songs real. She can make a song an indivisible part of dramatic expression, of character, of situation. You don't think, when she is singing a world-famous song, that it's ever been sung before, or that it's even been written down, and learned. You feel it's being created, imagined, felt, by that character at that moment. Frankly, I feel it's the same thrilling conjuration that great actors can achieve with Shakespeare… it's not recitation, it's not delivering a 'famous text', it's language emerging from them at that instant.

Not so long ago, I was privileged to be in the audience at a concert given by Kerry. Again and again, with songs of every style, every age, on every subject, she made something entirely thrillingly real – so the concert wasn't delivering numbers, it was creating an extraordinary succession of micro, one-woman, one-act plays.

I think Kerry is what it's all about. Kerry is where it's at.

Trevor Nunn

CHAPTER 17

Within the National Theatre complex there are three separate theatres, and we were in the Lyttelton, the second largest, which is a conventional proscenium arch theatre. The place is huge and has this incredible community feeling to it with its own canteens and bars, where I admit to spending quite a few nights. I shared a dressing room with all the other swings which was brilliant and had separate little cubicles so each person could have their own space. They are arranged around an internal lightwell, designed to overlook the courtyard so all the actors in the shows can see each other and hang out of the windows to shout across to each other. I think it's a bit of a tradition to all bang on the windows at the same time half an hour before curtain up. Another of our ensemble David Shaw-Parker, or DSP as we called him, would often bring his guitar in and play for us all. It was so magical and unique but I didn't realise and was unaware that these things didn't actually happen all the time.

We previewed at the National for what seemed a long time, roughly four weeks. Previews are a time where you can try things out in a show to see if they work, so basically the show is up and running but its a great chance to put it in front of an audience and change bits of dialogue that perhaps don't work, tweak some choreography, adjust costume changes or even re write whole scenes that don't work. It's almost like a full dress rehearsal and the audience can get reduced price tickets to account for that. I remember going to see *Martin Guerre* in previews and loved it but it changed completely after that. *We Will Rock You* also changed dramatically in its preview period. We would do one scene during the day and it would be totally different in the evening. Our brains would be frazzled.

With *My Fair Lady* it only changed a little bit although when we transferred to Drury Lane they had to cut half the ball scene as it was too long and the curtain needed to come down much earlier. I think it may have been to do with different musicians' rights but it was definitely a much longer show at the National and by moving into a West End theatre, it was cut quite a lot. It was during previews that Martine became sick and the first understudy Alexandra Jay, went on for her a couple of times. She was only 19 and it was her first job out of college.

This one particular morning I got a call from Shaun Kerrison the resident director, sounding worried, *"Kerry you have to get yourself here immediately. Martine is still poorly, and Alex has lost her voice and is exhausted. You and I need to run through the show. You're on as Eliza tonight."* There were literally only a few hours to go. I wasn't even officially meant to be a cover until we transferred to Drury Lane after three months. At the National they don't have second covers so the only reason I was in place at all was because we were going to do a transfer. I'd had no rehearsals at all and had only sat in to observe a few of Martine's rehearsals and watch everything, hence I wasn't really 'rehearsed in' as such, as that was due to happen later, nearer the time. I knew the show and knew her dialogue after watching it avidly over the weeks. I also knew the traffic and her songs, but I had never actually rehearsed it with any of the other actors, let alone been on the stage doing it. I had been on for a couple of the ensemble tracks so I had the experience of being on stage in the show a bit but that was it. Shaun and I got together in this one tiny studio and we literally ran through the entire script on our own. He played every other character and I had to become Eliza. I think the matinee was in progress at the time so we couldn't use the stage, and when that was finished they took me to rehearse a couple of technical movements so that basically I wouldn't get hurt and that was it. I didn't even have a chance to try on any costumes or rehearse the quick changes. It was all we had time for really and a couple of hours later I was on stage as Eliza Doolittle facing a packed house at the National Theatre, London, at the start of my career, thinking *"I'm ready and I've got this"*. Still to this day I think to myself, *"How on earth did I do that?"* but I did, and it didn't faze me. If I had to do that now I would probably freak out.

I had so many quick changes, that I had never done before and I had all these costumes just thrown at me as I came off stage. Jan Johnson was the number one dresser for Eliza, a seasoned and professional dresser, and she was brilliant. She got me through it saying... *"You just stand Kerry and let us do everything. Trust us, and we will get you ready"*

She was right of course, I literally just stood there as she shouted instructions of what I had to do which I obeyed and it all happened miraculously. There were some crazy quick changes one of which was sixty seconds or something ridiculous, but that wonderful team of

90

dressers made it happen. The backstage staff as a whole were incredible, ushering me around and literally placing me where I had to be. Jan would wait for me to exit the stage, get me changed and run me to my next entrance and push me on. That is how the whole show went and I don't really remember much else about it, I think I was so pumped with adrenalin.

The audience were tricky as I heard their reaction to the announcement that the role of Eliza Doolittle would be played by Kerry Ellis. It was like a collective groan and was quite daunting. In those days they would make the announcement just prior to curtain up. I'm not sure they do that now as I believe they put a slip of paper in each programme or a sign, front of house for that very reason. I knew they weren't reacting to me personally, but the fact that Martine wasn't there. Secretly it provided me with the drive to prove them wrong and gave me that kind of spirit to go '*I'm gonna make you enjoy this show*'. Of course I get it, and I've had it myself, if you go to see a show in order to see someone specific and then they're not there, it is disheartening, but then if you get somebody who is great that is brilliant. I have also experienced the flip side of that, where my name is above the title and people have come to see me and then if I'm not in it for whatever reason the feeling of guilt I have is enormous. I understand it from both sides now.

It's a fact that understudies do go on, and have done for years. It's not a shock, and that is the whole point of having them. Nowadays you're almost pre-warned as everything is on social media and we forget about it very quickly. The only time it happens now is if it is a huge star like Sheridan Smith or when illness forced Glenn Close to pull out from Sunset Boulevard at the Coliseum, and my mate Ria Jones went on for her. She ended up with an amazing standing ovation. It is different with musicals. For example, if you are going to see Sheridan Smith in concert and Sheridan Smith isn't there it is a completely different situation from if you are going to see Funny Girl with Sheridan Smith. It is the responsibility of the producers of the show to cast somebody equally talented if not equally well-known and someone who can fulfil the role.

As for me, the press went absolutely mental. This was a headline story. A huge celebrity from Eastenders and a household name, who had recorded her own albums and who was leading in such a massive show

91

suddenly became ill and couldn't go on stage and this young unknown stepped in to take her place. It could have happened to anyone and whoever it was would have got some press coverage. Because I was the second one to go on, it was an even bigger story and I got a lot of attention. There is a well-known quote from the first day I went on when Jonathan actually went out in front of the curtain and said something like:

"Ladies and Gentlemen, you're about to see the debut of Kerry Ellis. This is your first Eliza, it's my second today and my third in two days. If there is anyone in the audience who would like to apply for the role, please pick up an application form at the stage door" This made all the papers the next day! In fact, the press did me a huge favour as it put me on the map and there followed a big double page spread with Baz Bamigboye, a well-known entertainment writer and theatre critic. My big regret is that it is the only role I have played where I don't have any photographs of me at all in costume. We had no smart phones then and had to rely on cameras which weren't allowed backstage.

My reviews were quite favourable and I got some lovely write-ups including a big double-page spread which I think was in the Daily Mail and another one in the Stage which was all new to me, and of course I've kept them, along with so many others. My Mum has most of them but I still have boxes of 'stuff' which I keep promising myself I'll go through one day. When I first went on as Eliza, because I wasn't meant to be playing the role at the National, the only wigs that I had were my 'swing' wigs which were all blonde and they had to be re-dressed. There's a moment in the show where Jonathan had to describe Eliza's hair and eyes which of course were usually brown and he really struggled to force out *BLONDE, BLONDE, BLONDE, BLUE, BLUE.* It was so funny and quite a memorable moment. When we transferred to Drury Lane, I got a brown wig. I think I was the first blonde Eliza which I quite liked.

I try not to read reviews these days and Daniel, my manager will read them first. If it's good he will send it to me and if not he will give me the gist of it if I ask. I don't tend to look at them because I don't think they are helpful. They can end up influencing you so much, as you can't help but take on board the comments, and then go on stage the following night loaded with all that information going round in your head, almost inhibiting your present performance.

Martine was always very nice to me. I in turn was hugely respectful of her. She'd done her training having gone through Sylvia Young's Theatre school but then went straight into television, and a lot of people didn't realise she was a singer. She was in EastEnders for so long that to come out and do a musical of that status was a lot of pressure for anyone to take on even someone who had been in the business for years. It really wasn't easy and I have complete and utter respect and sympathy for her as she was genuinely poorly.

Between Alex and I, we covered Eliza on numerous occasions and essentially shared the role throughout the whole time as Martine was struggling so much with illness and as a result was in the press all the time. They would see her out having lunch one day and the next day she'd be in the paper which all added to the hype of it. It was really tough on her, as she hadn't done a musical for years, and the attention was relentless. She was such a lovely girl and so brilliant in the role when she was there. When it was her birthday she invited us all to a posh nightclub in Chelsea to celebrate with her which was so exciting for me as a nearly 22 year old girl being in London and getting invited to all these special places.

Martine went on to win an Olivier Award for best actress in a musical. When it was announced, they panned the camera round to Jonathan, and so much speculation followed about him looking annoyed because she had won. Personally, I think it was more in frustration, as he was so brilliant and never off. He basically led and carried the entire show, and he didn't get the recognition for it, which I think was sad and a bit unfair. I'm not saying Martine shouldn't have won but he put in a lot of hard work. For her to have been under that enormous pressure and play that role for eight performances a week I think was too much anyway, and would have been for anyone.

We officially opened in March 2001 at the National and transferred to Drury Lane in July. I was called upon quite a number of times, and began to get used to the role, although I found it quite hard as I'm not a soprano singer and never really was. I found '*I Could Have Danced All Night*' particularly difficult because the end of the song was right in my 'break' and to suddenly have to sing in a 'soprano-esque' voice and expose myself was really challenging. On the other side I loved doing it, I loved the pressure and excitement, and I remember feeling like I had won some award. There's a bit in the show where Eliza walks into the library for the first time in her white gown and her entrance is quite high up on the set past the bookcases and she walks across this corridor and then she comes down the stairs to centre stage, and each time it felt like I was at the Oscars, it was so special. That particular scene always stays with me. The sets, designed by Anthony Ward were incredibly authentic and certain items were especially bought from antiques shops, one such item was a crystal whiskey decanter.

In one scene as Eliza, I had to throw my slippers across the stage and on this one occasion I must have thrown them so hard, and so badly, that they hit this crystal whiskey decanter and it completely shattered everywhere. Jonathan Pryce was just a genius in that moment. My face must have been a picture and for a start he had to stop himself laughing, but then he just carried on with the scene as if that was meant to happen, pushing the fragments of glass under the desk or out of harm's way and seamlessly kept going. I learned so much from him and all of them as they all really helped me. It was such a team effort in what could have been a really tricky time. They have all seen me grow up now and whenever we've met up since, we reminisce about that incredible unique time.

When Trevor Nunn eventually saw me in the role, he came up to me when everyone else had gone, took my hand and said "*Thank you Kerry, you've done a brilliant job, thank you.*" I remember those words to this day. To have Trevor Nunn congratulate me and thank me meant so much. We've done lots together since, then but that was such a special moment. He is such an inspiration to work with and in fact I did a workshop with him a couple of years later called '*Way Beyond Blue*' based on Eva Cassidy, which was very script dominated, with a couple of acoustic songs. This stretched me in a way I didn't know was possible and I felt it was some of the best acting I had ever done. There were only a couple of us in the play and we were in the room with Trevor for five days. To have that intense time with somebody of that calibre and doing something that wasn't 'showbiz' felt very real. I couldn't believe how much I learned in such a short amount of time. I had all my words down. The text had gone in and I felt very creative in that moment.

I got opening night tickets so my family were able to come and see me. Mum and Dad needed to come separately so having to choose was tricky and who I invite on such a special occasion has always been an ongoing problem for me. My Dad and brother came to that one and to this day my brother still talks about sitting behind Anthea Turner! We had this amazing massive opening night party at the Waldorf Hotel, which they loved. As time went on the family came to see it on a number of occasions, and they all saw me play the lead role. It was always quite last minute though and not always easy as my Dad was in Suffolk. Soon after the opening he took early retirement at 50 and decided to go travelling.

When he returned from his travels Dad brought Sal to meet me for the first time and I'd arranged to meet them in between shows at the nearby pub. They were then coming to watch me that night playing Eliza. Now I don't remember this, but Sally tells me I ran in to the pub still in pin curls with a stocking cap on my head and all I could talk about was something that was wrong in my flat at the time, which she seems to remember was a plumbing issue, that I needed my Dad to help me fix.

I adore Sal, she's just the best and is always very supportive. She hasn't got any kids of her own but she is so close to my two and is like a second parent to them. Dad stayed in the family home when Mum left him but sold it when he met Sally. They then moved to Newmarket and have been there ever since. Neil and I went to their wedding on 4th October 2003. I've always been really close to my Dad and there has never been a period of time when I haven't seen him.

Apparently our first meeting was all lovely, but a bit of a whirlwind, and Sally just couldn't believe that in another hour I was about to stand in front of two thousand people to do a West End show, and all I was concerned about were the pipes in my flat and asking my Dad to sort it out. It freaked her out, and I don't even remember it. Sal can never understand or quite believe how I remember all my lines. Thinking about it I honestly don't know how I remember them either and it kind of freaks me out too if I dwell on it too much. I do tend to put the work in to start with in respect of learning lines and songs, and usually, once it's in, I've got it. Every time I get a new job that has a lot of dialogue and songs, I always believe I'm never going to learn it all but somehow it all sinks in and happens.

That said, I do like to have a bit of quiet time to myself before going on stage and don't like to be fussed over or have too many people around. I like the half hour call before the show which I use to get dressed and take a moment to gather my thoughts. It's usually just me and gives me time to calm down and think about what I've got to do without any distractions. I like to focus and go over anything I need to.

Musicals are slightly different because you're doing them for so long and you do get into a routine. Even so I do like five minutes to myself. If I'm sharing a dressing room I usually have my own little 'station' so I can still zone out and do my make up

I partied quite hard during the run of the show and would enjoy going out most nights with the cast. There were a lot of gay men in the show who introduced me to gay clubbing, taking me to some the most iconic clubs in London till god knows what time.

I was experiencing loads of things I perhaps shouldn't have done so early on, and made the most of every moment and opportunity, which I think is another reason why now I'm not bothered by all that stuff. I could certainly dance all night and more, and would often be out till six in the morning dancing on speakers and worse. I abused my voice as I would scream, shout, and sing over the thumping music in the night clubs, and in a way learned my lesson fast, as I would be so tired the next day that I seriously doubted my ability to step on that stage and give my all in that evening's performance. Luckily being young I was able to but came perilously close at times.

After we transferred to Drury Lane, I had my first experience of recording a cast album at Angel Studios, of which I was a very small part. I'd done a little bit of studio work before when I was at college. We'd recorded a song for a special Pudsey The Musical which was released for Children In Need. They'd also had a mini studio at Potters with which I'd toyed a bit. This was proper stuff though and it was such great fun all being together, and so different from how I record nowadays, but it definitely sparked an interest for me. It only took two or three days to do. It was all scheduled, so we weren't there when Martine was recording for example, and we came in to do the group songs together.

As well as my own stuff, I've since had some brilliant recording opportunities come my way including featuring on '*Somebody To Love*' with Only Men Aloud fairly early on during my time in Les Mis. I'd performed in a big concert in Wales at the Millennium Centre and from that spent a day in the studio with them. A similar opportunity presented itself with Alfie Boe and I recorded '*Come What May*' with him in London which went on his *Bring Him Home* album after the 25th anniversary of *Les Mis* and went massive. I feel so lucky to be on that album.

CHAPTER 18

We all settled into our roles and the show was going really well. I was happy alternating between off stage swing, ensemble and covering for Martine. I was getting a massive amount of experience and loving the show and the social life that went with it.

One night as I was nearing the end of my contract, unbeknown to me Brian May came to watch the show with Mike Dixon, the Musical Director of *We Will Rock You*. I still don't know why they came; they might have been looking for people to cast or just to see the show. Whatever the reason, I was in the ensemble that particular night and Brian spotted me. The story in the papers has always been that I was on for Martine when he first saw me, but in fact I was standing in for an ensemble member. I had no idea that Brian was in, let alone that he had seen me, but I often wonder what would have happened in my career if I hadn't gone on that night. He came back a second time, with Pippa Ailion the Casting Director, and this time I was covering for Martine, and it was from that they asked me to audition for *We Will Rock You*. I have no idea though how he picked me out to begin with. He has since said that he saw something in me. As far as I was concerned I just got a random call from my agent telling me I had this audition. I didn't know till a long time after that Brian had been in and thought for ages that it came from the casting director, who incidentally went on to cast me in *Wicked* later on.

Jorg Betts was now my agent as I'd only stayed with Jonathan Greatorex for about six months. I seem to remember he was going through a particularly bad time in his personal life and was closing his agency. It was Jonathan himself who had suggested Jorg to me and to several other artists who were on his books, as he knew Jorg was branching out on his own after working with another agent previously, and it was a relatively new business for him. I subsequently met with Jorg, we hit it off and he took me on, which was how it was for pretty much the next ten years. He was hugely influential over my theatre career and was brilliant at what he did.

Auditions for *We Will Rock You* were held in the Dominion Theatre in Tottenham Court Road, where the show was going to be staged, and I remember going down these dark, dingy, musty-smelling red-carpeted stairs to the audition room.

In my first audition I sang '*Holding Out for a Hero*' and '*Total Eclipse of the Heart*', after which I was sent a call back along with the script and the music for '*No One But You*' and I remember learning the song in my dressing room at Drury Lane, knowing I was going to be singing it for Brian May. Prior to the show I was familiar with the music of Queen and knew all their big hits as my Dad had played their music a lot. However, I didn't know '*No-one But You*' and had never even heard of it. I remember Freddie Mercury passing away and being at Potters when I heard that news, so I was fully aware of what a big deal this was, even though I was only sixteen at the time and didn't have that connection. Brian vividly remembers me singing this at the audition and apparently he said to someone 'that's the girl for the role'. However, despite this I just kept being called back and ended up having seven auditions in total, with various other people all over a period of a few weeks. I never let Brian forget that he could have saved me a lot of heartache!

One of my auditions was with Cameron Jack who then became the understudy for Nigel Clauzel, who played Britney opposite my character. Cameron has gone on to great things and done loads of movies and television, and Nigel is Head of Drama at Bedford University. Years later I went to see another show he had put on there which was great and another full circle.

Up to then I had been going into the auditions fairly neutral, mainly wearing black. However, in the penultimate audition, Pippa asked me if I could rock it up a bit and come in a bit more dressed up for the part. I did as she asked and I wore these black leather trousers and a red leather halter neck which were just horrible, but the outfit obviously screamed rock chick and I was given the role of Meat so it can't have been that bad! To this day I thank god there are no photos of that audition because I'd die.

If I'm being really honest I don't remember much about the audition process or having any sense of how big this could be, nor did it register that I was auditioning for Brian May, who wrote the song! I don't think I even knew he was going to be in the audition room. Although I knew who the show was for and what it was I only really expected to see the casting director and director. However, each time I went in to audition there was a panel of about twenty people amongst whom were Arlene Phillips, Ben Elton, Christopher Renshaw, (the Director at the time, who only stayed for six months before Ben Elton took over and changed everything), Mike Dixon the MD, Pippa, Brian and Roger. Robert De Niro had money invested in the show so there was always a video camera set up to film in order for it to be sent back to him. In my mind it was just another audition and I didn't take on the gravity of it. I had the comfort of still being in a big show, which really helped. My thoughts were, *"If I get this then great, but if I don't I could maybe stay on in My Fair Lady for another year"*. There was a bit of an option there and I think that's what gave me the confidence to be a little more relaxed. I had been working a fair bit by then too so I was starting to build up an inner confidence and security in myself. I've gone through my whole career with the attitude that if this doesn't happen then something else will, and I think that sparked early.

By now they'd brought in Joanna Riding to take over from Martine, as Alex and I were going on too much, and Martine needed to leave the show. This was towards the end of my contract and I only had about a month to go. Jo was like a workhorse and she just didn't go off which was probably just as well as this all coincided with my auditions for '*We Will Rock You*' and I was already on a different path.

I actually left *My Fair Lady* two weeks early. They released me from my contract on the understanding that I would be on standby if I was needed. As I was a swing it didn't affect the show as such. The two shows overlapped for a bit and I was only called back for one performance. Shows by their very nature do sometimes get themselves into predicaments where they just don't have the cover in place. I remember once in *Mamma Mia* when they literally didn't have anyone to play the role of Donna when my mate Caroline Deverill was injured, but luckily Steph Parry, who had played it before was only a few minutes away as an understudy in *42nd Street* and was able to step in. That was pure luck though and not the norm!

In those days you used to be able to take the odd day off as holiday and I think people used to space out those little days and perhaps take a long weekend here and there. Nowadays you have to book in a block of three days minimum at a time, which is really difficult when you've got a big company of 30-odd people trying to arrange all those holiday dates. It's a logistical nightmare.

Neil carried on in the show for a while when I left. He had always been incredibly driven and was an experienced dancer, but during the run began to suffer a few health issues and found his body wasn't taking it any more so decided he wanted to find another route in life. The pounding a dancer takes can be quite brutal, plus he was getting a bit older and his hip began to play up. I believe he now has a studio at Chelsea FC but back then once he'd qualified he began with a studio in Soho teaching Pilates.

The fact that I was going from a brand new show to another brand new show was pretty big in itself, but this was also a step up because now I was going to be creating a role which no-one else had played before and it was a huge deal.

Now that Brian has been in my life for twenty years and I listen to all the stories he tells me about Freddie, I find it heart-breaking that I didn't get to see them play. If a documentary comes on about them and Freddie's life it breaks my heart and I wish so much that I had been able to have the opportunity of seeing them.

Some years later Brian put together a brilliant book of the show, which contains a few of the first early rehearsal photos which were held in Alford House, or as we affectionately ended up calling it Awful House. I think it was a school or youth centre in the middle of a huge council estate in South London, with nothing else around it apart from a big Tesco's. It had plenty of room for us all including stage management and all the creatives, which we needed as we were a big company and a lot of people were involved. We must have been there for six or seven weeks, which is a long time for a rehearsal period.

On the first day we were due to have a read-through of the script, which prior to this we hadn't been given. This in itself caused me massive anxiety and took me right back to those school days. Not being a brilliant reader, I was terrified that I would start to stutter, or mess it up, which made me very nervous, as I didn't want to look stupid and not be able to pronounce a word in front of a room full of professional industry people. As we walked in we had a meet and greet and introduced ourselves over a cup of tea, then all sat round in a big semi-circle where we were handed the dreaded scripts. Everyone was there including Brian and Ben, Roger and Arlene and suddenly I had to read this script. Just thinking about it now brings back all the anxiety and makes me shake. I started scanning through that script as quickly as I could, to see where my lines were and to check I knew the words and that I wasn't going to mess it up, desperately trying to highlight it quickly. Luckily I was fine, and this is the thing with me, it's not an issue, it's just my brain and my mind panicking but it's always fine. It's something I've only really managed to overcome in the last five years.

Brian and Ben were really hands on, in fact Brian was in on almost all of the music calls during this time. On the day I got to work on '*No One But You*', he was in the room along with Mike Dixon and after I sang it through we had this discussion about how it wasn't really exposing me enough or fulfilling what I was able to give, so I jokingly said, "*How about a key change?*" which was probably a bit brazen of me.

"*Oh my god yeah, let's try that*" Brian replied immediately. So we did, and it was put in the show. If Brian hadn't been in the room that just wouldn't have happened. Just a brief suggestion and he was able to jump on it and make the decision there and then.

After the read through the adrenalin buzz was amazing. Hearing the show for the first time was great. As rehearsals went on they wanted my character to be harder, and sound a bit harsher because Hannah Jane Fox who played Scaramouche had a very South London accent, Galileo, played by Tony Vincent, was American and I think they wanted a bit of diversity. They asked me if I knew any accents which I didn't as I was never really good at accents at college, so they suggested I try a Scottish one, as it would sound quite hard. I didn't think I was any good but I worked closely with Cameron, who was a real Scots in the show, and he helped me so much to make the character a lot harsher. They also got a vocal coach in to help me.

I found it quite a challenge but at the same time enjoyed it and it just completely changed who I was. I'm not that brassy, harsh character but the accent gave me the confidence to play it in that way and the freedom to be a bit sassier and harder. It was almost like adding another layer to the character which I hadn't done before and was really useful. I remember that being quite a big thing as far as I was concerned. They kept the accent for the role for the first five or six years and then if someone was cast who already had a strong accent they went with that. I think the idea initially was because Hannah and I were very similar and they needed that change, as they thought it was funny for her to have a South London accent!

CHAPTER 19

I would drive into London each day for rehearsals as it was before the congestion charge came in. I did the same when I was in *My Fair Lady* and would just park on a single yellow line, which was madness and I can't believe it now.

We rehearsed long hours, often working 9.00am to 9.00pm, and working with Arlene Phillips was a joy. I mean, she was completely nuts and bonkers but we all loved her.

The last run through we had in Awful House was in front of Robert De Niro with no set or anything. He sat in a chair in front of us and we all freaked out at this prospect. Here was *THE* Robert De Niro about to watch us all perform in our rehearsal space, in our sweaty rehearsal gear, with no set. He seemed to like it though and made a speech afterwards saying well done to us all. He also attended the opening night and we all had our picture taken with him backstage. He really only swooped in and swooped out again which is probably just as well as we were all terrified when he was there.

This was followed by a two or three week tech run in the Dominion Theatre. Roger was the total rock star, he wasn't perhaps as vocal as Brian but he would always be there for the chats and any announcements. The two of them are just very different people. He just led the typical rock star life, whereas Brian is different and incredibly hands on. He knows exactly what he wants and is very strong-minded, but in getting there he is very open to suggestions, although I didn't know that back then. He will sit back and listen to what everyone has got to say and digest it before making his own decision. Brian and Roger are so clever and two of the loveliest guys in the industry, and they both appreciate talent in others.

The show changed dramatically during that time. Big bits of set were cut, big scenes were cut, even a whole flying scene went. I used to sing '*Tie Your Mother Down*' and that was cut out completely. There was also a little side story of Meat and Scaramouche that didn't really work, as it wasn't particularly relevant and didn't help move the story along, so that was axed too. The show changed constantly. Ben would come in forever changing the dialogue. In previews we would be rehearsing one show in the afternoon and performing a different version of it in the evening, only for it to change a couple of days later. Luckily we were young enough and resilient enough to deal with it. If that happened to me now it would freak me out, but at that age I just got on with it and my brain was sparkier. It was tiring though, again with twelve-hour days often finishing at 11pm. It was such a big technical show in every aspect, and I remember us falling asleep in the auditorium sometimes with exhaustion. Tony Edge was our Resident director and such a nice man, so brilliant at his job of maintaining the show, which can't have been easy.

The sitzprobe was held in the loft space at the Dominion Theatre which has since been converted into lovely studios, but at the time was really tatty with a hole in the roof. The sitzprobe is basically the first time you run the show through with the band, usually at the end of the tech run and probably about three or four days before the show opens. For eight weeks or so we had rehearsed with just a piano and suddenly we had the full band and all the singers coming together. It was electric and I will never forget that day. It was just incredible, and it all felt right and special to the show as the room felt a bit rocky. It was edgy and grungy with black cloth everywhere. Perfect!

Previews went brilliantly well and we really thought we were onto a winner as it ticked all the boxes. A huge lavish show with the most amazing music and also incredibly funny. There wasn't one night where we didn't get a standing ovation. The music constantly had a huge reaction and the laughs and engagement were changing along with the script. Ben had been changing the scenes around if they weren't working and by the time we got to the official opening night I was in such a good place knowing how it had been received, that I felt comfortable, and don't remember any nerves for the actual show. Any I did have came from pure excitement. The response from the audience on the opening night was unbelievable. They were going nuts from the minute the show started with that unmistakeable intro to *Innuendo* rumbling through the auditorium. Everyone started screaming and barely stopped throughout, it was like being at a rock concert. By the end of the show they were on their feet. It was exactly the reaction we were hoping for but never imagined. The standing ovation seemed to go on forever and we were all on an incredible high. We then celebrated at the opening night party with a line-up of celebrities and stars at the London Astoria, now demolished but then a proper grungy music venue with a sticky floor. At Brian's suggestion, because it had been cut from the show, he and I sang '*Tie Your Mother Down*' together. It went down amazingly well and everyone went nuts for it. It was mental, this crowd of pop and rock stars were cheering and stamping for me!

I think the company got one extra pass each for the party so Neil came along too. He'd been in the business for years and was used to these occasions having done the whole musical theatre thing, so he wasn't as excited as I was, but he was nevertheless pleased for me and fully supportive of everything I was doing.

A couple of days later, we were still on this massive adrenaline high from such a memorable evening, and I remember us all being called together in one of the bars in front of the auditorium, for what seemed like an emergency meeting. Apparently the reviews had hit all the papers and the show had been slated. They wanted to discuss what next, and what the plan was. It was decided to advertise and put out some good publicity to hopefully counteract the bad reviews which is what happened and we appeared on Parkinson to promote the show.

What struck us as particularly strange was that those reviews didn't seem to affect the sales at all. People were coming in their droves and we were full to capacity every night. Bad reviews, yet we were still packed, it was so weird.

2002 was the Queen's Golden Jubilee, and Brian kicked off the Party at the Palace concert with his iconic performance of the National Anthem on the roof of Buckingham Palace, which of course was extraordinary. Afterwards the press surrounding the show suddenly increased, ticket sales went mental, audience reactions nearly lifted the roof off the Dominion and blew those bad reviews out of the water. All these years later the show is still touring, having been all around the world.

As a company, we also took part in the Golden Jubilee celebrations. After our matinee performance at the Dominion, we remained in our costumes and all got on a bus which took us through London in full stage gear. As we went into the designated stage door entrance at the back of the Palace, we had to go through full airport style security with metal detectors, and literally every single one of us set off the alarms as we were

106

all wearing bullet belts with metal and chains draped all over us. It was a constant 'beep, beep, beep, beep, beep,' and we were all laughing so much. It took us forever to all get through.

It was a great day and we were all gobsmacked when Ozzy Osborne stormed our rehearsal. Halfway through he just walked on the stage looking confused and asking if it was his turn yet. Here was Ozzy Osborne just casually bumbling about amongst us. My character's name changed over the years to Ozzy (Osbourne) and I'd love to think it was because of that!

The cast were also invited to appear at Party in the Park where this time I got to sing 'No-one But You' in front of 70,000 people, which I'm sure was probably Brian influenced. We only had a twenty-minute segment, and the songs we were about to perform took up 15 minutes, so the fact that I got to sing something that wasn't really a well-known Queen song, must have been pushed by Brian. He would come and watch the show a lot in the early stages and he had a real interest in that song as it was so special and personal to him.

Dealing with Freddie's passing, his subsequent funeral and then his absence on a daily basis was really difficult for Brian and all the band. It is something they are still dealing with now, every day of their lives in their different ways. In November 1996 the band all went to Montreux for the official unveiling of Freddie's statue. Brian had written the inscription on the statue which read, 'Freddie Mercury, Singer of Songs, Lover of Life'. A few hundred people had gathered around the lake on this rainy November day and Brian told me he suddenly felt an overwhelming sense of anger that Freddie was no longer with us and that he'd lost his dear friend. Anger turned to sadness and tears but he couldn't tell if anyone else was crying because of the rain. It was then he began to hear the song forming in his head. He started wondering if Freddie could hear it too, and if he would want us to cry which inspired the lyric, "Do You Want Us To Cry".

The song refers to Freddie living a life that was very daring and very intense and likens him to Icarus flying too close to the sun It was the first song that Brian, Roger and John recorded without Freddie in 1997, and subsequently released early in 1998 along with a video. It was also John's last recording as a member of Queen. Apparently there were a few disagreements about the pitch of the song and the tempo and how it should have been a bit higher or a perhaps bit quicker. It ended up with a lot of little Queen trademarks in there and unlike the title might suggest, isn't morbid at all and very positive. Brian always says that Freddie did a hell of a lot of good stuff with his life, and the song kind of reflects that.

Brian always reminds me about the day that I went in to sing the song for him at my audition and how I went in with my sheets of music, walked over to the piano, quite nervously brushing my hair behind my ears, and going a bit red. He said there was a kind of breath that I put into the song that suddenly gave it a whole new lease of life and from then he felt that it became my song. Years later he has said to me many a time,

"*This is your song now, it belongs to you*". I have sung it all over the world, with him, without him, in all different scenarios and I'm really grateful for this beautiful song.

I think though that to see it performed during that earlier time offered some comfort to him. He would come and give me notes and suggestions every so often, some of which I would rebel against and some I would take on. I remember in particular he would try and get me to take a bow after the song and I resisted it. I never really did it. I couldn't, as I felt it broke the mould and I couldn't bring myself to take that moment, which he really wanted me to have. The song got such a reaction, and he wanted me to have that moment to thank the audience. He gave lots of people notes and we would see him every few weeks. Ben was the same and we all got to know them quite well during that time.

Mazz Murray came into the show about six months in, to take over as the Teacher. We hit it off straightaway and were mates from day one. She went on to play Killer Queen for years, after Sharon and I left the show. Mazz has been a big influence in my life and supported me through break-ups, babies and weddings, everything really. We talk through stuff and rant at each other a lot. We are totally there for each other and can get stuff off our chests which you need to get rid of sometimes. We don't see each other a great deal as she is always working and also has a family, but we do try, and we talk a lot.

Around the same time that Mazz joined, the cast album was recorded off the desk as a live album. As such, there were certain moments where they needed to do a few drop ins or covers for times when there was too much audience noise. These were done at Brian's studio in his home outside of London.

I will never forget going to Brian's that first time with a few others. He has this amazing tree-lined driveway leading up to his house which changes with the seasons and is stunningly beautiful. I've been driving up that same driveway for nearly twenty years now and it always feels like the magical forest and a pathway to optimism.

It's so exciting and such a buzz as I just never quite know what we're going to create on that particular day, or what we're going to come out with.

The studio set-up was upstairs, and then downstairs, at the bottom of this big staircase, was where the vocals were recorded. I remember standing there singing 'No-one But You' and thinking, "Oh my god I am in Brian May's house singing one of his songs". As a company we knew him really well but I hadn't yet started working with him and we certainly hadn't formed a friendship.

The show gathered momentum and was beginning to be really successful here. It was due to open in Spain and they had a Spanish celebrity, Eva Maria Cortes, lined up to play my character Meat. She recorded 'No-One But You' in Prague as a promo for the show and to make it a bit of a big deal. I remember Brian bringing the new and lovely orchestrated version of the track back from Prague and insisting I do the vocal on it. I recorded it in the studio, and it eventually ended up on my *Wicked in Rock* album, released when I went into *Wicked* some three years later. I think it was from that point, Brian realised I had something else to give, and asked if I wanted to explore a bit more studio recording and work on some songs. That is where it all sparked from.

It all happened really slowly though and was a gradual process. I didn't even get to go in the studio again until a couple of years later when I would go along in the day for a few hours and we would play around with different songs, different arrangements and different styles. It was very sporadic even then, perhaps once a month, and we would have to fit it in

109

with when he was back home and I wasn't busy with the show. I always took the studio stuff with Brian with a pinch of salt, and whilst I thought it was great I didn't think it would go anywhere and expected nothing from it. Why would I? He had worked with Freddie so why would he be seriously bothering with me? I just thought he was helping me out a bit. I never forced the issue either, and it has always been quite organic and a pleasant thing for us to do, which I think is why we have worked together for so long now. There has never been a label breathing down our necks waiting for us to deliver another album, so it has always been as and when we wanted to. In the early days I just thought it was a brilliant experience, and I was grateful for all the information and experience Brian was giving me. I was learning so much, but I had no expectations at all. I didn't even realise that he wasn't working with and inspiring other young singers and performers, or that the studio wasn't filled with tons of other artists. He was always incredibly supportive and subsequently came to see me in Miss Saigon and every show I've done since. Our working relationship ramped up a level when I was in Wicked, which is when I became the driving force behind the album. It was a case of I wanted an album now, so let's deliver.

CHAPTER 20

A year in, when my contract was up for renewal, I had a good chat with Jorg as I wasn't sure if I should move on or not. At the time, there wasn't really anything around that I wanted to do, and Jorg was of the opinion that as I had created the role and was on good money, I should give it another year before coming out, which is what I did. It was great, as this meant I had a bit of security and regular money coming in for a couple of years. I was able to live life, pay the bills, and even go on holiday to the Maldives at one point, without giving it much thought.

I did all my partying and drinking when I was very young, especially at Potters, and, as such, got it all out of my system. During my two years in *We Will Rock You*, as a cast we would go out on Thursday, Friday and Saturday nights after the show until the early hours, getting up to all sorts. Most of us were in our early twenties and here we were in the centre of London, feeling like rock stars.

After each show we were just so pumped and ready to hit the town. I partied really hard but I still managed to get up and do the show next day with no problems at all, and bounced back really quickly. I was young, and although I had a part in the show, it wasn't a massive responsibility and I only had a few songs, which enabled me to party as well, and I made the most of it! No matter what though, work came first though, I always had an eye out for my next challenge, and I did a few solo gigs over that time in a small grungy rock bar in North London.

I definitely wouldn't be able to do all that now. Apart from having the kids to think about, I find alcohol quite tough on my voice so if I'm singing I just won't drink. It really does ruin my voice and it's too difficult to recover from. My family aren't big drinkers really, in fact my Dad is teetotal and always has been. I still enjoy the odd night out and I'll have a few glasses of wine but then I'll pay for that. My tolerance for alcohol is rubbish and no longer do I go out after a show. Having said that, I have certainly been drinking more in lockdown!

I had a few auditions towards the end of that second year which came to nothing, but then I heard there was to be a second national tour of *Miss Saigon* and they were auditioning for the role of Ellen. I went in to meet Cameron Mackintosh and Trevor Jackson, the Casting Director, at the

American Church in Tottenham Court Road, which was only down the road from the Dominion. I did a bit of a workshop first with Trevor, feeling quite confident and buoyed up by the success I was currently enjoying. After the workshop they turned round and said no to me straightaway, and that I wasn't right for the role which I was ready to accept.

Jorg couldn't believe it though and really fought for me, insisting they gave me another chance and saw me again, as, with the right amount of encouragement and direction, I would be perfect as Ellen. He reminded them that I'd worked with them before and had proved what I could do, plus I was currently in a big show. His insistence paid off and they called me in again. This time I worked with them, listened carefully and took direction, and they gave me the role. I think sometimes casting directors can be influenced by the show you are in at the time. There I was in a rock show trying to go into something a bit more traditional and maybe they didn't want that sound. I had previously auditioned for *Miss Saigon* when I left college and didn't get it, so I'd already been through it before with this show. The show had been out of London for a while and to be honest I wasn't massively sure about going on tour again, but I desperately wanted this part and I just felt this was my time to get this role, and luckily they gave me the chance.

There was only a matter of a week or two from coming out of *We Will Rock You* to going into *Miss Saigon*. A few of us were leaving as our contracts came up for renewal at the same time. On my last performance Brian came on the stage, and thanked myself and Sharon, who was also leaving, and gave us flowers, which was lovely. We had a big leaving party and it was a bit emotional as I was leaving the show that had become such a big part of my life and people who I had become close to over the two years, but I had the luxury of going straight into another show.

Brian and I will often talk about the highs of a big show and the sense of loss you feel afterwards. I have never really had that because I am always looking forward to the next thing I am planning or doing. I do however, experience the immediate comedown the day after. Whether I've been in a big show for a year or been part of something massive that's just for one night, it's the comedown period the very next day that's so tough, and is what I based my podcast on, to see how others in the business deal with it. I could have been on stage the previous evening playing to thousands or starring in a West End show for the last year, and then suddenly the next day I'm in the supermarket or doing the dishes and have a reality check of how normal things have suddenly become. When it gets to that time of day when I would have been doing the show again it's a bit strange and takes a little while to adjust. So although I'm always ready for the next thing in my career, the comedown period is an immediate thing that hits quite hard.

That really was my life whilst doing musicals, I always had something else to focus on next and another show to work on that I could look to; even it wasn't a big show, I made sure I had a performance, or a concert or even a workshop to fully focus on. Of course I can't orchestrate it but I do try and influence it. If I didn't have anything I think it would be quite frightening for me, and I would have to face that comedown head, on which I don't want to do.

It came as quite a surprise to me when I had a complete meltdown at the beginning of lockdown which came out of nowhere, and I completely lost it. I can see now that it was the fact I had nothing in my diary and nothing to go to. Suddenly, there were no opportunities and nothing to look to or plan for next, and it broke me. It was what sparked me to do my podcast and write this book. I needed to do something and focus on something. It's quite possible I would never have done either of these things during 'normal' life as I just didn't have the time. I'm not very good at just sitting still and doing nothing. I need something constantly going on in my life, which is loaded with so many things. I need it as a creative outlet as well as for my self-worth, and of course I need it to provide and earn money for myself and my family. It's something I have always done and is a huge part of who I am. If I didn't have my career I really don't know how I would feel or what I would do.

I think it is a positive thing in life generally to have that next focus. So yes, *We Will Rock You* was fun and I'd loved it, the show had brought me so much and some great friendships, but I was more than ready to go and face my next challenge.

Before I knew it, rehearsals were underway, but this time, thank god, there was no read through as such, because the show is completely sung through. The part of Ellen isn't that big and quite insular, and she doesn't make her first appearance on stage until right at the end of Act One. Consequently, they all rehearsed for about 6 - 8 weeks and I joined for the last four. It always feels a bit strange if you're not in right from the beginning so although I was eased in gently, I didn't have that big first day like I'd had on other shows.

Some of the cast had done it before but there was no one from the original London cast. They split the part of Kim between two girls, Miriam and Jen, both lovely with great voices. Hugh Maynard, who I've gone on to work with a lot since, played John. It wasn't a long process for me. It may have been a smaller part, but it was integral to the show and I was so excited to be there. The music is great and I remember Claude-Michel Schonberg who wrote the piece was around a lot and he was lovely; again, being around those sort of people was a privilege. We had a change of Director within the first few weeks. Lawrence Connor was brought in to shake things up a bit; he was originally the Assistant Director so it was natural he should take over, and came as no surprise. Before we knew it we were off on tour. We didn't stay long in each place, perhaps two or three weeks, and we covered the whole country. It was a big tour and it was the first time they didn't use the helicopter on stage, using a projection instead which some people liked and some didn't. It was generally accepted though, because the show is so magical and the music is so powerful.

It was great touring with a Filipino cast, they were like a family within themselves and a really strong unified group. They clubbed together, as some lived in London but most of them had come over from the Phillipines and they created their own social gatherings, and would cook on Sundays and invite each other round. Being on the road with tons of young people was almost like going back to being a student. It was great fun but also hard at times moving around and living in different digs. There were no sat navs back then so finding the digs wasn't always easy and I'd have to get an actual map! We were responsible for arranging our own accommodation; some I would do in advance, and some I would sort whilst on the road.

Over the years I've stayed in some of the best, and some of the worst digs, ranging from the most incredible hotels in the world when I toured with Brian, places I could never have imagined that he had stayed at with Queen, to the comedy B&B's during Magic of the Musicals. Mind you, anything that came after my caravan at Potters was better, so I was never disappointed. Now I'd be horrified, but if I hadn't had those earlier experiences I would have had nothing to compare them to.

I enjoy driving and would always drive myself to each venue, because of the independence and freedom it gave me to take control of my own time. It meant if I wanted to pop out to perhaps get a sandwich or go back to the digs for something, then I could do so without having to wait for a tour bus or rely on someone else. I didn't share digs either, again for the same reason, because I value being in control and independent.

It was quite hard playing the role of Ellen because people don't like her, and the audience doesn't want her to be there, so it was down to me to create that empathy for her. A lot of people who had played her in the past have said how lonely a part it is. You are on your own in the dressing room for virtually the whole first part of the show, as everyone else is on stage, then you come on and do your number. We didn't have smart phones then so I couldn't get on the internet, and instead I started to get a bit obsessed with competitions. I bought loads of magazines and entered everything I could, winning a whole bunch of stuff such as cosmetics and even a holiday. I was quite happy to sit and chill for a bit, and didn't mind filling my time at all, as I'm quite content with my own company. I mean of course I wanted to be on the stage, but I was okay with it. I was just happy to be in a big show and play my part. And of course, I had those moments, and got to sing two brilliant songs. I liked the challenge of Ellen and the fact I needed to make people like her. I made it my driving mission to make the audience feel compassion for her and I like to think I got it right.

When I'm in a show I am usually immersed in the story itself, but just occasionally it doesn't happen. This was especially so on the Saigon tour because they used local kids and as such they would vary considerably. If Kim's son was played by a really cute little kid who looked vulnerable it would break my heart and make it easy to bring out all the emotion. We needed about five children to cover the role in each town and city, and I remember in one particular area we visited, they struggled with this so had to cast the best they could. At one point we had a lad that was almost my height and I had to pick him up at the end which made me chuckle to myself and I had to really dig deep for that performance!

Steve Houghton played my husband 'Chris' in the show and we also had a lot of giggles. There is a scene in Act 2 where Kim and Ellen have just met and Kim goes running off stage crying. It's a moment of high emotion. Chris then comes on stage and has his breakdown, at which point I am facing upstage and have to turn to face him, and we have a bit of a shout down. Now, Steve and I were great friends, and had a similar sense of humour, and we were both a bit giggly on this one performance from something that had happened during the day. For some reason we completely lost the plot which resulted in the best kind of laughing but at the same time the very worst as we tried to contain this hysteria bubbling up uncontrollably, and all the while he is meant to be having this dramatic break down. We simply could not afford to lose it. It was one of the funniest moments I've ever had in my life but it was horrific. When I came off stage I was just mortified but I think we just about got away with it.

I had good reviews, but more to the point I WAS reviewed, and mentioned in most of them which was great in itself. The tour went on for a year and we managed a couple of breaks during that time. Neil and I had been really strong for the first couple of years but the cracks started to appear. I would try and get back home whenever I could, if I wasn't too far away and he came to see me occasionally on tour, but by then he was quite busy starting up his business. He went from working at Third Space, which is a swanky gym in Soho, to setting up his own Pilates Studio, so circumstances started pulling us apart from each other which I believe was the beginning of our eventual split. Being so young I was unaware that I wasn't perhaps getting the support I needed from him, although admittedly I probably didn't behave as well as I should have done. It was probably a combination of all those things which led to our break-up further down the line but at this point we were still making plans and continuing on as normal. It's always a weird situation anyway being away on tour and coming home just for that one day. It is so difficult, as you are slotting into somebody else's rhythm and that is tough. You need a good couple of days to adjust usually, but by then it's too late, and you're back on tour again. Also, I only had to think about myself on tour and was used to doing everything I wanted to do when I wanted to do it. Suddenly when you get home you have to readjust to compromising and sharing, a bit like being a kid again.

I still find that hard now, but I make sure I don't go away for long periods of time any more. Everything changes when you have kids and now the boys are at school it is even harder. I'm not gunning for a show any time soon, because it can consume your life and I would no sooner be picking them up from school before I'd have to leave to go to the theatre. I wouldn't get to have a Saturday with them, and we would only really have Sundays together, which is not enough.

We make sure there is always one of us here, or my parents, or James' parents. We've also had three amazing au pairs recently who all stayed with us for roughly six months, and a couple of comedy ones who didn't stay very long at all. The boys would always come on tour with me but once they started school it became such a juggling act, and as our parents are both forty-five minutes away we needed that extra support. The problem with what we do, and our lifestyle, means it isn't standard babysitting hours, so one day we might have needed someone to pick up Fred from nursery at midday, then go and pick up Alfie from school, then have them both for a few hours and then we'd be home. At other times they wouldn't do anything for a week. We keep weird hours but childcare has always been a constant and we are both here as much as we can for that reason. I don't want them to ask, "*Where were you?*" in the future. The boys are my priority and always come first. It probably helps that I had so much of my career by the time I had my kids and had done so much already, so by the time they came along I didn't feel like I was sacrificing work for them. My choices are a little bit different now, and we make it work as a family. I sometimes wonder if I'd had kids in my twenties, if it might have been a different story.

Six months into the tour of *Miss Saigon*, Neil and I bought a property together. I sold my flat to put the money in, and Neil re mortgaged his flat, and we bought an amazing house in Brockley just round the corner. It was an incredible house and we loved living there, but on reflection it was almost a case of too much too soon and in the end we were only in it for just over a year. How we managed to do it all, and move in, whilst I was still touring, I'm still not sure, but we did. I seem to remember it was quite a quick process, although I was only moving from my first home, which was tiny and I didn't have a great deal of stuff. The show ran smoothly and despite being apprehensive about touring to begin with, it turned out well, and I was quite happy doing it.

Notes from…

24th April 2008. That was the day I first met Kerry. A day I'll never forget – and just in case I do, I have it tattooed on my chest, by my heart!

The stereotypical "best man" meets "bridesmaid", but it was so much more than that from the very beginning.

I had no clue who she was, or what she did, even when trying to chat her up at the bar at the wedding, she was very modest, humble and reserved about what she did for a living. *"I'm in a show called Wicked in the West End"* …that's all she really said

It wasn't until our 'official' first date a few days later when I rock up to the Apollo Theatre in Victoria, to see her face all over the billboards… she is not only IN wicked, but she is the bloody green witch in WICKED!!

I loved that about her, still do. She leaves the song and dance for the stage, not for parties or dropping it into conversations in the gym, or at dinner with friends. She is a superstar and doesn't feel the need to brag about it at every opportunity like so many others do in her industry.

Never have I met anyone so committed, driven and focused in achieving all that they can in the crazy business called 'show'. She sacrifices time with friends and loved ones, dedicating her life to doing what she loves, and what she is amazing at… performing!

She is an inspiration to her fans, her family, myself and our two sons… a real role model, an example of *'look what you can achieve with hard work and a kick-ass voice.'*

People don't always get what they deserve in life, but my big wish is that Kerry does… to prove that you can be nice, you can be normal, and you don't have to "step over granny" or "brown-nose" your way to the top.

I love that she's doing this book, to let a few people in, people who don't know her like I do. Hopefully everyone will see she has an amazing heart and soul, she is beautiful inside and out. An amazing performer, an amazing mother and above all, a brilliant human being.

I love her. x

James Townsend

CHAPTER 21

We were in Bradford when Jorg called me to tell me I was wanted for the role of Fantine in *Les Miserables*. My immediate reaction was *"Oh my god, I have wanted this part for years"*. As luck would have it, Dan Bowling, who was the Musical Supervisor on *Miss Saigon*, was also doing the same on *Les Mis*. We hadn't seen him for a long time as musical supervisors don't tend to hang about with the show and are usually off after rehearsals. Jorg told me that Dan was going to come along and audition me the following week, which he did. I basically just sang through *I Dreamed a Dream* for Dan in one of our rehearsal rooms and that was it, a few days later I was told I had got the role. They knew I was capable of singing the song, it was just a case of him wanting to hear me sing it.

People are shocked when I tell them that I still have to audition for parts and I'm often asked this when I do workshops or Q&A's. I may be called in a little later in the audition process for some roles, so might miss the initial rounds but in others I won't. It totally depends on the production. Very occasionally I will just get offered a part but that is quite rare.

Auditions are the only time where I may get a little bit tense. For a live performance, if anything, those nerves aid me, the adrenalin kicks in and makes things happen. I am capable of doing things in a show that I could never sing in my kitchen. Ten years ago I could walk into an audition, and not know anybody, whereas now, guaranteed, I'm going to know half the panel if not all of them. I feel as if when I walk in the room they are basically looking at me as if to say, right, come on then, show us what you've got, and I find that really unnatural and a real pressure which I don't like. I literally feel the weight of expectation. I think it's harsh and not a particularly effective way to see if people can do the job. I do believe that as you get older and have more experience there could perhaps be another way of how you're dealt with in an audition, or a different way of going about it. Your CV and workload should count for something and perhaps afford a bit of respect, which I don't think it always does. You are purely judged on the audition day, unless of course you are a massive celebrity, and just offered a job because of the type of role.

This was a brilliant audition though and so relaxed. *Miss Saigon* was carrying on, yet again, here I was at the end of my year's contract, moving on, another farewell with drinks at a big London hotel, and the next big thing to look forward to.

Les Mis at the time was firmly established and running in London at the Queens Theatre. It had transferred the previous year in 2004 from the Palace Theatre, which is where I had seen it all those years previously aged 13 with Mum and Dad. We were more or less a brand-new cast and had four weeks' rehearsal period. I was there for the meet and greets over coffee from day one and met John Owen-Jones for the first time, who was to play the role of Jean Valjean, having played it before. It was wonderful to work with someone so experienced and he is absolutely fantastic in the role. It is another sung-through musical which was great for me as it meant we were straight into music calls. For me, this was a show I had grown up with and to suddenly be in it and start singing these incredible songs was unbelievable. I had literally lived to play that role for as long as I could remember, and I really felt I had achieved something at that point in my life. As a child this was the one show I had dreamt about doing and now, here I was, actually in it. It was a real moment for me. It's funny though, although I had a bit more confidence by then, I still didn't feel like I had really made it in the business yet, and it wasn't until I was well into Wicked that I began to feel that way and walk in with that sense of ownership as I probably do now, depending on the show of course, and who you're working with!

We rehearsed in a church at King's Cross and after a few weeks we moved into the theatre to get on the revolve, the famous staging that *Les Mis* was known for, which, ironically, they have now taken out. James Powell, the Director at the time, helped me no end. He gave me such a lot of invaluable information and advice, and directed me well. Claire Moore and Tracie Bennett split the role of Madame Thenardier but Claire started it and she became a bit of a mum to me, Shonagh Daly who played Eponine, and Julie Moller who played Cosette. I was in awe of Claire. She was someone I had listened to on the Saigon cast album whilst growing up. I had just come off *Saigon* and now found myself working with Claire who originated the role of Ellen. Another full circle! We all looked up to her, she was so inspirational and put us all at ease. The situation was surreal. It was a great and talented cast which included the amazing Shaun Escoffery and David Thaxton.

The icing on the cake was that I now got to go home every night. As before I drove into London most days and this time would sit on the boundary until 6.00pm to avoid paying the congestion charge and would then fly in from the Elephant and Castle quite often by the skin of my teeth. I'm never usually late for a performance but there is a moment I remember in My Fair Lady, when I was on as a swing one night and from my dressing room I suddenly heard the music of the scene I was in and was meant to be on stage. I literally felt sick and that panic gripped hold of me. It was a tiny little moment where I was on and off and I was part of a group so it wasn't the worst thing in the world, but I felt horrific, terrible and sick, all those things. It's a moment that stands out for me and I guess taught me a bit of a lesson, although I was still taking a risk with the London traffic! By the time I was in *Wicked* I stopped driving myself as I was provided with a car home!

As we were just a cast change there were no previews as such, although we did get reviewed after a few weeks in. They called it a preview so although it wasn't really an official opening night, they put on a few drinks to mark the occasion. We were well received, and it was quite something to hear that opening number for the first time and all those amazing songs, and I felt quite emotional. In October 2006, *Les Mis* became the longest running musical ever in the West End and I was involved in a special performance to commemorate this where they invited lots of young people to be the new generation of all of our parts.

I always love being backstage, which is almost a show in itself, and becomes a very important part of it all for me. The backstage staff are definitely the unsung heroes as nobody gets to see the well-oiled machine that happens behind the scenes. The company is so far extended, it kicks out to dressers, crew, stage management, lighting and sound technicians, it's massive. The cast is only actually a third of the company, it's the stage crew who make the show happen, and keep it going. I've had brilliant dressers who can make such a difference in your show, especially one like *Wicked* where they are with you virtually the whole time. If they are really attentive and have everything you need they can make your life so much easier.

You meet people throughout the show that you have a chat with, anyone from stage management to other cast members, to dressers, crew and musicians and I quite like that you see the same people at the same points during each show and you kind of catch up day to day as you run past them. People talk about shows being like an unconventional family and they really are. You see the same people every day for a year or two, and you become very close, very quickly. One minute I'd be on stage singing *I Dreamed A Dream*, the next moment I was offstage talking to someone about their dogs or what they had for lunch that day. It's very normalised, very quickly, but I love that. I also love the grunginess of the dressing rooms, none of which are ever really great apart from maybe ones that have been renovated, like the Palladium has recently. They are generally a bit grubby but I like that because it gives them a bit of history and makes them feel authentic. My dressing rooms become like a second home to me for however long I am there and I like to make them feel a bit homely. I put family photos up and take my own mug, just to add those little home comforts and make it as comfortable as I can, simply because I spend so much time in them. I've seen them all, believe me, from the smallest shared room to the number one dressing room and it's a complete difference. It's not really right that because you are in a bigger role, you have this huge dressing room all to yourself, but that said, I have been fortunate enough to experience both. Claire, Shonagh, Julie and I had to share as the Queen's Theatre is so tiny. Fantine is a big role, but I was on at the beginning, and then it was done. We were all playing relative parts and on the whole everyone respected each other's privacy and space.

I know many people in the business have little rituals they perform before a show, to bring them luck or avoid bad luck. I try to steer clear of that because I don't think they are helpful, and can even get in the way. If you have a routine that you do, and then something goes wrong in the show you'll blame the fact you fluffed your lines on the fact you didn't put your left shoe on first. I try not to fall into that and try to mix it up, although sometimes that is really difficult, particularly in a musical, because the very nature of it means you fall into a routine. You are doing the same show eight times a week and will naturally go past people at exactly the same point in the show or change a costume at exactly the same point in the script, even though you try and fight it, sometimes you can't. In my own shows it's always different because of the venue or set list. My only slight obsession is drinking water and being hydrated.

I've had loads of wardrobe malfunctions over the years, but I think one of the most memorable ones for me was when my wig fell off in *Les Mis*. It's funny now but was awful at the time. There's a bit in the show where Fantine is forced into selling her hair and then her teeth. The character has a lovely long blonde wig, and I would go round on the revolve, then do a super quick change at the back whilst still on the stage. There was a little team waiting for me and I would have to bend down, flick my head over and they would switch my wig. They quickly took off the blonde wig and put on the short one. Because it was so fast there was only time to put two pins in it to keep it secure, ready for coming round on the revolve for the next scene. On this one performance, the pins obviously hadn't been secured properly, and in the next scene where I was being thrown about by David Thaxton as Bamatabois, there is a bit where he would grab my hair, and throw me to the floor, and as he did so, my wig flew off and hit a woman in the front row. The girls around me immediately started laughing and giggling and the woman in the front row didn't know what to do and just placed my wig on the front of the stage. The girls managed to grab it and shove it back on my head. To this day I don't know what it must have looked like but it was absolutely hilarious.

Another time my corset fell off in *We Will Rock You*. I was wearing a bra top, thank goodness, with the corset on top and for some reason it just pinged and flew off, leaving me to do the whole scene in this little bra top. I was only twenty and mortified.

I often get so emotional on stage, but I always try to use those feelings for the role. Fantine demanded a high level of emotion and if I didn't actually feel it myself, the audience knew. Some nights were easier than others, depending on what I had been through that day, and if I had anything to tap into. It can be tricky night after night, feeling that emotion, and if I couldn't naturally 'go there' I would tap into different experiences I'd had, such as losses, hard times or my parents' divorce, just to spark that emotion. Of course, the music is so powerful anyway and whenever I hear those opening bars, I kid you not, I'm an emotional wreck. Its usually an overture that will get me going.

The process gets a little bit easier as you get older because you naturally have more experiences to draw on. Of course, it's wonderful that when I was younger I didn't have loads of tragedies or sadness in my life, not

Two awesome guys.

Brian and Jack.

Above: Me as Meat in WE WILL ROCK YOU
Below: Changing things up by starring in THE IMPORTANCE OF BEING EARNEST

Above: Myself and Kristin Chenoweth

Left: A still from my time as Elphaba in WICKED

Above: Starring as Fantine in LES MIS

Below: Taking direction from Trevor Nunn on the set of CATS

Backstage with Alfie during CATS

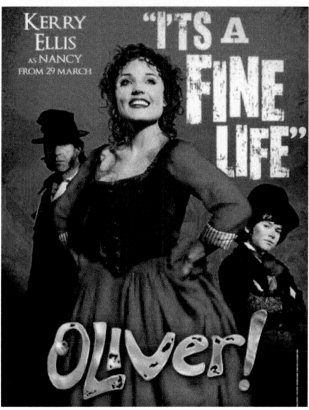

Poster from OLIVER

Strike a pose!

Family.

James, Alfie and Freddie.

A swish and a smile at Verona Arena, Verona, Italy

that I do even now, but with losing my Nan, and my dog, plus having kids, I'm able to touch on those emotions.

During the moments when a character breaks down on stage I get rid of all my own pent up emotion and let it all out, which is quite therapeutic and by the end of the show I'm buzzing with adrenaline and the audience reaction. Yes, I am also exhausted but that comes later. At first it's like I've had ten coffees without realising, and I almost forget until I get home and begin to switch off and wind down, then the exhaustion hits me. It's one of the reasons I don't mind touring or doing concerts, as I get that down time in the car afterwards which I quite like. I love my drive home.

During *Les Mis* I started working with Brian in the studio a little bit more and it all started to kick off. It suddenly became possible because I wasn't off touring all the time and was based at home. He had come to see me in *Saigon* and *Les Mis* so he was still very supportive of me and we'd stayed in regular contact. He was as busy as ever touring, but every so often when work schedules allowed, I would drive to his studio in South London for a few hours then get back in time for the show in the evening. At this stage we were just trying things out and working on different songs and styles to see what worked. One song we tried was *Song of the Earth* or *Canto Della Terra*, an Italian song by Andrea Boccelli which we had translated.   Brian was also keen to try out rock songs like *Stay With Me Baby*. There's loads of recordings from that time that have never been released. Maybe one day some of them might surface. We tried writing together as well but it just didn't gel to start with. I certainly didn't have a clear view at the time of who I was or what I wanted.   That didn't come till much later, which is probably why it was such a slow process. It was a pipe dream when I was younger to be a recording artist and to play arenas, but I had never really thought it through or how to get there and I certainly didn't know what type of music would take me there so I wasn't instigating anything because it was all so new to me. I knew about musicals, and covers, and how to sing and interpret a song, but I was so used to being a chameleon and fitting into a role that I didn't know who I was or what I wanted to say or sing.   Brian was trying to give me lots of options and at one point he introduced me to Chris Kimsey, another producer who was most well-known for co-producing a couple of the Rolling Stones albums, and I went along to his studio for a day and recorded a song. Brian must have seen something in me and was really

125

trying to help me see it too, but it took a while to come out. It wasn't until I knew who I was and who I wanted to be as myself, before our working partnership could then grow, which didn't happen till *Anthems* was released further down the line. I think that is partly why our journey has been so interesting as neither of us really knew where we were going with it and it really became a journey of discovery.

It was whilst I was in *Les Mis* that Neil and I finally split up and we then had to go through the process of selling the house that we had only been in for a year, which was all very traumatic. For a lot of the time I hadn't even been there, and Neil had set up his own life within it. I was only twenty-six and to be selling a big house which I had bought with somebody was quite difficult, and extremely stressful. What was especially hard was the fact that when we had originally met, Neil had resisted getting into a relationship, because he felt he was too old for me and that it wouldn't last, but I was the one insisting it would. Not surprisingly, it turned out we were in different places in our life. Not that he was putting pressure on me to get married or have children but I wasn't ready to settle down at all. I just wasn't there yet even though he was so important to me during those years and I loved him dearly. He was probably my first true love and it was hard to let him go, and I think regrettably I did hurt him a lot.

CHAPTER 22

Towards the end of my time in *Les Mis* I auditioned for the part of Eva Peron in *Evita*, which I desperately wanted. They were about to do a new version of it which was going to be a massive production, and at that point I had never worked for Andrew Lloyd Webber. Here it comes, this is it, I thought excitedly; I really believed that this was my time and this was my big role. I auditioned a couple of times for Simon Lee, the MD, I had learned loads of the music and it was all going well and I was feeling really positive about it until suddenly I was rejected and didn't get through to the final audition to sing for Andrew and the Director, Michael Grandage. I was gutted and I remember walking back to *Les Mis* that day wearing a black dress with my hair in a bun and bright red lipstick and just feeling like I'd been punched in the stomach and had all the wind taken out of me. This was the first time I had really wanted anything quite so badly. By the time I got back to the theatre I had pulled myself together and knew I had a show to do.

As it happened, auditions for *Wicked* came up not long after, and I ended up auditioning about seven times, on and off. Initially it's to see if you can actually do it, and that they like you, but then like with *We Will Rock You* it becomes more about matching you up with various other performers to make sure you work well together and that the voices blend. Again I met new people along the audition process and I was paired up with other witches and Fiyeros.

Ironically the first time I went in I sang for both witches. I think because I am blonde and blue eyed they had me down as a possibility for Glinda but once I started to sing, it became apparent that I would go the one particular way, because on the second audition I just had Elphaba material to perform.

My final audition was just before I had a matinee for *Les Mis* and I remember having to sing *Defying Gravity* two or three times, *I'm Not That Girl*, *No Good Deed*, *Wizard and I*, and then run through a few scenes. My adrenalin was pumping when I came out and then I had to do two shows back-to-back. About a week later I got a call from Jorg between shows, whilst I was walking down Old Compton Street with my hair in pin curls, as you do. I just remember screaming in the middle of Old

Compton Street which obviously in London nobody gave a monkeys about, and then ran all the way back to the theatre and told everyone that I was going to be in Wicked!

I needed to find somewhere to live quite quickly as the house sale was going through. Knowing I had *Wicked*, I didn't want to move too far as I didn't want a long commute. I knew Brockley but I was looking at surrounding areas as well like, like Forest Hill, Greenwich and such-like. Things have a funny way of turning out and a one-bedroomed chocolate box style maisonette in a little mews came on the market, just around the corner from the house, which was perfect. I'd seen a few before this one came up, but I immediately fell in love with it. The sellers had just renovated it but they needed a bigger place, and it was just perfect for me, ticking all my boxes. On the day I moved in I remember sitting outside the house with my Dad waiting for the go-ahead for the keys. It was kind of a bitter-sweet feeling because of the situation, but I felt like it was a fresh start on my own now and that felt exciting. New job, new home and life was good. I had moved into the last place with very little in terms of possessions and came out with much the same so sad as it was, it was all very amicable. I later converted the maisonette to two bedrooms and I still own it to this day and rent it out. It's turned out to be the best investment I ever made. To top it all off I also got a gorgeous little Jack Russell puppy who I named Jack. I'd missed having a dog as JJ had died whilst I was at college, so it had been a while. I loved the American drama 24 with Kiefer Sutherland as agent Jack Bauer at the time so my Jack was a little bit inspired by Mr Bauer!

About a week after I'd been told that I had the part of Elphaba, I had another call to say I that still had the role, and I was still going to be the first British girl to play the green witch, but there was a slight snag, because the American girl, Idina Menzel, who had opened the show on Broadway, was now going to come and open the show at the Apollo Victoria in London for three months. My heart sank to begin with, but I soon realised it made little difference to me, and I was still really excited once I'd got over the initial disappointment. I was still going to be around for all the original rehearsals and would work with Joe Mantello, the Director and the MD. I would be in all those rehearsal rooms; I just wasn't going to open the show. I knew how massive the show was, but also what a big deal Idina was. She had got the Tony award and was hugely celebrated for that show and I really don't blame her. If *We Will Rock You* had suddenly opened on Broadway and they'd asked me to go and open it, then of course I would have leaped at the chance.

When Idina came over I was her standby and although I had to be in the theatre, I was completely off stage. I didn't really get to know her very well, as the nature of it meant that if she was there, I wasn't, and if I was there, she wasn't. We were around each other a little bit during rehearsals but not very much. I had costume fittings, and the first time I was greened up was brilliant. To suddenly see myself transformed was very exciting. Annalene Beechey was the the other standby for Glinda and once the show opened we would hang out in our tiny little dressing room where we could watch a bit of telly or run through the show. We were together for the entirety of that first three months until I took over.

My first appearance came about a month in, part way through one of the performances, when Idina very suddenly got sick. Talk about being thrown in at the deep end. In Wicked, it was quite normal to go off mid performance, which isn't ideal, but as it is so horrifically hard, you can start off believing you're ok, and after the first three songs realise you are not going to get through the next nine. Idina got to '*The Wizard,*' when I got the message that she might be going off. Someone started frantically chucking green on my face. By '*I'm Not That Girl,*' which was another couple of songs in, it was definite that she was coming off just before '*Defying Gravity*'. All hell let loose, and I was suddenly surrounded by people dressing me, doing my hair and finishing my make-up.

We literally switched as Idina ran off from her exit and I ran on for the next entrance to carry on the rest of the show. I don't think the audience were any the wiser because they don't stop the show to make the announcement, although I think they may have announced it during the interval. It's such a crazy moment in the show anyway, and such a massive one, and there is so much going on that maybe an audience member who had seen it fifteen times may have spotted me, but the majority probably wouldn't have. The buzz in the building was excitable though. My adrenalin was through the roof and my heart was racing. I was beside myself with excitement and I was so ready for the moment, I just wanted to be on that stage doing it. What an introduction to Wicked! I went on a good ten or fifteen times again until, a couple of months later

129

I officially took over the role and had my own opening night and press night. Going on as understudy was like having my own previews, which was good and took the pressure off a little bit, but in a way you want that big bang, as that's what we are geared up to do. However, it gave me a taster of it, and a bit of an insight into what it was like. It was a big, full-on role, and a tough one to play.

By the time I opened in London I was fully prepared, so any rehearsing by then was more just tinkering with the performance, and fine tuning it. Initially my make-up was done for me, but I had phases of doing it myself once I had been in it for a long time, and it took me about half an hour to do which wasn't too bad, and I was even quicker as time went on. Backstage was so chaotic and as I've said before is like a show in itself. Because I was on stage pretty much the whole of the time, I didn't see that many people, and when I did come off I was getting changed or someone was shoving a water bottle in my mouth. It was pure chaos, but organised chaos, and is as organised, if not more so, than the show itself. It is a well-oiled machine where you know exactly who is putting your right boot on, who is putting your left boot on, who you are passing at the exact same place on the exact same lyric, and who you will be sat next to for five seconds while you have a breather. The volume of traffic backstage is unbelievable.

My opening was great but there was quickly a lot of pressure on me, as suddenly, I had to perform the show eight times a week, which was quite scary as I'd only ever done two performances in a row before. I've been lucky in that I have never really suffered with stage fright, but I know a lot of people do. I've had moments where I have had slight anxiety but I think that happens to most performers. With me it can happen for a period of time and then disappear, but never enough to make me not want to go on stage. I have experienced a sudden grip of fear in a few shows which is mainly when I have a big responsibility, so I experienced this a little bit in *Wicked* and also during *We Will Rock You*. When you do something for that long it becomes so much a part of your skin, and second nature, that every so often you question yourself, and that can be dangerous. I would have wobbles where I didn't know what I was saying or singing, and I have fluffed many lines and had total blanks along the way. I sang the same verse of *No-one But You* three times once because of pure fear. I had totally forgotten how it went. I've had similar in all shows and it is quite panicky but luckily I have always managed to get through it. However, I have seen people suffer with it on another level and it's horrible. I think I would question if I really wanted to continue in the business if I got to that state.

Eight shows a week, in a role of that intensity, was pretty daunting. Shona White was my understudy for that first year, and, ironically, two or three shows in, I had to miss a performance which to me was heartbreaking. My voice had gone and exhaustion, combined with the pressure, had taken its toll. It was the first time I'd gone off so early even though I had been on loads of times already. I felt sick making that call to say I couldn't do the show that day but I had no choice, I literally had nothing to give. It was the excitement, the pressure and the expectation of the opening which all contributed, and my voice just needed a day to rest. The next day was fine but I do think that show is a constant battle.

It's an insane schedule, and anybody who has played Elphaba will say the same thing as we've all had trouble in different ways. It has literally broken so many people and I think it's insane that there isn't an alternate with a role this huge. I've never been so physically, emotionally and vocally drained in all my life, and this led to a few issues for me vocally. It is such a brilliant show but at the same time so tough and was the first one to make me struggle.

CHAPTER 23

I was experiencing vocal problems right from the start, but it wasn't too extreme to begin with. It was only during the last three months of the initial London run that it became more dramatic. I got really tired and my chords were swollen from over-singing. It's happened to a lot of Elphabas because of the nature of the role and the sheer amount of dialogue, singing, shouting and general use of the voice. I think you need a bit of specialised training when you play Elphaba, and I don't think anyone gets enough, as it is such a big thing to take on. I had a couple of lessons during the run but they came at the wrong time really as I was too far into it, and ideally I should have had them before I started.

People are often surprised to hear I've only had a handful of singing lessons in my life and little or no vocal training. Before I went to college I had a few vocal lessons locally in Suffolk with musician and opera singer Olive Quantrill, sadly no longer with us but who had a long and successful music career performing and conducting, amongst other things, a number of successful choirs. I also had a few more whilst I was at college but not loads. As for vocal warm ups before a show, I guess I should say for all those musical theatre students training hard at the moment, that yes, I do them religiously before each show, but the truth is, it depends. If I'm doing a gig I might make a few noises to check I haven't lost my voice overnight and that's about it. I figure that I will probably be singing for two hours on stage and if I sing or warm my voice up too much beforehand, it could be counter-productive. That's the way I see it anyway. With any of the big orchestral concerts I do, there tends to be a lot of singing and rehearsing on the day with the orchestra anyway, so I definitely don't warm up for something like that. With a musical it is all part of the process and the cast all come in at the same time each day to warm up together, which you are kind of conditioned to. I think you can easily tire your voice too much. Yes, you have to move your voice a little bit to make sure it is there and you still have a voice, but then I just kind of ease into it. I know a lot of singing teachers who seem to teach a certain way these days, and when I go into theatre schools or colleges, I notice the young people coming through have a definite style which stems from how they are being taught. They all have a high twang, and this mixey, twangy sound, which is quite incredible really, but the danger is, a lot of them sound the same, and are missing out on their individuality.

My voice has definitely changed and evolved over the years and I've learned a lot from each job that I've done along the way. In a lot of shows I was quite fortunate in as much that I could just sing without thinking too much about it, but in *Wicked* it was down to me to almost retrain myself to sing in order to sustain eight shows a week. I was always quite a gutsy, hell-for-leather, bolshy just let it come out full pelt type of singer but if I had gone into *Wicked* like that I would have properly blown my voice out very quickly. I admit I don't have a great 'mix' voice as such. A lot of singers can switch between their head voice and chest voice effortlessly but I am not one of those, it's all or nothing with me and I find it hard to take my foot off the gas with it. That period of time educated me so much on how to get through songs by just easing my foot off that gas a bit, but still having the same effect. I'm still learning now how to sing different types of songs, and my voice is constantly developing. It's interesting because I remember singing '*If I Loved You*' from Carousel with Brian not that long ago, for our *Golden Days* album, and I remember saying to him,

"*It's really not my kind of song Brian*". I'd heard Katherine Jenkins singing it and thought it was more for a soprano voice and not my bag at all. It was quite on the edge for me as it required a place in my voice which I found quite difficult.

"*The vulnerable parts of your voice are what people find interesting Kerry. If you embrace that vulnerability, you will connect with people more*", he explained.

I took that, and went with it, and it's stayed with me ever since. It's amazing how being brave enough to show that live on stage does you so many favours, and he was right, it allows you to 'find' your voice in a weird kind of way and allows that deeper connection with the audience.

I got through those first six months in *Wicked*, and then I think fatigue kicked in, and I found it really hard to get back to feeling and being really strong and would have good and bad moments. Once I got into the swing of the run, I would have a couple of months where I would be fine doing my eight shows then I would have a month of doing seven shows and then maybe six shows then back up to eight again which would be fine for a while. Eight shows took its toll on me and its not really sustainable, and

133

I strongly believe it should be a five or six show week. In other shows like *Phantom of the Opera*, the girls do four shows a week, and in *Miss Saigon* the girls do four each. Even in *Mamma Mia* it's seven a week.

It was quite hard to deal with mentally too as I really didn't want to call in sick. I desperately didn't want to let anyone down who had come specially to see me, only to find I wasn't there. My chords were incredibly swollen at one point and I got to a stage where I wasn't talking at all during the day and was having to write everything down. That was also around the time we were just starting to get into twitter world, and social media was coming in a bit. I was reading tweets reacting to when I wasn't there, which for me was devastating to see other people's disappointment. Obviously I had called in sick because I physically couldn't perform my part which was bad enough, but then to read the disappointed people's comments on twitter was heartbreaking. That was really tricky for me.

Just before I went to Broadway, I saw a vocal specialist on Harley Street who Brian had recommended to me. I'd been to my own GP initially, which was a waste of time really as I knew it was a very specific and specialised problem which wasn't within his realm of expertise. The Harley Street Doctor gave me anti-inflammatories in the form of steroids to take the swelling down in my throat, which is what I needed by that point, and which, to be fair, did help and took the swelling down a bit. He also said I should go on complete vocal rest and try to recover, which I did for a few days but it's kind of tough to stay off, and there is a loaded pressure to go back, which I also put on myself to a certain extent. I think I managed five days of rest but I wanted to be back on stage, I didn't want to miss out on this amazing experience any more than I had to. Apart from anything else, I was being paid to be there, and as a professional my attitude has always been the show must go on. Every day that goes by when you're not there gets harder, and you feel like you are letting everyone down who has paid good money to see you. I'd never had that pressure before to that extent and I was able to properly empathise with how Martine felt in *My Fair Lady*.

It was awful, I felt really defeated and like a bit of a failure. I wanted to be strong enough to do what was required of me without thinking about it but I couldn't. I just didn't have any time to recover, it was relentless. I know so many people who have played the role since who have survived it on paracetamol and Nurofen and basically self-medicated to get themselves through it. Everyone you speak to about it, has their own coping mechanisms. A few people were obsessed with Throat Coat tea, a herbal tea with lemon, ginger, liquorice root and loads of other ingredients which I would drink in the interval all the time. I'd try anything to soothe and calm the stress of it. There were various steamers that were on trend at the time. I would use a Nelson's Steam Inhaler which I was obsessed with and did use a lot on that show. We had a physio, Physio Ed we called him, who although independent would work on a lot of the shows and he would give me vocal massages, digging into my throat to try and release the tension. Initially I would go to visit him but by the time I came back from Broadway he was on site.

Idina had never done a show here before, and the very fact that she came over paved the way for me to go to Broadway. How it often works is, if somebody comes here from Broadway and does three months in a show, an English actor can then go to Broadway on just a straightforward exchange without having to have a green card or be sponsored. Her being here opened that door for me and I believe it was meant to be as so often happens in my career. It was after I'd been doing the show for a while here, when Joe Mantello the Director asked me if I wanted to go and perform it on Broadway. Did I?! Did I what?! I almost bit his hand off, all vocal problems forgotten. This was another dream coming true for me. A couple of phone calls later from Jorg and it was all arranged. It all happened so quickly and there was no audition process of course, as I was already playing the role. I was scheduled to go at the end of nine months. I finished in London on the Saturday night, flew to New York the following day, rehearsed for four or five days then I was in straightaway. It was such a quick process and really was the stuff of dreams. I was a young girl in New York for the first time and about to star on Broadway.

CHAPTER 24

Six weeks before I was due to go to Broadway, it was my best friend Caroline Deverill's wedding and I was to be chief bridesmaid. She was getting married on the Sunday, so I finished the show on the Saturday and drove from London straight down to Bognor Regis, where her parents lived, arriving there at around 2.00am, and we all sat up for a while, generally catching up and excitedly talking about the next day. I was meant to be singing 'From This Moment' by Shania Twain at the ceremony but by this time I felt completely knackered. I'd been on steroids, had just finished the show, then driven all the way here, had this swollen throat, was going to Broadway in six weeks and now had to sing at my best friend's wedding ceremony. I was really freaking out thinking I just could not do it. I had no voice. The following morning, I woke early in a panic, so with virtually no sleep, I was hanging out of the bathroom window of Caroline's Mums house, so no-one would hear me, phoning Louise Dearman, my dear friend and a brilliant singer, begging her to sing this song instead of me. I just couldn't let Caroline down totally and this seemed the obvious solution. *"Louise please I've got no voice left you've got to sing the song please..."* I begged.

"I can't Kerry, I don't know it that well and I don't know the lyrics."

I started getting ready with Caroline, trying not to show how worried I was. It was all lovely and going to plan and we finally all made our way to Amberley Castle for the ceremony. The castle itself was absolutely beautiful, about 900 years old complete with portcullis and luxury hotel facilities, and was just perfect for the occasion. I walked down the aisle just ahead of Caroline and sat down opposite Craig Adams who was playing the piano. I had met Craig in 2005 during *Les Mis* when Steven had first introduced me to him. Although we'd known each other since college, Steven and I became incredibly close when we were tour buddies on *Magic of the Musicals* and have remained so ever since. He was in town one day and arranged to meet me for coffee, saying he had someone for me to meet. He'd previously had a long-term boyfriend at college who we all knew and assumed they'd get married, so I was quite intrigued. Apparently he and Craig met whilst both in *Mamma Mia* with Caroline, when Craig was playing Sky and Steven was the resident Director. Craig was quite a performer at the time and had done a lot of shows including

Joseph and *Zorro* before giving up in favour of writing. I could see Caroline making her entrance which was my cue to stand up and sing this song. All the while I was muttering to myself, "*I can't do it, I can't do it...*"

As always happens, I went on auto pilot, stood up and sang, and it was absolutely fine. Little did I know that at that moment my future husband James was watching me sing for the very first time. He was the best man and sat next to Caroline's fiancé Ian. Coincidentally, James had already met Steven and Craig as Caroline had been on tour with them in *Mamma Mia* along with quite a number of my old college friends, and Ian had taken James to see the show where he also met quite a few of my college friends.

Once the ceremony was over, Caroline and Ian walked back down the aisle together and James and I filtered in after them. Craig and Steven were nudging each other and giving me the wink whilst nodding towards James, and I was shaking my head back at them. As we were walking behind the bride and groom, James said hello and hooked my arm and I immediately slapped his hand away as we had done it the wrong way round. A memorable first meeting with me telling him off and slapping him. It can't have been too bad though because we pretty much spent the whole day chatting to each other, flirting and then danced the first dance together. I thought he was cute, but he wasn't my usual type, not that I really had a type, but I would normally go for tall, dark haired, slightly unusual guys and he is five foot eight and blonde. We laughed all day and I found him hysterically funny, so there was a spark, but I think I was resisting it. I stayed over in Amberley Castle that night and headed back to my room. The next morning James knocked on my door to say goodbye just before he was leaving. I felt absolutely gutted as he hadn't asked for my number. I frantically tried to think what had gone wrong or if it was something I had said, then about ten minutes later he returned and asked for my number. The following day he called me and we got together on and off. For quite a while he didn't really know what I did. I'd told him at the wedding that I was in a musical, and I was currently playing a green witch. He knew nothing about theatre and didn't even know what a stage door was. I think he thought I just had a small part and maybe was one of many green witches. I found out later that he put in the wedding book 'I love the green witch', which we always laugh about now.

James and I had six weeks of getting to know each other, and going out, before I had to go to New York. He'd been to see the show for the first time, and bawled his eyes out, which I thought was really sweet. When we met up at the front after the show, he was almost lost for words. He just couldn't quite believe it. "*I had no idea…*" he admitted as he hugged me.

He was blown away and would cry every time he saw me on stage in the early years. Now, however, he has become a bit more opinionated and tells me what he thinks, which can be quite interesting. Not so much if I'm doing a musical, but if I am doing my own stuff he will definitely tell me what he thinks, which is great sometimes, because he knows me so well, and as an everyday punter he can see things from an audience perspective, so it's quite good to have that opinion… Sometimes! I don't always agree, and I don't always want to hear it, because he tends to offer the opinion too early and I'm not ready.

I want to be able to come off stage and for him to say, "*Darling you were brilliant, it was fabulous,*" but then talk about it properly the following day. Not to tell me where I went wrong as I'm walking back to the dressing room, as it's too raw.

I like to do things to the best of my ability and to the best they can be done on the day. Of course I get annoyed if something doesn't quite go how I hoped, but I can get rid of it. If I've had a bad show and it isn't great and things haven't really gone to plan, or if Craig and I have done a gig somewhere which hasn't gone to plan, I will be annoyed, but we will chat and rant about it in the car on the way home, and then it's gone, and I'm okay with it. I can let things go.

It is difficult though, because if I come home from a show, and debrief the performance or rant at James, I'm not really looking for a response, I just need to offload what's happened. If I've had an issue with the sound or an issue with the costume or whatever, I just need to let that go but he likes to comment, which again I'm not ready for. I'm kind of used to it now and I know it comes from a good place. He is my number one fan and he does support me even though he can't come to everything these days.

The day before I left for New York, James and I spent the day together, hanging out in Richmond Park, just walking along the river and having a few drinks. It was such an emotional day and a bit of a double-edged sword. We tried to keep it light, all the while saying and thinking that it could be make or break, but it was done with a heavy heart. I was so excited about this huge opportunity and my dream coming true, but suddenly things had changed slightly, as I had met the love of my life and had to leave him. I was devastated, and I was also upset over leaving my puppy Jack, who was only eight months old, despite knowing my Mum would look after him well.

James took me to the airport next day and I sobbed all the way, it felt like such a wrench. For the first time I had 'stuff' to leave behind. Previously I'd had no ties, now here I was with a new house, a boyfriend and a dog. Alongside that, I was still worrying over my voice, and if it would hold out. I was flying first class which had all been booked for me and I made my way into the VIP lounge which was all wonderful, but I didn't want to eat, I didn't want to drink, I was still sobbing and it was a complete waste of a first class flight. Plus I had a dreadful headache by the time I arrived. I curse James now of course!

My accommodation had all been arranged for me, and I was staying in the same apartment block as Stephen Schwartz, the composer of *Wicked*. It was a small block and he was on the top floor which was amazing as I'd get to see him in the lift occasionally. He was fairly quiet but a sweet man and knew me from London having seen me in the show there. I was actually staying in Christian Slater's Mum's apartment which I thought was pretty cool at the time.

When I arrived I had the rest of that day to settle in, followed by four or five days of rehearsals before stepping into the role. It literally was me stepping into the role, as the show had been running for ages and the rest of the cast hadn't changed. It was really quick and I was slightly jet-lagged, plus I hadn't had any break at all. I felt like I was on a fast train that wasn't stopping, constantly trying to catch up and not getting any rest. My body just didn't have time or the energy to catch up. Aaron

Tveit, who has gone on to be a bit of a superstar and success story, played my Fiyero and Kendra Kassenbom was my Glinda, a really solid and lovely girl. She had been in it for a while and had done the show with Idina a couple of times early on as well. In fact there were some really lovely people in the cast who reached out warmly to me, to make me feel so welcome. It was just a shame I wasn't able to be more sociable because of the restrictions of the role, but if I had, I would never have got through it.

On the opening night at the Gershwin Theatre I was excited and of course it was an incredible experience. I had thought about and dreamed about starring in a Broadway show since I was a child. The most memorable moment was my first entrance at the beginning when Elphaba runs forward on stage and then stands there. I remember thinking *"Oh my god I'm on Broadway."* It really was the stuff of dreams and a real moment for me.

The audience went absolutely mental, and it was quite an incredible feeling which I will always cherish. The end of *Defying Gravity* when I was levitated in the air was another moment. I was on top of the world and despite everything felt invincible. It's strange because I was so connected with the audience and yet so alone on that stage. It all rested on my shoulders and the audience would go mental when I got it right. The pressure is tough, but the rewards are greater. Jorg came for the opening, so I had some support. We hadn't travelled together and maybe if we had I wouldn't have sobbed over James as I'm not that kind of person. I would have held it in!

I didn't get home during that period as there just wasn't time, but my Dad came out and stayed with me as I had a two bedroomed apartment. There was no way he was going to miss it. James ended up coming out to visit every three weeks or so, which I think might be partly why he eventually lost his sales job, as he was spending so much time coming out to see me and not enough time working! That, and the fact his heart just wasn't in it.

Notes from…

I wasn't really aware of Kerry Ellis until I met my husband Steven, and he took me on a 'date night' to meet her/watch her in *Les Misérables*… *now* I realise he was just showing off!

I kind of missed the whole '*We will Rock You*' thing… I know! I don't know how, either! Thinking about it, I suppose I'd never been a fan of Queen (am I allowed to say that?) and therefore not been to see the show. These were the days before 'Insta' and 'Twitter' and YouTube, so if you didn't see a show, you weren't really aware of who was in it or what it had to offer. And the other thing I'm learning about myself, as I get older, is that I'm often late to the party, in everything I do — and that was certainly the case with Kerry Ellis.

Anyway, years passed, I met Steven and… dot, dot, dot! (Little clue there as to what show we met on for all those Musical Theatre fans!)

Back to Kerry: Steven and I were both on breaks from the shows we were in, we were at the early stage of our relationship, that 'still meeting each other's old friends' stage, that horrible 'can't quite be yourself yet', 'still on best behaviour' stage…

I told a mate of mine, Martin, who I was working with at the time, that I was going to meet a friend of Steven's and see her in *Les Mis*.

'*Kerry Ellis?*' He said, with a jealous rage.

'*Yes?!*' He almost fell off his chair!

Cut to 15 minutes later and tonnes of fangirling from Martin, I realised there was a buzz about Kerry Ellis that I hadn't been aware of.

We met at a Starbucks on Wardour Street before the show. I remember thinking how effervescent she was… but she also had this unassuming charm at the same time. I was probably an idiot as I always am in moments like that!

But it wasn't until I heard the beginning of '*I Dreamed a Dream*' that I realised what all the fuss was *really* about. That voice. That ease of sound. That effortless control of an audience. It was like a lightning bolt. I suddenly sat up. She made it look so easy.

141

It wasn't until a few years later that our working relationship was forged – and at a very unusual place – the wedding of our friend Caroline.

A few special relationships were formed that day; mine and Kerry's, over a very last minute rehearsal on the phone, with me at the venue, sticking my head out of a window in the rain to try and get enough signal, mine and Ian's – Caroline's husband – who I went on to write with and of course Kerry met her husband, James. It's funny when you look back at certain events, you suddenly see how seismic they were to the rest of your life; that performance for Caroline's wedding – I forget the song, one of those iconic wedding anthems I think – was the starting point of a relationship that has been a special part of my career and brought me endless moments of joy and fear and creativity and laughter in equal measures.

Craig Adams   B.A (Hons)

MD / Composer / Head of Music – Laine Theatre Arts

CHAPTER 25

Scarlett Strallen was playing *Mary Poppins* on Broadway and opened about a month after me and not long after I started we somehow bumped into each other, which became my saving grace. We would regularly have breakfast together and as we had similar pressures, both with these huge roles and both missing home, we were able to connect and really became a lifeline to each other. Julia Murney, an American actress who had also played Elphaba, also contacted me, and was brilliant when I was over there. She reached out to me with an email saying "*I know you're on your own out here doing Wicked and just want you to know I'm here.*" We spoke back and forth over email quite a bit and I really did find that supportive and helpful. She understood what it was like being in the role and the vocal pressures.

Other than that, I didn't really do too much because of the demanding nature of the role. I just didn't have the energy or enthusiasm to go out much. It was wonderful when James came out and I had a lot of visits from other people too, which perked me up. However that was always weighted, as I then had the pressure of them seeing me in the show and being up to standard for them, but also the pressure of them being around as they stayed with me, and wanted me to show them the sights and generally entertain, which was exhausting in itself, and really hard. I really wanted to do all that, yet at the back of my mind I knew I had to look after myself and deliver a good performance every night. I was constantly running on empty. They'd all want to go out for drinks and dinner but I couldn't do any of it. It was the talking that was detrimental more than anything, and I remember just not wanting to speak. Even when James came over I pre-warned him that I couldn't speak to him and would have to write everything down, which he probably thought was great! It worked out ok though, and when he wasn't there, I would be quite self-contained and not do much, but when he was with me, we did all the touristy things such as walking round Central Park, over Brooklyn Bridge, down to Greenwich or up the Rockefeller Centre. I saved up the time and although I wouldn't speak loads we would go walking and explore the city and sights together. One thing I could do on my own though was shop and I managed that with no problem. I bought loads of clothes whilst out there, and definitely had excess baggage when I came home, as is always the case when I go to New York! It was a dream to shop on my own and not speak to anybody. I loved nothing more than being by myself during the day and walking down to Greenwich for a leisurely coffee, allowing me some peaceful time to just reflect and wander around, taking it all in.

I remember going to a tiny spa in an apartment block in Greenwich on a Sunday and just sitting in a steam room all day not speaking and just relaxing, which enabled me to switch off entirely. I also tried yoga for the first time, which sparked my interest, and eventually led to my love of it today. I would go in between shows which really helped, and I also tried Hot Yoga which I'd seen advertised and looked interesting. There was a class literally down the street from the theatre, which couldn't have been more perfect and I loved that one. I was quite religious with it as the teacher was wonderful and just to have that escape and something to quiet my mind really did help. Anything that would take my mind away from it, or distract me, would be helpful. I didn't know at that point how significant yoga would become in my later life. I got really down, and what should have been one of the highlights of my career, and a joyous time, was probably one of the toughest points in my life and was spent exhausted and constantly worrying about my health and voice. I was terrified I would lose it totally. New York was so loaded for me but it still has a special place in both our hearts and we've been back so many times since and love it.

While I was there, *Wicked* entered its 5th year on Broadway and as part of the celebrations I got to turn the Empire State Building green with Stephen Schwartz, in honour of Wicked Day. There is a brilliant picture of me doing that. As you go up the Empire State Building, there are lots of photos off various moments and I think that one may still be up there. After the 'green ceremony' we rushed off to continue rehearsing for a one-off show to celebrate the anniversary with previous Elphabas, Shoshana Bean and Stephanie J Block. They also put together an anniversary CD of which I was a part singing '*I'm Not that Girl*'.

There were loads of these type of opportunities connected with the show and I managed to do various press and work stuff along with a few publicity bits and pieces. I performed in Times Square, and an outdoor festival at Bryant Park, singing *Gravity* and the *Wizard and I*. I was also seen for a breakfast television presenting role whilst I was there. After performing in Times Square I was approached by one of the producers to see if I'd be interested in going along to meet them at their offices. I saw it as a potential opportunity, as you never know what will happen with these things, so I went along to meet them. Once I was in the building making my way to their office, I passed Daniel Radcliffe in the corridor and remember doing a double take to see Harry Potter, it was so surreal. Once there, I had a chat with them, and they seemed very nice, but I heard no more. I often wonder what would have happened if I'd been offered the job, although part of my contract with *Wicked* was that I had to go back into the London show after six months. There were always opportunities in New York, and that's what I loved most about being there. Here, you have to get yourself out there and find the work, whereas over there they find you. I could have started the process for a green card while I was there but decided not to. James, my dog, and the house were still pulling me back home, plus I had no strong desire to stay there anyway. I also felt under enormous pressure, so that was the last thing on my mind. Maybe if I went back again, things might be different, but who knows.

Just prior to this trip, Brian and I had been getting in the studio more and more, at least as much as we could whilst I was doing the show. We'd recorded various bits and pieces including *Gravity*, *I'm Not That Girl* and *No-One But You*. There's a brilliant video out there of me singing *Gravity* in his studio with him filming it. It was a three song EP but I'd wanted to have something to take with me to New York to sell front of house. We released it in the UK just before I went and did a little bit of promo for it. The EP kick-started, and became, the introduction to *Anthems*. I now had some momentum, and needed to get something out there, and it gave us a kick up the bum to do that, which was great, because when I did eventually come out of *Wicked* and went into *Oliver*, I had the *Anthems* album ready to go.

James continued to come out as much as he could, which was about every three weeks for a long weekend. On one of those visits, I was invited to Miami, Florida to do a video for some film students. They must have found my version of *Defying Gravity* with Brian, and they wanted to make me a video. They arranged to fly me to Miami and I asked James to come with me as it would be brilliant, and give us a bit of a break, which he did. We stayed in the Hard Rock Hotel and it was all a mad whirlwind and such brilliant fun. Everyone seemed to know who I was, and that I was there and it felt like quite a big deal. I spent two days filming this crazy video for *Gravity*, just outside Universal Studios, with all these film students. They had loads of green screens and I was being virtually flown around everywhere.

While I was there I won an award for Broadway World's Best Breakthrough Performer. I have been so incredibly lucky in my career to have been nominated for several awards, and even win a few, but this one felt quite special. It was all very informal and casual. I'd made a bit of a splash while I was over there, and to now be recognised for that was really nice. I had a message through from Jorg telling me I had won this award. I suppose there must have been someone from Broadway World who came and watched one evening, but I wasn't aware of it. The show was probably being reviewed and it stemmed from there. The Broadway World representative came on stage one night and presented it to me at the end of the show, which was lovely. I'm also so proud of my WhatsOnStage award for Best Takeover In A Role in 2008 and 2015, both for Elphaba. To be honest though all my awards and nominations are special. It's just really humbling to be recognised for something you love doing.

Whilst I was there it was the height of the summer, and living in our climate, the air conditioning was something I wasn't used to. It was on constantly in the flat, and the theatre, and I think that probably contributed to my vocal problems. Another issue was that opposite my flat, there was a construction site where a big tower block was being demolished, and the work went on for the whole six months I was there. They would start so early in the morning that I was barely sleeping. The show finished fairly late, then, by the time I got back to my apartment, wound down a bit, spoke to James on the horrific skype connection, which was soul-destroying in those days, and then finally get to sleep, it was only a few hours before I'd get woken up again at some obscene hour, to the sound of the bulldozing that would carry on all day.

The whole of my time there I seemed to be playing catch-up. The flight, the change of environment, the change of aircon, new flat and surroundings, along with the pressure and the fact I was so tired, had all set me back further. Ideally I could have done with a month off to recover before embarking on Broadway and then start afresh, which would have been fine, but that's just not how things pan out. I did manage to see an American doctor a couple of months in, for another course of treatment. I had overshot my voice and my chords were swollen up again. I was taking part in all the structured vocal warm ups and doing everything I could to take care of my voice. I even had a couple of lessons whilst I was there with quite a well-known vocal coach who had taught Idina and Stephanie J Block for a while. She must have been coaching Jeff Goldblum also, because I would see him coming out as I was going in. It helped a little bit, but I was singing on a tired and slightly damaged voice and you can't repair a tired voice or swollen chords. Looking back it can't have been too horrifically bad because it didn't actually stop me, and luckily it didn't damage me.

When I left it was with a weighted heart, and with not so much a sense of regret, but with a sadness that it had been the best of times and the highlight of my career so far, one that thousands of young musical theatre students would die for, and yet the toughest time of my life. It really took its toll both health-wise and emotionally.

I've never really talked about this before and whenever people have asked how it was, I have always given the same response of, *"Oh wow it was amazing, such a dream come true, I loved it, it was brilliant to be there."* And it was, but people don't know the depths of it and everything else that was going on. Others who have played Elphaba agree that we are all a bit damaged by it. It seems everyone who has played the role has been through some kind of problem and we all understand each other. We're almost like an Elphaba self-help group! An AA meeting of green girls where everyone has their story about it, as it is so incredibly hard. It's not something that's publicly spoken about.

The whole experience was a whirlwind, and when I look back, it was gone in a heartbeat although at the time it didn't seem that way. I would desperately love to go back with an easier show like *Oliver* or *Les Mis* or something, and be there in a different mindset, so I could enjoy it more and experience all that Broadway and New York have to offer. Don't get me wrong, it was amazing but ultimately I couldn't deliver my performance as well as I wanted to, and that was really hard to deal with.

On the last night when the curtain came down, the cast did the traditional celebratory clap and cheer. It was announced in the theatre that I was leaving the show and they brought on flowers. We had a few drinks afterwards but it was fairly low-key and I was ready to come home. I was emotionally and physically exhausted, and just totally drained. My time was done and I was excited to get on that plane and come home to see James. This time I could enjoy my first class experience and I think I ate for most of the way! James was there at the airport to meet me and, unbeknown to me, had picked Jack up from my Mum's, and brought him along too. I just absolutely sobbed when I saw them both. I would have loved to have taken Jack with me as I'm sure he would have been a massive comfort. James drove me home and from that point never really left!

CHAPTER 26

As soon as I got home, I was more-or-less straight back into the London show. Alexia Khadime had been brought in specially to play the role in my absence. The cast by this time had mostly changed again, so we had a slightly different ensemble and covers, although Dianne Pilkington was still in her role as Glinda. I was looking forward to returning because I loved the show itself, but it was the audiences who made it so special for me as they were so responsive. Broadway had taught me how to be around different people. It had been invaluable to be with the people who had created the show, as New York was where it all began. I was able to bring some of that back with me and I did feel I could hold my head up high and come in with more experience, as I'd been doing it a bit longer. I felt I had a right to be there.

Maybe it was because of my renewed sense of self-worth, I don't know, but there now seemed to be a little bit of a power struggle between myself and certain people involved in the show. The company were a really nice team, and initially, everybody had been lovely; however, certain individuals were keen to express their roles, shall we say, and I think they wanted to mould me back to the way they wanted me to do it. We weren't working together and I wasn't being supported. It was such a high-pressured show and you need a level of support to get through it, more than you normally would. People don't really talk about this, but anyone who is in that show, or has been in it will know what I mean. I've gone on to do other shows such as *Oliver* and *Cats*, which were a completely different experience. The people were so lovely and I was treated with such respect.

The good thing was my voice was a lot better by now, partly because I was stronger and I was getting used to singing the show. I'd learned little tricks to help me along the way, and I knew when to stop. For instance, I would have a night off when I felt tired as opposed to pushing through, which I liken a bit to running. If you keep on going, providing you're not actively damaging yourself of course, you can get stronger and for me to have done it for two years without stopping must have strengthened my voice somehow, or I would have failed and given up. I was gaining control and also respect from others and for myself and was learning how to navigate the role properly.

Again on that first entrance back in London, the audience went nuts. It was obviously news that I was back, and had been publicised, as there were a load of fans in the audience. This is where I really felt things start to change for me, and I began to notice that people were supporting me. This sudden reaction from the audience was a bit of a game-changer and it just felt different. Whether that was because I'd been on Broadway I don't know, but suddenly I had a bit more of an impact.

I have worked with some really naughty people over the years who have made me laugh so much, which isn't really difficult to do as I am such a terrible giggler. I just find things really funny and it is worse when you know you shouldn't. Ollie Tompsett, who was playing Fiyero, was one of these people. I am not sure what happened on this particular performance but we knelt down to sing our duet, 'As Long As You're Mine,' and despite having done the show for over a year I just blanked and completely forgot my words, which was ridiculous. I was looking at him in fear and I think he knew that I'd forgotten the words and just started to sing my verse, but in my key, and I found it one of the funniest things I'd ever heard. Not because he couldn't sing it, because he was brilliant, but we both found it hilarious and we giggled throughout the entire song. It was one of those moments where I came off afterwards, and I was mortified, and annoyed with myself. I think Ollie felt the same and we couldn't look at each other for a while and had to get cross with each other, to get over it. We were such good mates but because we'd had this horrific giggling fest through this song we then had to get angry because this couldn't go on. It still makes me giggle to think about it.

During my final months in Wicked I was given the opportunity to appear in the 2008 *Royal Variety Show*. The producers of the show approached Brian and I to be on it, on the back of the *Wicked In Rock* EP, which for me was beyond exciting.

It all tied in perfectly as the cast of *Wicked* had appeared on it the year before with Idina, so the fact I was now in *Wicked* was something a bit different. I think the producers were obviously excited to get Brian on there as well.

We performed *Defying Gravity*, and Roger's son Rufus, who was only seventeen at the time, was our drummer. He was so nervous that he was sick before we went on, but of course as you'd expect was brilliant. This was his first gig and he subsequently came on tour with us, and then with Queen where he split the show with his Dad. He now plays for The Darkness and I feel so proud that we gave him his first shot, and he is now this massive rock star. We try and stay in touch and send the odd message and he came to my wedding. I've seen him backstage at various Queen gigs and would definitely love to go and see The Darkness at some point.

I was beside myself, as I'd always wanted to do the Royal Variety Show. It was something I grew up watching, enjoying seeing the big musicals of the day feature on it. I often talk about things happening when they're meant to, and how sometimes you're not meant to do a particular job or role at that time. I didn't do *Les Mis* for a good few years but when I got it, I played Fantine and it was the right time. It was the same thing with the Royal Variety. I didn't get to do it with We Will Rock You which I think they did the year after I left and I just kept missing out on it. When it came along it happened in a big way. I got to appear as myself, but at the same time was representing Wicked, and performing with Brian, plus it was the build up to our first studio album coming out so it was all perfect timing.

I remember standing on the stage, and the curtain coming up, then hearing the rumble of the intro to Gravity and my adrenalin was off the scale. I was and still am so proud of that performance, it felt great and seemed to light up the auditorium. The Royal Variety audience was quite an interesting demographic though, because they're not raucous, and not what you want them to be. They're generally quite reserved, and really you want the fans there for the big reaction, but of course it is what it is and I get that, and it's such a worthwhile charity. The television broadcast and exposure was what we really got from it which was brilliant.

There were so many massive superstars there and Brian knew everyone so it was like I had my very own backstage VIP pass. I remember saying to him, "*Oh my god there's Cliff Richard*," and he said, "*Oh I know Cliff let's go and say hello*," and he was like that with everyone. It was the same with Prince Charles, "*Yeah I know Charles let's go over*". It was mind-blowing and I was thinking "*Oh my god what is happening... this is bonkers."* Those kind of nights are just the best but I really have to pinch myself. Brian is just so generous as an artist, and always takes time to introduce me to people. As he did later on with *Anthems*, he wants to push me forward, and does it in those situations. It was absolutely mental backstage and so so busy. I think Rhianna was there that year and Take That and Michael McIntyre very early on in his career. I just remembering passing them all in the wings. It's like a conveyor belt of celebrity, but it's like a military operation and there is no time for chatting as time is so tight.

We lined up on the stage afterwards, and met Prince Charles and Camilla, although it's all such a blur and I can't remember what they said, which to this day really annoys me. I've been quite lucky and have sung for royalty quite a few times over the years, including the Queen, William and Harry at her jubilee, but also at the Royal Albert Hall later on. In more recent years, I had the honour of singing at the launch of the Royal Princess, a new ship in Southampton, which the Duchess of Cambridge christened. I love the Royals and used to absolutely adore Princess Diana, who I could relate to as I can with Kate.

I was quite excited about her being there because we are similar in age, had our babies at the same time, and were married in the same year, so I felt we had certain things in common. Kate and I were both pregnant on this launch day and I remember her coming in looking beautiful as always and sitting down to watch me perform. I got to sing a new song especially written for the launch which was quite a moment, and singing for Kate was very special as there was an air of magic about her and I felt it. Sadly I didn't get to shake her hand. I would love to have met her and hopefully I will at some point.

Another opportunity that came my way at this point was of being a mentor on a television show called "*I'd Do Anything*". The premise of the show was to find someone to play the role of Nancy, to star in a brand-new production of *Oliver*. This was the second such show in the series following on from the success of *Any Dream Will Do*, and it was quite early days in reality television. The production team of *I'd Do Anything* came along to the theatre and I filmed a few bits with them. They came on stage and we did a bit of a workshop which was featured on the programme. I wasn't heavily involved and it was just a day or two of filming. I think I featured on one of the episodes, where I watched the contestants' performances, and gave some feedback, then they came to see our show. Ruthie Henshall was another mentor so it was lovely to see her again, although I'd been to see her in shows, we'd only done a couple of corporate gigs together since college.

In this business I think we all have to have an ego to a certain extent. By that I mean some kind of self-belief, and I do think I am confident, especially on stage. Unfortunately though, ego is invariably thought of as a negative trait in the types where the ego walks in before the person, and I don't think I am like that at all.

I'm sure I wouldn't be like that and can only relate it to myself and someone like Samantha Barks, who was a contestant in '*I'd Do Anything*'. Sam was from the Isle of Man, and eventually came third in the show, but from that she kept working until she got the part of Eponine in the *Les Mis* film, for which she won loads of awards and is now massively successful. When I was a mentor on '*I'd Do Anything*', she was virtually unknown and I was doing really well in my career. I've interviewed her recently for my podcast and I am genuinely pleased for her success. If I want something, I find my own way of getting it, new ways of being ok with things, or navigate towards something else that is new or exciting or positive, rather than competing. That is the trouble with our industry, it is so competitive. I believe that if you can find a way to get through it, without the negativity and competition, you can protect yourself and survive a little better.

My time in *Wicked* was fast coming to an end. It had always been a bit crazy at the stage door entrance, with barriers up where we would sign autographs. That was normal in an abnormal way, but now, it was very different, and by the time I was due to leave the show, people were camping out to get tickets, and on my last night I literally could not get out of the stage door. It was mobbed and I actually felt like a rock star.

There's a line in the show that goes "*For the first time ever I feel Wicked*" and on my very last show James suggested I should say "*For the last time ever I feel Wicked*"

"*Don't be so stupid, I can't change the words*" was my immediate response, but he managed to persuade me and I actually did it. The crowd went absolutely mental and all stood up. It was such a lovely and memorable moment. I made a speech at the end of the show, which was a first for me and quite something. I'd never had that moment in any shows before, of being able to speak at the end to say thank you to the fans, and everyone involved, and it felt good, as I'd been on such a journey with it all. The wonderful producer Michael McCabe and his associate Nia came on stage to present me with a gorgeous bouquet of flowers and then we all had a few drinks afterwards to mark the occasion, but inevitably it was quite low-key as lots of people were still staying on

It was incredible, but I was so overwhelmed and I don't think I took it in properly at the time, because, believe it or not, it becomes the norm very quickly, and you are dealing with the job in hand, as opposed to enjoying the moment. I think that as much as I enjoyed it, it's not until I look back on it, that I understand the scale of it and how incredible it actually was. It was such a special time but you are loaded with so much other stuff and information and exhaustion and all I wanted to do was get home. The relief when I finished the show, that I wouldn't have to sing it again, or so I thought, was immense. At that point I had never been back to a show so for me that was it. As such, it was mixed emotions and of course it was a bit sad as it was the end of that pretty epic chapter, and the end of being the green girl, but I was done.

When I returned to the show five years later it was a vastly different experience as I was in a completely different vocal space, but more importantly, head space.

CHAPTER 27

When I first met James he was working in the City, in sales. He lost that job through coming to see me so much in New York, and there followed a few more sales jobs working locally. Each time, he seemed unhappy as if he wasn't going anywhere, and had no real drive. As our relationship progressed, he could see how much I, and everyone I was working with, loved our jobs and I remember having a conversation with him.

"*If you could do anything, what would you do?*" I asked him.

His immediate response was "*I'd work in football*" to which I replied "*Well why don't you work in football?*"

He thought about that, but not for long, and initially began to train as a personal trainer. He enjoyed it, but it still wasn't driving him or motivating him, so he took the plunge and started training as a football coach and has never looked back. He started off in Brentford, went to Cambridge and Stevenage then ended up as a coach for Luton Town where he has now been for the last seven years and loves it. He'd love to be a manager of a first team one day which is quite tough to get into but I'm sure he can do it. I'd like to think I inspired him but I think it was just suddenly being around my friends and people in an industry where they are passionate about their jobs, so I can't take full credit. I did make him give up smoking though!

I always think James should be the showbiz one though, as he is far more dramatic than I ever am. I'm definitely not a show off in my normal everyday life and I can be quite shy speaking to people sometimes. In fact, if I'm out socially I'm quite reserved and take a step back in that situation, whereas James is Mr Saturday Night if we go out. In my career however, I am front centre stage and confident in that place. I step into the role of being *Kerry Ellis* or the *West End Performer*, whatever people expect of me on that occasion. I notice it more when I do workshops. It's really nerve-wracking walking into a room full of young people but I can step in and teach with confidence, it's almost like flicking on a light switch. If, for instance, we go to a wedding where I don't know anyone, I just sit back and don't instigate any conversation. It's not shyness, because I don't consider myself shy. Maybe it's because when I am working I have to be on the front foot, to be confident and sociable, which can be tiring, albeit enjoyable, so it's good to sit back and let others take the limelight as it's not always about me. I admit I do enjoy being the centre of attention though. If I haven't worked for a while and I'm at home, my husband tells me I'm unbearable. It's like I need to go out and be that person and do that thing, then I'm all right again and can chill. I love the simplicity of being away from all that though. One of my greatest pleasures is walking the dog. I also love my yoga class. I appreciate the simple quiet things which are such a stark contrast to the hectic entertainment business I work in.

After my stint on Broadway, James moved in with me and we eventually decided to buy a place together. Steven and Craig were now living in Hitchin together, and we would often drive to visit them at weekends and we both just fell in love with the place. It seemed every time we got off the M25 we would say to each other how amazing it was, and how green and calm, and that we should move there one day. We would sit in Steven and Craig's garden on many occasions having BBQ's, and be able to totally chill and relax. On one of these glorious summer evenings whilst enjoying a glass of wine, their neighbours, Astrid and Steve, popped over and joined us for a drink. During the course of the conversation it was casually mentioned that they wanted to sell their place. We jokingly said we would buy it, and they immediately invited us to have a look round. We instantly fell in love with it and put our offer in, which they accepted. Something changed, and they didn't sell it in the end, but it gave us the impetus we needed to start looking around Hitchin and we've now been here for twelve years.

Firstly we put an offer in for a little house in St. Ippolyts which we lost. We then found another property which I completely fell in love with and ended up losing it twice. We were gazumped the first time, then it came back on the market as it had fallen through, so we put another bid in and got it. All the searches were going through and I was so excited, until the person at the top of the chain pulled out and I was devastated. The estate agent then told us he had another property which had just come on the market and hadn't even been put online yet, and did we want to view it before it was advertised. We went along and I liked it but didn't want it as my heart was still with the other house, and I wasn't ready to move on and let it go! I just couldn't get excited about this one, but James thought it was brilliant and explained it was a really good house, that yes we would have to do a bit of work on, but it would be worth it and it would be a great investment. He persuaded me to go back for a second viewing, which we did, and although I still wasn't that keen, I agreed he was probably right and we put an offer in there and then and we are still here today.

I would say James and I are both alpha males in our relationship. We often discuss this and agree we are both equally dominant and as a result are often at loggerheads. I don't class myself as a feminist. I think the pay gap is ridiculous and of course we should all be equal in that respect. However, I do believe if someone is better at a job, then they should be paid more, whoever they are. I admit I like chivalry and I like guys to be gentlemanly but it's more about respecting each other as humans. We're not equal because we're not physically equal. Yes, some extremely strong women can be stronger than some men but on average, and in general, we are different. My son Alfie is strong and I explain to him that if he pushes his friend, a little girl of the same age, it will hurt her as she is not as strong as he is. We've gone way too far the other way these days, and I think we have to now create the right balance.

I kept my flat basically because I could. I have always been quite good with money and I had managed to save a lot whilst in Wicked, carefully putting it away and investing in the right places. We'd had plenty of holidays along the way and enjoyed ourselves, but I had still saved enough to put down a deposit on our new house, meaning, I could keep Brockley. I knew I would never really have a pension as such, and I had always thought if I could have an extra property at some point, it would be brilliant, and that was the ideal opportunity. I'm not saying it was easy and if I'd sold Brockley it would have been so much easier financially, but as we had no other responsibilities at the time I knew that was the time to make it difficult.

Once I'd committed, I was ready and excited. We completely ripped out everything, which we hadn't intended to do as we thought it would just need a bit of cosmetic work, but one thing led to another, and as we started taking things away we would see another job to be done, or the electrics needed doing, and so it went on. The entire bathroom came out, we extended the loft and over the years we have just gutted the entire house. It was fun when the two of us moved in as we did it mostly ourselves with a bit of help from Craig and Steven. We got experts in for the stuff we couldn't do ourselves as we're not particularly good at DIY, but we weren't afraid of getting our hands dirty and getting stuck in. We could rip it all apart but then we weren't so good at putting it together or the finessing! We gave it a good go though. Steven is really handy and put in both our kitchen and bathroom, which really helped us keep costs down. Sadly my Grandad was too old to help by then, plus it was too far for them to travel really. He was so handy and they were forever doing their own house. Nearly every time I went round they'd painted another room. They were so house-proud.

As soon as we moved into our house we decided to get another dog. It was always on the cards as we are both massive dog lovers and we really wanted a dog that was ours. When we first met, James had a Beagle called Honey and I had Jack. Sadly, Honey died before we moved in together so we wanted a buddy for Jack, but nothing too big as we both worked, so another Jack Russell seemed the natural choice. We looked online and it wasn't long before we found what we were looking for. A registered breeder in North London had a couple of eight-week old Jack Russell puppies who were looking for a home. Luckily one was sold or we would probably have taken them both. We named him Ocho, which is Spanish for eight as my husband is obsessed with that number, which has a lot to do with his early childhood and memories of football. He has got much better recently but he used to have to touch the door handle eight times, turn the light on and off eight times, those sort of things. Although he is better, the number eight is continuous in our world. If we go to Vegas for example he has to make eight out of all the numbers in the casinos whenever he is placing a bet. He just can't rest if he hasn't done it or if it isn't right in his eyes. He also is a little bit obsessive with the house and if it suddenly becomes a bit of a tip, he can't rest until he has sorted it out. I wouldn't say he is really bad with it but I recognise it.

When we brought Ocho home Jack was very stand-offish with him, not aggressive, but he would just turn his back and basically ignore him. They were best buddies eventually and would play all the time. He actually did the same thing with James when I first met him. For the first six months Jack remained aloof and did not take to him at all. It was so funny because James is a real dog lover and was all over Jack, giving him loads of love and attention and trying to play with him and get him on side, but Jack would not have any of it. Every time James came to my house or wherever we were, Jack would just wee all over him. James couldn't quite believe it. "*What the hell's going on?*" he would say each time.

Jack was very much my dog and it was like he was saying to James, no, this is my woman, you are not taking her. So for six months James would pick him up and Jack would wee on him. He was never aggressive and would only wee the once when James first came in. He was marking his territory as it had just been me and him since he was 8 weeks old. Why be aggressive when you can just wee on someone? He did eventually relent and got used to him.

Poor James really went through it to begin with as my brother was also quite harsh on him too when we first met, and he'd not really been hard on anyone before. I think with Andrew he probably knew that James was here to stay before I did, and he did give him a bit of a tough time and lots of banter which James took really well. Now they are close and get on brilliantly. Apart from that and Jack weeing on him, everyone else welcomed him into the family really well. James is so sociable and friendly, it's hard not to like him really.

Not long after we got Ocho we decided to move into Craig and Steven's. It was freezing cold one night, we had no heating system no hot water, and no electrics. James and I were in one bedroom with all our belongings stacked up around us and just the two dogs keeping us warm. There was brick dust everywhere so we had that constant feeling of being dirty and we couldn't live like that any longer. We moved lock stock and barrel with Jack and Ocho to Steven and Craig for what we thought would be a week and ended up as two months, but it was all worth it in the end. They are like family to us so it all worked really well and they loved having us there. They were such brilliant times.

CHAPTER 28

For once I didn't have a musical to go into immediately after *Wicked*, but it so happened that the Shaw Theatre, a tiny theatre in London, which holds about 500 people, approached Jorg about the possibility of me putting on a one-woman show there, for one night only, which was something I'd been thinking about and had wanted to do for a while. I jumped at the chance and from there it just escalated. I called upon Steven initially to help me creatively plan the show and give me a few directions. He asked Craig to MD for me, and that was the first time we all came together as a little team. Craig put together some new arrangements of covers, in tribute to some of the shows I had been in so far, which I performed in the first half. The second half was more rock numbers, which I really enjoyed singing. I'd performed a few odd gigs on my own before but this was now on another level.

Craig has given singing lessons for many years and coincidentally now teaches at Laine. I will often ask him about my voice and vocal technique generally, to which he will always say, "*I don't want to talk to you about it Kerry, because you have your own way of doing things, which is very natural, and your instinctive way is how you have sung all your life. If I now try and mess with that, I don't think it's going to do you any favours.*"

I understand what he means but there are times when I do want to know the answer on how to do something. "*You'll find it,*" is his response and yes, I suppose I do eventually, in my own way.

We asked Brian if he would join us as a special guest, which he was happy to do and he played with the full band at the end, much to everyone's complete surprise and delight. The size of show we managed to put on in that little theatre was quite unbelievable. We had even brought in our own sound system. Steve Sidwell, who had been the orchestrator for *We Will Rock You*, did some of the other arrangements for me, which was a pretty big deal as he is such a massive arranger, composer and orchestrator. We really were just meant to be trying it out to begin with, but it just kept growing, ending up being hugely successful and a sell-out and I put on three or four of these types of shows over the next few years. I loved the freedom of being able to sing what I wanted, and say what I wanted, and just be myself. It was liberating and such a buzz, but at the same time it was terrifying.

Much as I loved it, it was quite a testing and nerve wracking time for me as I'd never really done anything as myself before. All I had done were shows where I had scripts, costumes and direction and knew where I had to be on stage, at any given moment, as someone else. In a musical you become someone else and can hide behind that character, their persona, and words, but suddenly I couldn't do that and had to be myself as there was no one else. I was the anchor for the whole show and couldn't just sing. It was a bit like ripping off a plaster. Okay, I'd done a couple of concerts where I was part of a line-up, but to have to speak as myself, choose which songs to perform, book the band, and basically put it all together was quite a responsibility.

Back in the days of Potters I always found the prospect of talking to an audience as myself really weird, although luckily I didn't have to do it much then. Everyone else was so brilliant at being funny and the patter they came out with, they were just so confident. That weird feeling stayed with me whenever I had to be myself and I just felt odd and totally insecure. I couldn't turn into this Saturday night 'here I am folks', type of person. I think I was so nervous about saying the wrong thing and sounding stupid or making a mockery of myself, that I just couldn't do it and it stuck with me.

I've done tons of these types of shows now, but this was a really significant turning point for me, as I found it so difficult to speak. I'd never really had to do it until this point where it became a vital part of what I was doing. Once I started, much as I was nervous I began to get used to it and it was all right. I always knew I could confidently go out and deliver a song, which was a doddle, but the communicating was a different skill I had to learn and ultimately conquer. That part alone has been a massive progression for me over the last ten or fifteen years.

When I first went on on tour with Brian not long after, I would just sit on stage, learning from him and watching how to communicate, and then be brave enough to do it myself. Over the years doing a succession of shows at venues such as the Hippodrome, The Pheasantry in Chelsea and Crazy Coqs meant I could really hone that skill and use those more

161

intimate venues almost like a playground, where I was able to experiment with new songs and new patter. It was doing these shows in these venues that I truly learned to be ok with myself. I'd learn what worked and what didn't, so in later years, when I put on my one woman show at the London Palladium, I really was ready for it. It has always been a recurring problem for me, not wanting to look stupid. It is definitely a process where I have evolved over time. I love it even more now to just be able to talk to the audience and say hello and sing how I want to, as opposed to how someone else wants me to or how the character dictates. I am still evolving as a performer, although I am in a different place now and it doesn't worry me anymore

When I was recording my podcasts during lockdown I was talking to personal trainer, blogger and best-selling author Alice Liveing about posting on social media as yourself. I mentioned the fact that I loved that she posted with no make-up on sometimes and showed her other side. She replied that she didn't care anymore but wouldn't have been able to do that when she was building her brand, which I found really interesting. I really think that it takes time to get to a point where you are secure with who you are and secure with your following, and only then can you allow yourself to be vulnerable.

I think age and maturity has helped me and I am a bit more self-assured these days, although I was always confident so it's not a confidence issue. When I was younger I just didn't want to make a fool of myself, or come across as stupid or unknowledgeable, or say the wrong thing. I was so aware of what I was saying that it restricted me, whereas now I am more comfortable in my own skin and my attitude is, if I say something that's not the right thing, or it doesn't get a laugh, I don't care, and I'm all right with it which is quite liberating. A lot of stuff changes when you become a parent and it's not just about you anymore. Obviously my career is about myself, but I am kind of okay with being me now in front of people.

It was bitter-sweet that I had been asked to be a mentor on the '*I'd Do Anything*' television show, as Nancy was a role I had always longed to do. However, I wasn't prepared to go on the programme myself and do a musical theatre audition in front of a live television audience. The irony was that when Jodie Prenger left in 2010, they asked me to take over as Nancy. They basically offered it to me but had to go through the motions of asking me in to read for Lawrence O'Connor, who was the Associate Director and who I'd previously worked with in *Miss Saigon*. I went along to Cameron Mackintosh's offices in London, and it was very informal. We all sat round a table, I read a little bit of script, sang a bit of a song and that was it. I knew I had the job and that this was more of a courtesy. It was just myself and a couple of others going into the show at this point so it was quite a small rehearsal period of a couple of weeks at 3 Mills Studios, Bromley-by-Bow, which was quite a mission to commute to, but I didn't care as I was excited to do the show.

After such a responsibility with *Wicked*, doing *Oliver* was a light relief and gave me my love of performing back because there was no pressure with it. I loved it so much because of that, and it was a joyous time. I knew I could deliver the show, and sing it easily with no stress or strain. The music was fun and the kids kept all our energy levels up. Everyone in the company was lovely and it was great being back at Drury Lane but this time in a role. Again, my entrance on that first night will never leave me. As I came down the stairs the audience went nuts. This was the first show I had done since *Wicked* and it was so good to get that reaction. There was a lot of expectation in the auditorium and everyone could sense it. I think it even took the producers by surprise. I don't think they were expecting that reaction and neither was I. I thought it was a *Wicked* thing. *Wicked* was such a unique time and we gathered momentum and support along the way. So when this same reaction happened in *Oliver*, I started to believe I had that momentum and support, which reinforced the feeling that I'd earned my right to be there and the sense of self-worth I now had. I loved working for Cameron; he is always really decent and lovely to work for and I loved everything about being in that show. Griff Rhys Jones was my Fagin and then Russ Abbott came in for a spell. It was just a fun show to be involved in and working with such big teams of kids who had such energy was a real lift. Eight shows a week with *Oliver* felt like a doddle. I'm not saying it was easy but it was just a breeze and so enjoyable. In fact my general health and voice improved so much once I was in the show, and I could have performed it twenty times a week. It was a completely different demand.

By the time I came to the end of my run in *Oliver* I was ready to do something else. I remember being asked to go up for a few auditions, Ghost and Rock of Ages being two of them but I didn't want to. I needed

163

a break from musical theatre. This was the first time I had started saying no to things and turning opportunities down. Before now I'd gone along to any audition even if I wasn't sure I wanted it. I had got to the stage where I knew what I did, or more importantly, didn't want. Plus, I really wanted to try pursuing the music thing for a bit, or at least be able to focus on it. Brian and I had been working on this album more or less for ten years now and I needed to give it a go. It needed to be my focus. That was my plan.

TOP TIPS WHEN STARTING OUT

- Take every opportunity and don't be frightened to do so. If there is an audition that you don't like the look of or you don't think you are right for, I would say go along anyway because you don't know who will be on that panel and who might be casting for something else. They may agree you are not right for that role but might remember you in the future and think you are perfect for something else. Do the audition and give it your all, even if you don't want the role. Do the best you can because it just might serve you well in the future.

- Remember that if you are turned down for a role it is not personal. You just don't fit and that is okay, you might fit next time. I auditioned for *Les Mis* at college and desperately wanted it but was turned down. I auditioned a couple of years later for the show and got through to the workshop stage, but still didn't get it. Then years later I got to play Fantine in London. The time just wasn't right before. Don't get bogged down with the rejections. Pick yourself up and move on.

- Use social media in a positive way. It can be quite consuming and influential for younger people, which makes me glad I didn't experience it in my early 20's. I feel the pressure of it even now in my 40's. However, I wouldn't have been able to do my podcast if I hadn't been connecting with people through Instagram. It enables you to reach other like-minded people, there can be a lot of positivity and it's a brilliant tool if used in the right way. Follow people who make you feel good or inspire you to try something you hadn't thought of. Don't follow people who perhaps stir up negative feelings within you if they are doing something you really want to do.

- Try not to engage with trolls. Those people want a reaction from you and it's not worth a response. I would never say anything unkind or provocative on social media as you never know what's going to come back and bite you, and you may regret it. I would say just be careful. Social media is like having your own little newspaper, so put out that positivity.

- Be respectful, especially to those who have been in the business for years. You will gain people's confidence if you respect them. Treat others how you wish to be treated yourself. Everyone wants to work with nice people, so just be nice and be kind.

CHAPTER 29

We would often go away on holidays, and long weekends with Craig and Steven, so in November 2010 it was nothing out of the ordinary when we all decided to have a little break in Padstow, Cornwall. We stayed in Rick Stein's beautiful luxury hotel which only had about ten rooms, making it a perfect place to relax. As we were getting ready for dinner on the last night, which so happened to be November 5th, I stepped out onto our balcony overlooking Padstow harbour, hoping to see a few fireworks going off. It was so picturesque and tranquil and I stood there just taking it all in. We had these Chinese lanterns, which were okay to use at the time, and James was really insistent that we set them off there and then, whereas I wanted to wait until after dinner, as it would be something lovely to do afterwards and we wouldn't be rushed. I eventually gave in as he was so insistent, and after trying to light this thing for what seemed like ages he released it into the night sky, although it might not have been hot enough because it was all lopsided and looked like it was heading for an early landing in the bay. We were both in hysterics by now and as I turned round to James still laughing, he was down on one knee fumbling in his pocket for the ring and asked me to marry him, which made me laugh even more, but this time it was that type of giddy nervous laughter. I said yes of course, but still kept laughing and couldn't quite believe it. He'd had the ring specially made and had designed it himself. Apparently he'd kept checking in with Steven and Craig to make sure it was all right, which of course it was, I loved it. Craig and Steven were in on the whole surprise and had been listening intently from their room next door, then excitedly popped their heads round the balcony to congratulate us. So, newly engaged, we all went down to dinner, and to top it all, Rick Stein came over and said hello, and signed our menu for us, which we still have on our wall at home.

The following day Steven drove us all home, but we broke down on the way and ended up being towed the rest of the way. It took us five hours, as the recovery driver kept having to stop for breaks, and we were in a service station for what must have been two hours. Not exactly a romantic end to the weekend, more like a comedy, but we'll never forget it. We were married less than a year later on September 8th 2011; it had to be the 8th of course, and Steven was my Man of Honour. It was lovely because Craig and Steven returned to Cornwall for their wedding in 2017, which of course we attended.

We were pretty relaxed about our wedding arrangements and wanted it to be quite laid back. At one point we even thought of just going away to a little villa in Spain or something like that, but, because I wanted my grandparents there, it would have been really tricky as they were quite old by then, and it would have been hard to get them there.

I hadn't really planned on a big wedding dress shopping day. I casually mentioned to Steven one day that I was thinking of popping into Hitchin to look in the little bridal shop there, and, as my Maid of Honour, asked if he'd like to come along, which he did. The first dress I tried on, I immediately knew was 'the one'. It was perfect, although I did have another shopping session in St Albans after that just to make sure.

I think that was tough for my Mum. I often wonder if she wants the whole mother-daughter experience. My friend Bobbie and her Mum Jane, who was like a second mum to me growing up, are super-close and always do girly things together whereas I've never really had that kind of relationship with my Mum, and I do think it was hard for her. I wasn't that bride, and I wasn't that person. We just weren't in that place at that time either, so I didn't embrace it, and I think perhaps the stubbornness in me didn't feel I should do it for her either, which I struggle with to this day. The day itself was perfect. We were married at Tewin Bury Farm Hotel in Welwyn, in a little converted barn, with about ninety guests and it was as relaxed and low key as we'd wanted.

CHAPTER 30

Brian and I were getting back in the studio more now and had started seriously working on *Anthems*. Before I went to Broadway, I'd performed *Chess in Concert* at the Royal Albert Hall for the wonderful director, producer and lighting designer Hugh Wooldridge, the man behind *The Night of 1000 Voices* as well as many other worldwide events. I played Svetlana Sergievsky, alongside Idina Menzel as Florence. I only had a couple of songs to do but it was a big moment and a huge deal at the time, with quite a line-up of names such as Marti Pellow, Josh Grobin, Clarke Peters and Adam Pascal. It was filmed and subsequently televised in New York. Brian came to watch me in it and saw Josh Grobin sing *Anthem*.

"That's such a cracking song," he said to me after, *"I think you should try that and we'll make it a special arrangement for you."* I loved the idea but put it to the back of my mind and whilst I was in New York we were emailing back and forth, chatting about it and music generally and various bits and pieces. Brian proved to be a bit of a lifeline while I was there as I could talk to him about my voice and insecurities with theatre, and the pressure of it, as he understood. He could relate to everything I was saying and totally got it, which was quite a comfort to me. We would also talk creatively as well; Brian would offer a piece of advice or something to focus me while I was having a tough time vocally. By the time I came back we had loads of ideas for the album and were ready to record what was to become *Anthems*. It took us pretty much up until I finished in *Oliver*, approximately eighteen months later, to have it ready to go. I couldn't get much recording done whilst I was in *Wicked* so we took it gently. *Oliver* was a much easier show for me and I had so much more energy to give.

We recorded the orchestras for both *Wicked In Rock* and *Anthems* at Abbey Road Studios. Although I'd been to the studios before for other little recordings, to hear those orchestrations from seventy musicians being played for our own album, was quite emotional. Having that many musicians in a room, was, especially for me, quite something. I remember us both sitting in the studio with the orchestra as they were recording, rather than in the control room as it was so exciting. Steve Sidwell, who had previously worked on Robbie Williams' '*Swing When You're Winning*' album and the Carole King musical *Beautiful*, also arranged some of the orchestrations for the album. He'd been a mate of ours for a number of years and did us a bit of a favour by putting together all of his best players on it. I often think things happen at the right time for me. Being at Abbey Road and working on something that was so important to me felt like everything was coming together. We still say how brilliant that album is with all the wonderful orchestrations, musicians, arrangements and vocals. It's an album I am so proud of.

Once we'd finished recording we were signed by Decca records. I couldn't get my head round this big label signing me and I was beside myself. *My Wicked in Rock* EP had been released under Brian's label, but suddenly to be under this huge label was on another level entirely.

I was suddenly doing photo shoots for the album cover. Lots of clothes kept arriving for me to try on and I was surrounded by photographers, which was so surreal. I had discussions with the team at Decca over the kind of things I wanted, and I gave them a load of images for the look I was trying to portray, which was classical with a rock element mixed together. They then sent me a mood board which is a board with lots of different ideas on it, including colours, pictures, different ideas for outfits, hair and make-up and basically gives a feel of what you are looking for. The board can be a mixture of everything ranging from perhaps some biker boots and a net skirt to a rock tee shirt and a ball gown.

The shoot itself was amazing but Brian and I didn't agree on the cover at all. It was really pop and commercial and I loved the colours. They'd photoshopped my face but Brian kept insisting that it wasn't me and that it didn't even look like me at all. He much preferred the back cover and told me that my beauty came from my vulnerability, and my honesty, and by being myself. He didn't like it at all but I loved that version of me and I was adamant about it! I wanted to be this glossy rock star. Now I look back on it I can see that he was so right.

There have been several similar occasions where he has shown me pictures that he has either taken himself, or picked out for me, "*This is you Kerry.*"

"*No way Brian,*" I'd argue back. When it came to the '*Kissing Me*' single cover I really wasn't sure about it at all. Brian took the photo of me in the studio and to me it just wasn't glamorous enough, or worse, not interesting enough. He kept reiterating that this was me, and this is what was interesting to other people, so I gave in on that one, and again I look at it and think, yeah he was so right. It's really interesting how our relationship has developed over the years. The older I got, the more confident and opinionated I got.

That said, I'm not really an argumentative person. James and I bicker, but we don't properly row, and I'm the same with Brian. He is pretty headstrong and he knows what he wants so we have had our disagreements, especially as he has been quite opinionated about what I should or shouldn't do. It's always with the best intentions though, as he's always thought that I should have been this massive rock star and a music artist and to begin with, that is what he was trying to facilitate. I think because of where I came from with such a strong theatrical background, I knew that I could have a sustainable path in theatre, and that I could earn my living from it. Whilst I was happy to give half my career to developing what Brian and I were doing, I didn't want to give up the theatre work entirely which in many ways was my security. Brian tried to persuade me to concentrate on the music industry and much as I would have loved to have chased the dream of being a rock star, I just couldn't take that risk.

We've even disagreed about people I've worked with, only because he wants the very best for me and is always thinking bigger and better. In this respect he is like a parent, which I guess forces me to strive harder and think like that too. However, I know where the money is, and what I need to do to support myself, which is something I have always done. Of course, I know that he has facilitated certain things which would never have come my way if I wasn't with him. I'm not blind to that, but at the same time we have done a lot of it together and equally he wouldn't have done some of the stuff if I hadn't been with him. It's swings and roundabouts for us both.

Although I had done loads of press and promo with shows before, it felt very different with *Anthems*, because it was me as an artist, in my own right. It wasn't me being Elphaba or me being a character, it was suddenly me as me and it was weird. It was also a bit of a whirlwind as tons of television and radio followed, including a few *Friday Night is Music Night* appearances.

I was lucky enough to be asked to do quite a few of these over the years in various venues such as the Peacock Theatre, Wogan Studios, the Hackney Empire and Mermaid Theatre. Wonderful places and they were always a joy to do.

Anthony Cherry, the producer of *Friday Night Is Music Night*, was always a great supporter during the course of these different shows and is now a good friend. He had been following my career and asked me if I'd like to present my own evening in 2012. It was at the Colosseum in Watford with the incredible BBC Concert Orchestra. I had to do all the links, I had my own guests and it was all my songs. In hindsight, it was quite early on in my solo career, so although I was ready to do it was quite a daunting prospect and I was absolutely terrified. I think only Michael Ball, and perhaps one other person had presented their own show before, so it was quite a big deal.

We were also invited to perform Anthems at the annual televised *Festival of Remembrance* at the Royal Albert Hall in 2010, a day I will never forget. It was good to get to know some of the people involved and be around them on their special day and then to bring our performance to it and really feel we were adding something to the evening which was a lovely feeling. To be part of that, and watch the poppy drop, the Military Wives and the Chelsea Pensioners was an absolute privilege and special, and I felt very emotional.

During the poppy drop there was no music, just deadly silence for two minutes. It's so difficult to describe the emotion but to have that many people respectfully silent whilst thousands of poppies just dropped from above, flooding the Royal Albert Hall, was so incredibly moving and so dramatic, it just took my breath away. It's such an emotional day anyway, and up to that point I had watched so many things and listened to so many heartbreaking stories of triumph and disappointment. The occasion is highly emotive and I would defy anyone not to be moved, even if you had no connection whatsoever with the day. At the time I still had my grandparents and I felt proud, and that it was a good thing to do for them. Knowing they were watching made it extra special and I'm so glad they got to see me do that.

The poppy drop is the last moment, and like a release of all that emotion, and it is so powerful. Brian and I have shared a lot of those type of experiences over the years together and it was great to be stood next to him on that occasion. We often talk about it and agree it was one of our most poignant experiences. Our performance on the night went down well and had more meaning behind it somehow. For the first time I felt like I was doing something which was not just for me, which was really good.

Notes from...

I first met Kerry when she was in *My Fair Lady*; and later in *We Will Rock You*. I was totally stunned by her *No-One But You*. Although I recommended her for an Eva Cassidy workshop, we had never really worked together on a major project until *Chess in Concert* at the Royal Albert Hall in 2009. I tell this story in master-classes, as it is the perfect audition story.

Tim Rice was one of the producers of *Chess in Concert*, and, as he was keen to keep Benny and Bjorn happy, suggested that we look at a popular young Swedish singer to play the role of Anatoly's wife, Svetlana. Josh Groban was to play Anatoly.

We invited the young pop-singer to London, had dinner with her and put her up in a nice hotel, ready for her audition the next day. There is no doubt that as a pop-singer she was enormously talented and very pretty – which, realistically, the TV cameras would like – but her vocal range was limited. It was a pop sound rather than musical theatre, and perhaps might not have reached and thrilled the 5,000 people in the Royal Albert Hall. Also, although the 20-odd notes she could sing were terrific, the vocal range of Svetlana is formidable. Plus, we already had Idina Menzel on board as Florence.

I wanted Kerry.

Tim was not arriving until 2.00pm, so I asked her to come and meet the audition panel at 12.30pm. In the room were our casting director, musical director, choreographer, stage manager, and the MD of *We Will Rock You*, Stuart Morley, who was our Associate MD and auditions' pianist.

Kerry came in and I introduced her to those she did not know. It was all gloriously friendly – she is such a lovely woman. Eventually I said, "*What are you going to sing?*"

She said "*A song by a well-known US writing partnership.*"

To which I said "*Oh God, no...*"

Silence in the room.

I explained that their songs were not structured 'A A B A' songs and were more 'A A B Z P Q R C' songs. In other words, they had no shape and were interminable. Not good songs for an audition.

I asked "*Why?*"

To which Kerry brilliantly replied; "*Because it is a song about a woman who has been jilted.*" She had done her homework.

Remembering how she had moved me in *We Will Rock You*, I asked if she could sing *No-One But You* instead, to which she replied "*Well, I have not sung it for a year or so… but I'll have a go.*" Stu Morley popped up from behind the piano and went "*Show key?*"

And off they went.

It was truly magnificent.

As she left the room I popped out with her and explained that Tim was coming in after lunch (it was now 1.00pm), and would she mind coming back? She said she would. I said I wanted Tim to discover Kerry, so could she play along… She said she would.

Tim arrived on time and introduced himself to everyone in the room; striding over to the pianist and saying, "*Hello, I'm Tim*".

He came back to the table and said, "*OK, Huge, who have we got?*" I explained I had a suggestion for Svetlana whom he might not know but that she had the voice and acting chops to fill the Royal Albert Hall. Kerry entered and I introduced her to everyone – as if they were meeting her for the first time – with no hint of what had happened earlier in the day.

So off we went again: "*How are the family? What have you been up to?*" etc. etc. I then asked Kerry, "*What would you like to sing?*"

Once again she said, "*A song by a well-known US writing partnership.*"

To which I said "Oh God, no…"

Silence in the room. Tim said "*I say Huge that's a bit strong.*"

I explained that their songs were not 'A A B A' songs but were 'A A B Z P Q R C' songs. In other words, they had no shape and were interminable. Not good songs for an audition.

I asked "*Why?*"

Again, Kerry brilliantly replied, "*Because it is a song about a woman who has been jilted*". She had done her homework. I could see Tim was impressed.

Looking at Tim I asked Kerry "*By any chance, could you sing the song you sang from We Will Rock You?*" While I was 'desperately' trying to remember the name of the song, Tim chipped in "*No-one but You?*" I clicked my fingers exultantly and said "*Yes, yes, No-one But you*", to which she replied "*I have not sung it for a year or so... but I'll have a go.*" Stu Morley popped up from behind the piano and went "Show key?" And off they went.

The second time Kerry sang it that day was truly one of the most exciting moments in my career thus far. Because she had had time to think about it over lunch, and because she knew everyone in the room was rooting for her, she gave the performance of a lifetime. At the end, I think I can truthfully say that everyone in the room was either crying or damp-eyed. I sneaked a look at Tim who was truly shaken. And stirred. We had all witnessed something very special. All he said – very quietly – was "*Well, we have found our Svetlana...*"

To this day, I ask Kerry to sing *No-one But You* whenever we have the chance to work with each other.

As Rodgers and Hammerstein once said "*Once you have found her, never let her go...*" I adore her.

Hugh Wooldridge

Director, Producer, Writer

Notes from…

If anyone can make lockdown entertaining, Kerry Ellis can. Goodness knows what she's been up to, but these pages should reveal all. In the meantime we've got her recordings to remind us of that wonderfully distinctive voice, particularly memorable for me when she gets to grips with the *Anthem* from *Chess*, hers the definitive distaff version.

Tim Rice

CHAPTER 31

It was Anthony Cherry who again contacted my agent asking if I would sing at the *Olivier's* with Barry Manilow, due to be televised live at the Theatre Royal Drury Lane in March 2011.

"Oh myyyy goddd!! Why me?" was my response.

The answer was they needed someone who was known in the theatre world, who could come in independently and handle what was quite a pressured situation. Anthony was an Executive Producer at the BBC and I had worked with him on various Radio 2 programmes, including a few of Terry Wogan's shows. Terry was great, and such a big supporter of Brian and I. In fact we still maintain that, we were actually guests on one of Terry's last live shows for Radio 2. By this point I had also presented my own *Friday Night is Music Night* so I guess I had proved myself, and Anthony must have thought I could handle this.

I was sent this song *"Look to the Rainbow,"* from Finian's Rainbow, which I'd never heard before, and immediately freaked out a bit at having to learn a song and then sing it with Barry Manilow himself at the *Olivier's,* which would be filled with theatre folk.

I was called into a studio in London to meet him for the first time. As I went in, I remember seeing him in this Alexandra McQueen black jacket, with sequins on the back, and my jaw must have dropped. He had that proper, untouchable, super star presence, and I was a bit in awe, but he was so lovely and welcoming and instantly put me at ease and sat me down. He sat at the piano and talked to me a little bit about the song and what it meant to him, and how to perform it and interpret it. We then had a little go in the rehearsal room, and ran it through a couple of times, but running through my head all the time was *"Oh my god this is Barry Manilow, I can't mess this up."*

I was completely star struck. It may sound crazy as I know I've worked with Brian loads, and he's on that level, but it's because I didn't know Barry, and there was no proper introduction. It was a case of here you are, here's Barry, now you're going to sing with him, off you go.

All this alone made me quite nervous, let alone the calibre of the audience and on top of that live coverage by the BBC, with special guests such as

Stephen Sondheim, Cameron Mackintosh and Angela Lansbury. On the night of the awards though, Barry was so lovely, and he introduced me on stage as his new best friend. During the live performance he sang the wrong lyrics half-way through the song, and I had no choice but to follow him. It was fine though and I'm sure no-one noticed.

James works in football, and it is his life, so when I got a call one day that same year, offering me the chance to sing the National Anthem at Wembley, for the FA Cup Charity Shield and therefore do something that was credible not only to him, but my Dad as well, I jumped at it.

I hadn't done anything like that before, as in singing on the pitch to a packed Wembley, who weren't specifically there to see me! I'd only had a tiny sound check before the crowd started arriving and was given an earpiece so I could hear the music as there was a massive sound delay. Of course, we had to stay for the match and had the best seats. I was able to repeat the experience for a charity match sometime later and we were given a VIP Box for that which was even better. To do something like that and impress my husband was a bonus.

Whenever I talk to students or do workshops with them, I always say to them, your life can literally change in a phone call. During my whole career, I have never known what is coming next, or what is around the corner. Most of the time I don't know where it comes from, or who suggested it, but I get these incredible phone calls out of the blue which can change the course of my life. That is part of the excitement of this industry. I think my music has definitely helped.

I was having a chat with Hugh Wooldridge one day about the possibility of doing another concert for him. This prompted him to ask if Brian and I would launch 'Anthems' at the Royal Albert Hall and incorporate it into a *Night of 1000 Voices* with myself, Brian, a full orchestra, choir, and a bunch of dancers. He basically gave us his ready-made platform to launch our album and kick start the tour. Doing that performance and having the audience go absolutely crazy the first time I came on stage, just blew my mind it was unbelievable. It was quite a significant moment in my career and I will never forget those posters! I was launching my first album at The Royal Albert Hall! "*This isn't how it happens,*" I kept thinking to myself! It seemed like I just kept going up a notch in my career and it would take me by surprise. I was forever wondering what's next or what could possibly top this, and then something does. At the time, I didn't know how I could top going to Broadway and opening in *Wicked*, and then this came along. Each time though, I felt ready for the next challenge that was presented to me. Even though this seemed to come quite quickly on the heels of my own show at the Shaw, and I had done a few other smaller concerts where I had spoken and addressed the audience as myself, to suddenly be in a packed Royal Albert Hall and talk to that audience to promote my first album was mad. Leaving the stage door after the show that night was like nothing else I had ever experienced. I felt like a pop star. It was like a Take That concert and I just couldn't get out!

From that, Brian and I were pretty much on the road with the *Anthems Tour* around the UK for about three weeks, with a band and backing vocalists. It was amazing and almost like starting afresh with a whole new career path. It was then I had to make the extremely painful decision to part ways with Jorg, which was pretty dark at the time. Jorg had been so incredible, and we'd had ten solid years working together. We'd grown together and had become really good friends. He was such a brilliant agent and had done so well for me during those ten years but rightly or wrongly I just felt that I was moving into a different area, that he didn't have experience of, and although he wanted to help, I just didn't think it was his field. It was like I was moving towards a more commercial career and I needed someone to support the music, as well as the theatre, and to raise my profile a bit to enable me to sell out my tours. For me, this last ten years has had the same purpose, to create that profile, so I can continue making my music and to sell albums and concerts, which is a really difficult thing to do. However talented you are, you need an elevated profile to do that. It wasn't the easiest of goodbyes with Jorg sadly, and I was heartbroken.   I've changed agents three times in the ten years since leaving Jorg. Initially I moved on to Jonathan Shalit at Roar Global. I'd started looking at people whose careers I admired to see who they were with. Katherine Jenkins and Myleene Klass caught my eye. Myleene was with Roar and had done loads of shows and music and some radio, quite a variety of stuff, which was what I was keen to do. I set up a meeting with Jonathan Shalit and had a couple of other meetings as well, but Roar seemed the best place. As it turned out I was only with them for about a year as they just weren't right for me, or what I envisaged for my career.

The tour itself was amazing, and this time I got stay in some of the best hotels in the country, although we also had a big tour bus but we didn't sleep on it. We were playing 2000 seat venues and touring with Brian was a different ball game entirely. The people and fans who were coming out to see him were unbelievable but what was nice was, that it was a collaboration of fans. There were a lot of Queen fans who I felt had taken me under their collective wing a bit from the *We Will Rock You* Days and there was also a big theatre fan group predominantly made up of *Wicked* fans. We were merging our fan base which was kind of unique and it really seemed to work. Brian loved it, and I think for him it was quite a game changer because it was the first time, in a long time, that he was playing new music, and different music, and being on the road with something else other than Queen. So for him to be expressive and creative without necessarily playing Queen songs was great. He also loved being around different musicians. I think that is part of why we have worked together for so long and why he enjoys working with me. It is a different outlet for him and it is creative. He gets to write new songs and to discover new music and essentially to work with another singer. Initially, we had been chasing the drama of Queen, plus what I brought from my theatre work, and we were basing our work on that, but in actual fact it changed a lot over the years and we found our drama in our own way. *Acoustic by Candlelight* was one of our most dramatic collaborations but in a very different way. It wasn't big and grand, it was just dramatically simple, which I believe is when we are most powerful.

Since I met James I am always away doing short contracts of two or three weeks and each tour or trip is different. While he doesn't enjoy me being away, he is used to it now. Since having the boys though I won't go away for longer than a week or two maximum. I will either take them with me or get back whenever I can at the weekend, or on my day off. It was easier before we had the kids as James would just come and see me as and when. On the *Anthems* tour he would turn up all the time and think nothing of driving up for the weekend which was great, but now he can't.

We used to be quite romantic, certainly pre children. Now it is more difficult but we try and get the odd weekend away together and make time for each other. James is really good at the little gestures which I love, like bringing me flowers home or taking me somewhere as a surprise.

Childcare is always a difficult one due to our ever-changing routines and abnormal hours, but somehow we always find a way. James' parents Angela and Bob are brilliant and support us so much, helping with the boys whenever they can. Think Gavin's mum Pam in *Gavin and Stacey* and that is my mother-in-law Angela to a tee. When I first met James they would tell him that I was going to run off with a dancer which we now joke about.

I've opened up a whole new world to them as they hadn't really done a lot of theatre before, and they've come into this mad world and embraced it. They come and see me when they can and we try and see them as much as possible although we are about an hour away so not massively close. It's the same with his older sister Karen, she's great and we all get together when we can.

Anything I do that is open to the public, my Dad wants to come to, which is nearly everything. If it's a musical then great, he can just come along as a regular punter and watch it, no problem. If it's a concert, it's not so much that he makes a nuisance of himself, but he is just with me all the time, and much as I love him it can feel like 'take your Dad to work day'! It's a bit like being parented at forty. Although what I do is entertainment and fun, for me it is still work, and I have to focus on that. Sometimes it's brilliant, especially when I was pregnant. I had a couple of gigs in Wales and he would drive me there, so we could chat, and it was great company for me. I do so many concerts and so many different shows and workshops, my weekly schedule could be, for example, a workshop in Leeds on Wednesday then a concert in Southend on the Thursday, then perhaps a Voiceover somewhere else on the Sunday. He's helped me out massively when I'm trying to work the oracle and drive from say Manchester to Bournemouth to Plymouth, helping me with the driving, and I really do appreciate it.

Occasionally, I have put my foot down to him coming to things. We have a good relationship and if I really mean it, he does respect that. To be honest though most of the time he just turns up anyway even if I grumble. I've kind of given up these days and just let it happen, as I know he will just do what he wants. He made a good point to me not so long ago:

"*Kerry, if Alfie and Freddie were doing something would you go?*" and of course I would, I totally get it.

He's followed me all over the world now, especially since he took early retirement, and I think he felt like he was making up for working shifts when I was younger. He has quite a stubborn streak and if he wants to do something he will do it no matter what.

That said, Dad was pretty much on the Anthems tour the whole time and was always hanging about making a nuisance of himself, getting on the sound desk, then getting on the lighting desk. Suddenly it was very different, because it was mine and Brian's show, so we were the bosses. It was so good to have him around if I was really tired, as he was incredibly helpful. He loved it and just wanted to be involved. We're super-close, and really open and honest with each other so it's never been a problem. He's brilliant and he knows I love him. However, whenever he says "*I'll come*" I do hesitate, as sometimes I just like the peace of being on my own!

Further down the line, once I'd had my boys and was touring again with Brian, Dad and Sal came along and had the boys for me as James had to work. I just couldn't have toured without them as they did everything for the boys and it meant I didn't have to leave them.

CHAPTER 32

The Anthems tour ended up at RAF Cranwell and, where we did a big concert in collaboration with the RAF, using their orchestra and performing in their grounds. We raised a bit of money for the RAF and formed quite a good connection with them.

As a thank you to us for doing that concert, Brian and I were invited to fly with the Red Arrows. I still have to pinch myself now, remembering the day we spent with them. All the while I was thinking, *"How is this happening? How am I getting to do this? People just don't get to do this,"* which of course they don't. It's a real select few who get to go and fly with them, and we were amongst that elite few.

We had a health check to begin with, to make sure we were fit enough, then we sorted our flying suits out, did a bit of training in the morning which involved running through a briefing and watching a video on what to do if you come out of the plane! Oh my god! We were both so excited. I'm an adrenaline junkie anyway but that was something else, and I had never experienced anything like it, nor am I likely to again.

Brian and I were in separate planes because obviously there is only room for two in each, and we could wave to each other in the air. Three planes in total went up so we could fly in formation. There was a photographer in the third plane, who I think filmed it, but certainly took some great pictures. We did all the spins and the flips and rocketed up to Newcastle then rocketed back again. I have never felt anything like it in my life. I mean talk about a g-force. You feel it slightly if you go on a roller coaster but this was on another level. I had moments when we did the flips, where my vision would kind of cloud over and I literally couldn't move, it was like I was a magnet to the seat. I was also sick in the plane which was delightful. I was wearing a helmet, and an oxygen mask, and during our briefing our instructor had said it was more than likely that it would happen, and if it did, we had to take our oxygen mask off, be sick in the bag, tie it up and put it in the side of the door then put the mask back on. For some reason they gave Brian an anti-sickness tablet but not me, so he was okay. Probably because I was younger and they thought I wouldn't need it. Turns out that yes I did. Apparently it's quite common, but it didn't make me want to come down.

We were up there for about forty minutes or so, doing a bit of formation, backward flips, sideward flips. I even took control of the joystick at one point. I didn't have any pedals, so it was just the joystick in front of me which is so sensitive. Every so often the pilot would allow me to steer direction. I did a landing and pulling up and I even did one of the flicks. Luckily I wasn't near anyone else, apart from Brian, who was far enough away at that point. The moment we landed, within minutes of each other, there were loads of photographers waiting, and there was I having just thrown up with vomit spattered face and hair. Lovely! In the press photos you can't see anything but I do look a little bit peaky!

I was fine though apart from being a little giddy and wobbly, and high on adrenaline. It did leave us both a bit speechless that, one, we had been able to have this once in a lifetime experience, and two, the sheer physicality of what it puts your body through is something so unnatural to what we are used to. Everyone was so kind to us and the pilots of course were amazing. Sadly they lost two of their pilots quite soon after that. One of them Jon Egging, who I think was the pilot in the photographer's plane, lost his life whilst completing a display at Bournemouth Air Festival in August 2011. We were invited to his funeral, which was so sad. I think we were the last people to be allowed up with The Reds as I'm not entirely sure they take civilians up anymore.

It was just unbelievably amazing but such an intense and overwhelming experience, which requires your full concentration. I will remember it forever. I have a photo in my downstairs loo which I always look at and smile, thinking, "*Oh my god, I am in that plane.*"

I'm very much aware of some of the amazing things we have done because of Brian. I'm under no illusion about that, but I am also proud of what we have done as a pair for various charities. It is very much a two-way working relationship that we have. We can get together and do what we want, do any type of music, with no label and no pressure. Also there is no expectation for Brian to come out and play certain melodies.

I think Brian sees a lightness in me, and he likes the fact that I live in the moment and always try and put a positive spin on life. Since I've had my kids I'm even more like that as they give me massive perspective. I could be having a bad day, or I don't get a job I was after, or I mess up an audition or have a rubbish show or whatever it is, then I come back home and it's gone almost immediately I see my kids, which puts it all in perspective. I don't dwell on things too much, which is why my yoga has become incredibly important to me. It's all about not cluttering my mind too much and having a bit of meditation and time to empty my mind and get that perspective.

For me my cup is always half full and I blank out anything bad or remotely negative, preferring to focus on the good and positive in my life. I only remember the good stuff, which isn't to say I don't acknowledge anything negative, I just don't tend to dwell on it. Whenever I look to the future, as far as I'm concerned it will be good and I focus on what I want, never doubting it will happen.

CHAPTER 33

In late 2011, I was approached by the producers of a new television show called *The Voice*, who were looking for rock singers to appear on the first series. My agent Jonathan Shalit handled a lot of the reality stars of the day, and he was quite encouraging of me doing it. It sounded straightforward enough and meant I didn't have to have to do the rounds of auditions to get through or wait in line with thousands of others. I don't think I would have agreed to it, if that had been the case, but I was being given a chance to just go along and sing live in front of a studio audience, and I thought, '*Well why not?*', I was quite happy to do that.

I'd now come to a point in my career where I'd done a few shows, I'd recorded an album and yes, I was doing good, but I wasn't exactly selling millions of records. The way I saw it, this opportunity might be a platform to get to that next level, and I just kind of treated it like another audition. It turned out I actually knew a lot of the people on the production team and in the band, even some of the vocal coaches which was great, and I felt quite relaxed about the whole process. I was given a list of about a hundred songs and asked to choose my top ten and the idea was they would then choose the one for me to sing, which seemed fair. The only problem was, the song I actually ended up singing wasn't in my top ten.

'*Son of a Preacher Man*' is a great song of course but I really battled with the producers over it, as I didn't feel it was right for me. It was a killer, and I thought it would put me in that musical theatre bracket which I didn't want. I hadn't sung the song since college days and I just felt it was going to give the wrong impression of me as an artist. As far as I was concerned I should have been singing something more modern or lyrical, but that is what they chose for me and I had no choice.

During filming and prior to my performance I received a lot of attention in the holding area and leading up to the show I'd had a camera in my face the whole day. In fact, from day one the film crew had been following me around, constantly taking me away for interviews, wanting my whole back story and my theatre history. It was quite full-on. I remember explaining to camera:

"*This industry is all about taking risks so I'm taking the risk…*"

187

The weirdest thing of all though was walking out on that stage to no music. I had to walk out to the sound of my own footsteps. It's a very unusual situation, as there is usually a certain amount of noise or rustling, then intro music and hopefully a bit of applause, something, anything rather than silence, which was weird. Normally when you're performing, you're in front of people who have paid to come and see you and are happy and reacting a bit. Even in a regular audition the producers are still facing you, and you get some feedback. Singing to these four massive chairs with their backs to me was very strange.

For me that's not what performance is all about. Yes, it is about your voice, but it's also about engaging, how you tell a story and how you put the song across, so for me that's a massive element that you're then missing. Yes, it is about how you sound on the radio but it's equally about how we interpret songs and how we communicate. There were about 500 people in the audience and they were great, but again they are asked to be super-quiet which is not the norm. Theatres are alive and full of excitement, whereas television is very controlled which I do understand but that was so alien to me.

As I stood there in the silence, my mouth dry and my palms sweating, for the first time since agreeing to appear on the show, I thought: "*Oh god, what on earth am I doing here, risking being publicly rejected?*" but then the music began and the performer in me kicked in.

I was able to sing my song through and they didn't stop me, but I couldn't seem to just concentrate on singing and performing the song. I found I was over-thinking things, I was looking at the chairs, trying to perform to the audience and the nation, and all the time going through my brain was: "*What happens if they turn round? Do I even want them to turn round? Do I want to be involved in this machine? What if they don't turn round?*" My brain was doing stuff that it shouldn't be doing when I'm in performance mode. The cameras were right in my face and I couldn't ignore them.

Of course, as we now know, none of the judges turned for me, but when they chatted to me afterwards and asked me if I had done anything on stage before it was really funny as the audience immediately started shouting out all my musicals. That was kind of nice and made me feel:

188

"Oh well, I've done my job here, and at least the audience have had a good time and reacted positively which was great." The judges were all quite complimentary to me as well, and Danny O'Donoghue from the Script said he wished he'd turned. I took it all with a pinch of salt though, to me it just felt like another audition where I didn't get the part, so no big deal really.

Of course, the irony was, that a few weeks later, Brian and I were performing at a big corporate charity event and I ended up sitting in-between Brian and Tom Jones. It was really funny because Tom praised my performance that night and told me I was brilliant, but he didn't put two and two together, which I get because they see and hear thousands of people all the time.

I find it amazing how my appearance on *The Voice* affected people, and the impact it had, and still does to this day. It was quite something. On that evening in March 2012 when the show was broadcast, I found myself suddenly world-wide trending on twitter, I mean people were going nuts! I suppose by then I knew the outcome, and had time to get my head round it, but I just took it very much in my stride.

As I've said before I always try to be very positive and optimistic. In this business you have to be thick-skinned whilst taking all the opportunities you can, because it is an ever-changing industry and you're forever moving through different castings. You never quite know what is going to happen next or even if you are going to work again, so you have to give everything a go. You also never know where something might lead or who you might meet along the way. It might not be on that particular job but you could meet someone who remembers you, and then brings you something else in the future. I think it's really important to be resilient and open to new things. For me the hardest bit of being on *The Voice* was the fact that they film your family throughout the entire process, which I found odd. I can put myself out there, because that is what I have chosen to do, and I can deal with the response, and anything that happens as a result of that. However, suddenly, having my family in the room or backstage and knowing they were being filmed made me feel quite vulnerable for them, which I didn't like at all. I was used to coping with rejection, it's what I do daily and part of the job, but seeing

189

my parents and husband suddenly having to deal with it and watching their reaction whilst trying to gee me up was really tough.

I've never really watched it back since. I've caught clips of it but not in its entirety. I moved on very quickly and didn't really entertain it in my thoughts or engage with it.

My husband will always joke that I'm emotionally dead, or even slightly dead inside, and that I don't share easily. I know what he means but it's not an intentional thing I do. Being in this industry for so long, I have learned to brush things off quite easily. My upbringing was so stable and loved, and I believe that has stayed with me, and now I am in a position where I am trying to provide and create that for my kids. When I talk about my career I feel secure about it. I am quite a levelled person and don't tend to get too emotional. My brother will always say to me, "*The reason you have never sold albums or been a massive songwriter Kerry is because you've never had any real heartbreak to talk about.*"

In a way he's right. Yes I've lost my dog and grandparents, and yes my parents split up so I've had those moments, but I've always pushed through and focused on the positive and don't let it get to me. Maybe I have built up a bit of an emotional wall, but I haven't recognised it as such. I must have had knock backs and rejection very early on in my career but I genuinely don't even remember them and must have blanked them out. In such a fragile industry you have to be resilient or else you won't survive and maybe because I started so early and have been doing it for so long, it is just a natural default attitude I have. I have this conversation with Brian a lot. It's taken a long, long, time for him to understand me and he has often said he still feels he doesn't know me.

CHAPTER 34

When Brian produced *Anthems*, he did it because he really wanted to give me a platform to become a music artist, so I was very much the face of the album, but it was produced and supported by Brian May. During the *Anthems* tour he was still of this mind, so I would be front and centre stage, whilst he would almost be like my guitarist, which was insane. We would come together for little acoustic bits but essentially he was generously trying to give me that platform. If he wanted to do that there was no way he could be on stage because he was a worldwide superstar and we couldn't ignore the fact that he is there, so I felt very strongly that we had to do it together. He still kept trying to resist it but I explained to him that it should be just about the simplicity of the two of us doing our thing. Once the tour finished, we started to do little performances where it was just me and him, and we tried a few acoustic songs. To me it felt like we were at our best acoustically, with just the two of us, and it was that time which spawned the idea for our *Acoustic by Candlelight* album which was recorded live a couple of years later in 2012, during the first leg of what became the *Born Free* tour, a series of intimate and acoustic shows performed under candlelight, which we toured with just the two of us and a keyboard. The album was then released during the second leg of the tour in 2013. That's when it really felt that we were moving in a different direction. Where we started out, *Anthems* was a big rock sound, with me leading the vocals and Brian playing. He may have sung one song but it was predominantly me doing my thing, and him playing as he would do in Queen. It wasn't until that next tour when I really felt we came into our own, and it changed dramatically. We started looking at things very differently, and for me that was then it began to feel right. It felt real and reflected what we were about. We were quite literally discovering it along the way. It's only now on our most recent and what I consider to be our best album *Golden Days*, where we have collaborated properly and we have both found our feet.

I'd met lyricist Don Black when he came to see my very first one woman show at the Shaw Theatre. Brian and Don subsequently wrote a song for me called '*I Can't Be Your Friend*' which I recorded for the *Anthems* album. For our next album Brian and I really were keen to include our own version of *Born Free*, a song which Don had written in collaboration with John Barry as the theme tune for the 1966 film. Don wrote an additional verse for us with brand new lyrics, so the song would become ours, and we could make it unique. It is such a classic, well-known song, that we needed something different.

Not long after, Virginia McKenna, founder of the Born Free charity and of course starred in the film, was doing a corporate fund raiser in London, and we were invited to go along and sing the song at this event. I hit it off with her immediately, and from that night we stayed in touch and became quite good friends. Virginia is one of the most incredible women I have ever met. She is the sort of person who, once you have met her, affects you deep in your soul. She has this special undefinable spiritual aura about her which makes you hang on her every word. We made the decision to record *Born Free* as a single to raise money for her charity, The Born Free Foundation, and she in turn was quite invested in Brian's charity, the Save Me Trust. We also included a song she had written several years before about her husband passing, called '*Nothing Really Has Changed*', on what became the *Born Free* Tour, and recorded it for the album. All this meant we could raise awareness for the foundation.

Soon after, Virginia invited Brian and I to perform at the launch of Pride of Cape Town 2012, a massive public arts exhibition of fifty life-size fibreglass lions, before they were dotted around the city, which again was to raise money for Born Free's work to protect and conserve lions in the wild.

Before our performance Virginia invited us up to Shamwari in the Eastern Cape of South Africa where the Born Free sanctuaries are, to stay in the lodges for a week. It was unbelievable, and one of the best trips I have ever been on. It was incredible stepping out of these lodges and just seeing giraffes standing there. We would go on safari in the mornings and were taken round the whole reserve. We also filmed the video for the *Born Free* single while we were there, which we were able to play on screen during our tour.

Virginia's passion, knowledge and deep love for animals is like no other. She is also kind and considerate to everyone. She accompanied us the whole time and we had various lunches and breakfasts with her, and I could have listened to her talking forever. She is so passionate about the lions and has some incredible stories about what they have done over the years. She also keeps up to date with what's going on in that moment too and has so much information to share. At the time when we were out there, there was a big problem with rhino horns, which I think were being poached to be used in the traditional medicine system in many Asian countries as well as for status symbols. Virginia was educating me about it all, but not so I noticed, she was just fascinating to listen to and she would explain over lunch how some people believed the horns had certain qualities, which actually wasn't true, and that they could heal people, which they couldn't as they had no healing powers at all.

While we were there, we were involved in the relocation of two rescued lions at the Born Free Centres, at the Shamwari Wildlife Reserve. It was so moving. We watched one of them get darted, then eight of us had to pick up this beautiful, majestic lion and lift him onto the truck. Brian, Virginia and I, along with one of the rangers, sat in the lorry with the lion while we transported it. We then helped get him off at the other end and I remember putting ointment on his eyes just before he was due to wake up and touching his paws. It was such a unique and special experience that I still can't believe I did it. We spent a lot of time with Virginia while we were there and we would sing round the camp fire to her in the evening. We surprised her one night by singing the song she had written, and she just melted.

It was an incredibly moving trip, which ended with the amazing concert in Cape Town, and one I will never forget. We have since done various corporate events for them, where on one occasion I got to meet David Attenborough. I mean oh my god, I was dumbstruck. The cause has remained close to my heart and I will do anything I can to support it. Any time I get to go on *Pointless* or suchlike programmes where you play for charity, I will always play for Born Free, or Brian's Save Me charity. I have always had a passion for animals anyway, but it's all about Virginia, she's infectious, and makes you want to help. I can't explain, but there is just something about her that is ethereal and spiritual. She probably wouldn't agree at all, but anyone who is lucky enough to meet her says the same, that she is the most incredible and inspiring woman. She has supported me ever since and comes to see Brian and I as well as my solo concerts whenever she can and I am so honoured that we are still in contact.

Upon our return we released the single and later that year in November 2012, embarked on the first leg of the *Born Free* UK tour. The second part in June 2013 covered further venues in England, Ireland and Wales and the final leg a month later took us to mainland Europe visiting France, Austria and four dates in Italy. When we returned we were invited to appear in a star-studded evening at the Royal Festival Hall in celebration of Don Black and his music, where we performed *Born Free* and by which time I was so heavily pregnant that I was literally about to give birth to Alfie.

I get asked quite a lot to do charity shows so I have to be quite picky about who I do stuff for. I really think that if I did everything there would be no value in it. Charities such as the Born Free Foundation, Brian's Save Me charity plus anything children related like the Make A Wish Foundation, I don't have to think twice about. Another one is Pup Aid, led by Marc (the vet) Abraham, a non-profit campaign run by volunteers to raise awareness and influence legislation around puppy farming. As part of his Save Me charity, Brian puts on an annual Wildlife Rocks festival in Guildford, where we play a few acoustic numbers. It's like a country fair with various different animal charity stalls, dog races and all sorts of activities. I met Marc the vet through this festival. Brian was already friends with him and I got chatting to him, telling him how much I loved my dogs and that I was a big dog supporter. We kept in touch after that and he's invited me along to various events and to judge one of their dog shows. I've been to a few now and they are always great occasions. Another one I support is the Dogs Trust, the UK's largest Dog Welfare charity. I go along to any events that I can and do a bit of judging or announcing. It's all about raising awareness and using your voice to shout about it.

There are loads of theatre charities, which are probably the ones I get asked to do the most. I support the MAD (Make A Difference) Trust and have done for years, they have been good to me in the past and I've given back to them whenever I can.

CHAPTER 35

So many fantastic opportunities followed, including a small part in the *Les Mis* film. This was a new experience for me, and to be part of that film, of a show I loved, and to be on that set around all that craziness was a privilege. A stage musical is all very two-dimensional because the minute you go off to the side of the stage, it all stops, whereas on a television or film set there are no wings and you are surrounded by the set. Of course, with that comes the fact there is no audience, which I find weird as I feed off the crowd and the atmosphere in a theatre, or concert hall, and I am reactive to that. There were loads of theatre people involved in the film as they needed tons of singers.

We were all featured ensemble, and there were many of us who had been in the show over the years and there was a lot of waiting around, as there always is on film sets, but I didn't care as I just loved being part of it all. Helena Bonham Carter is a massive Wicked fan, which I didn't realise. I knew she'd been to see the show but when I turned up on the set in full costume she said straight away, *"I know you… you're the green girl in Wicked aren't you?"* She was lovely and a big fan of musicals generally.

On the Friday, Hugh Jackman came on set shouting something like, *"It's that Friday feeling…"* and he then produced a wad of lottery scratch cards which he was waving about and went around handing them out to every single person on set. I mean we're talking hundreds of people. There he was just toddling round in his opening convict costume handing out these scratch cards. I don't know if anyone won anything, but I just thought what a brilliant man. My part in the film took just a couple of weeks to film as I was only in the *Master of The House* scene, but it was something I will never forget. As there were so many of us involved, we didn't get invited to the premiere but instead were invited to a special screening which annoyingly I couldn't go to as I was doing something else. James and I just went along to see it at the cinema complex in Stevenage not long after.

Years later though I did get to do the red carpet for *Bohemian Rhapsody* at Wembley. Watching a film in a huge arena was weird, although the atmosphere was incredible and it was great watching everyone react to the film. People really did clap and cheer at the Live Aid bit. I had to watch it again not long afterwards because I'd found it difficult to get into as it was such a big environment and it was hard to take it all in. I was sat next to Hannah Jane Fox who I did '*We Will Rock You*' with originally, so we were able to have a giggle and a catch up. I also got to chat with Pete, Brian's guitar technician and Neil Fairclough their bass player. It was just nice to see so many familiar faces. There may have been some tickets available for the public to buy as Wembley is huge, but on the whole it was by invitation and there were a lot of famous people in that arena. It was one of those evenings where I looked around and just thought "WOW".

To me Brian is Brian. We collaborate together and he's part of the family, I've known him so long. As such I tend to forget how huge a star he is until I am in that type of environment, and when I saw him go up on stage at the end with all the cast and do a speech, then saw the whole of Wembley going nuts, that's when I realise, oh my god that's Brian May. It's not that I forget as such, but I take it for granted.

Earlier that year I'd been called up to go and meet Jeff Wayne at his house in Hertfordshire, to discuss the possibility of taking on the role of Beth in *War of the Worlds* that December. I grew up listening to that show, which I had on cassette tape, and I although I didn't realise what it was all about as a child I knew I loved it so this was a no-brainer. I'd never really played arenas before and this was to be a full arena tour starting almost immediately we returned from the first leg of the Born Free Tour, mainly in the UK but with a bit of Europe too, which was incredibly exciting.

This was such a different experience for me and an electric environment to work in. There is such a love for that show from such an unbelievable and loyal following. It shocked me really and it is almost a cult following of people who have seen it everywhere and follow it around. These are true fans who know the show inside out and love Jeff Wayne and all the different parts of the story and react to it. It was lovely that a lot of my fans also came to see the show along the way. Generally, fans like you touring as it means they don't have to travel to London all the time. Anyone who has seen me in whatever I've been touring in show-wise, concert-wise or solo tour-wise also came to see me in *War Of The Worlds*, regardless of whether they were fans of the show itself or not, so it was really nice for me to see those familiar faces.

It was a great adventure and to be in a tour bus on the road with Jason Donovan, Ricky Wilson and of course Marti Pellow, who I did *Chess* with years previously, was brilliant.

Jason and Ricky were both such great fun. Jason had a real theatre mindset and was totally focused on giving a good show. I worked opposite him as he played the Priest and we were on stage together all the time. He was such a hard worker, totally dedicated and committed as they all were. Ricky had never done anything musical-related before but he was so brilliant at it. Whichever town or venue we were in he would get up and go for a run early every morning then report back to us on what he'd seen around town. He also had a bit of an obsession with chocolate bars and would come in with all these random retro chocolate bars. They were really nice guys. It was a good team and a great bunch of people. It's so good to have very different people thrown together on one tour bus sharing different stories and experiences. We could all sit around chatting and drinking tea which may not sound very rock and roll but it was lovely.

I love the fact that I have been able to play all types of venues from the largest to the most intimate, although I think if I am being honest theatre is still my love, because you can have that connection. I love working small venues for when I am doing my own stuff because you can chat to the audience and create that sense of intimacy. Arenas are exciting because of the sheer amount of people but they are a bit distant and far away and I felt a real separation from the audience.

Everybody was on in ear monitors, which I'd used before but not in a musical situation. They're not fun because they close you off a little bit from the room. If you're singing with monitors, you can hear everybody and everything. With 'in ears' it's like having ear buds in and you can only hear your music and your voice but nothing else. I usually wear one in and one out which isn't particularly the best way to do it but at least that way I can hear the room, the atmosphere and the people which is really important.

I think audiences generally have changed over recent years. It used to be such an event to go to the theatre, people would dress up and treat it as an occasion. Perhaps it is more accessible now or it's the celebrity casting which taps into the Saturday night television audience, which is different. I used to get annoyed when people would film shows with their cameras, in the days before smart phones came in, and you would see that red light glowing in the auditorium. It used to wind me up, because, as performers, we weren't used to that and it was new. Nowadays, they film and take pictures constantly, and it doesn't worry me at all. In fact, if I am doing a gig, you want people to support you, and in a way need the content out there. I'm at a point now where I have seen every bad picture of myself at every bad angle, so it doesn't worry me anymore, and I'm kind of all right about it. I see other performers ranting on social media about it and I used to feel the same way, but I let it go now. Having said that, when you are offering live entertainment you really do want people to be in the moment and to enjoy the experience, which is the whole point of going to see something. What's the point of watching it whilst recording and distracting yourself and then watching it back later on a rubbish little screen. Why? "*Just enjoy the moment,*" I want to say to them.

What keeps me going and excited in my career is the variety of work I do. I like being creative and I like new challenges and working with different people. If I was just to do one thing for the rest of my life it would kill me. It is harder for me to do musicals now because of the boys but never say never, it will come back I'm sure. There's so much to do and so many musical roles out there.

Notes from…

My abiding memory of Kerry is that she was conspicuously hard working, exceeded expectations in every role she played and was never any trouble!

My particular favourite was Kerry's Ellen in *Miss Saigon*, which was as close to definitive as I think it can get. It is a profoundly difficult role to get right as, frankly, by the time she arrives, the audience are hardly well disposed to engage with her. She managed to deliver it with absolutely the right balance of dignity, courage and vulnerability and, when the Ellen can do that, it elevates the emotional power of the story by several notches.

Trevor Jackson

Associate Casting Director – Cameron Mackintosh

CHAPTER 36

Soon after *The Voice*, I left Roar Global and moved to Peter Brooks at Creative Artists Management (CAM). They represented me for about eighteen months, and I had a really good relationship with them. During that time, someone recommended Daniel Hinchliffe to me, who had previously done loads of PR work for Sony and was setting up his own agency, the Soundcheck Agency. There was a bit of a crossover for a while as Daniel came on board to look after all my press and music whilst CAM continued with all my theatre work. I eventually left CAM when Daniel said he could handle all of it. We got on really well and I agreed it would make sense for him to do that. Soon after Daniel called, *"Hi Kerry, I've been thinking, you've not done a show in London for a while, I think we should book the Palladium."*

"That's ballsy Daniel, that's really ballsy," was all I could think of to say.

"Well sometimes you just have to put it out there," he continued, *"and I think this is a good time."*

We subsequently booked the London Palladium for May 12th 2013. It was quite risky as you really don't know quite what is going to happen if you book the Palladium. I also didn't know I was about to become pregnant with my first child!

Usually when I'm doing a tour there is a promoter involved who deals with all the publicity and advertising. They also book the venues around the country, dependent on availability at any given time, which means it can be a bit hit and miss in terms of distance and travelling. Sometimes it's a buyout, meaning the artist pays for the venue outright, and sometimes its worked on percentage of ticket sales. All venues are different, and I think with the Palladium we paid outright. It was a massive risk to take in the hope that ticket sales covered all the costs including performers fees. Essentially, I was responsible for paying everyone and anything left over I would get. Brian and I had worked with loads of promoters previously and we hired one of them to help us out a bit with publicity.

I had about six to eight months from the moment we booked it to the actual day, so I wasted no time and immediately started putting the show together. I brought lots of my friends on board and called everyone I could think of. Craig was my MD and I put the band together from musicians I knew. I'd previously done a show at the Hippodrome Casino, Leicester Square when they first opened. I did a week there with a seven-piece band and three backing vocalists, and as it had been such a great night I used most of that band but made it bigger. Mazz Murray did a song, Brian did a special guest spot and we did a couple of acoustic numbers together. I also brought the four Elphabas, up to that point – myself, Louise Dearman, Rachel Tucker and Alexia Khadime – together for the first time, to sing *Gravity*. Everyone knew who had played the green witch, so to sing all together was a real coup. I also asked some students from Mountview to come and perform and booked the Bergesen String Quartet. Daniel sorted me out a gorgeous black spangly dress from a friend of his, William Vintage, an amazing designer. I was super excited as that hadn't really happened much before.

I love online shopping, and I'm constantly on the internet trawling through sites to get ideas for my stage clothes. I have got it massively wrong over the years and when I look back at some of the choices I've made, I've no idea what I was thinking at the time. There have been occasions when someone has taken a horror photo of me from the front row and as a result, I will never wear that outfit or dress again. I have an issue about my arms for that very reason, as I have had so many pictures taken from the front row at such a bad angle, that it makes me self-conscious, and I will always cover my arms up now. Mainly I choose my own stuff, based on what I feel will have a good impact, what I feel confident in, and what looks fantastic.

I quite like having control over that, as I know what colours and styles suit me – usually! I'm currently working with a girl called Claire from Claire Christian Couture on the Isle of Man who has made me a couple of lovely outfits for my forthcoming tour. I'm always changing and developing as an artist, and my style reflects that. Having my hair and make-up done is great if it is available, but I am just as happy to do it myself. As I do so many concerts, I like to have a ton of outfits to take with me, which leaves me the option to wear what I want on the day. I might not feel like a particular outfit on a certain day, as I don't feel comfortable or just don't feel right in it, for whatever reason, which is normal, right? I can get up in the morning and sometimes feel a million dollars in something, whereas the next time I don't. It's the same with concerts so I like to have a wide choice of say six outfits then wear two or three of them. I'm also a firm believer in giving the audience something to look at. Maybe that is because I have come from theatre, and I'm always thinking of the show as an entirety and not just about the music. For me it is about the whole production. The blue cat suit I wore for Jane McDonald and friends on television was a prime example. I just saw it on the internet, it popped up and I immediately thought, "*I have to have that in my life.*" I've worn it for so many things. I have definitely learned what works along the way, and more importantly what doesn't, and I have experimented with various looks over the years for who I think I am. The thing that always remains the same is that I love a sequin and I love a costume change. Even if it is something quite relaxed or small, I will always change. It gives a different vibe as well as something else to look at. For me, Celine Dion at the moment, is on another scale with her style and I just love what she comes out with.

I don't consider myself to be trendy. I look at the kids today and they all look so grown up and mature. I wonder if it's because they have access to YouTube and all the online content which we didn't have. We had to rely on magazines. I would always try and follow a trend but I wasn't really that interested. I still don't think I get it right all the time. I wear a lot of black and neutral colours although I'm quite adventurous on stage and some of my outfits over the years have been quite daring. Sometimes I get a bit of help and advice on that, and every so often someone will make something for me and I'll get sent stuff, but it's really not as often as people would think.

As for my hair, it very much depends on the venue or what the gig is. For instance, I did *Miss World* quite recently and there's a whole hair and make-up team there to do it for you, which was wonderful. Of course, that is a huge-scale production but if it's just me doing my own tour or solo concert, I'll just do it myself which I am used to. I still had very long flowing hair for the Palladium which I'd religiously curled for over 30 years. People would comment on it all the time whilst I was at college, and also when I first left. Then, when I was doing my own gigs, people would refer to me as the girl with the long blonde hair, like in the Timotei shampoo advert. It was really strange, I didn't have any other sort of crutch or superstition, but it got to the point where I worried that if I cut my hair would people know it was me and would I still be the same performer? It became like a comfort blanket and with my long hair I felt strong and good about myself. At the time of the Palladium concert, I was about three months pregnant with Alfie and eventually had it cut after he was born which was a massive deal for me, although I didn't go dramatically short at first, but my mindset changed once I had kids.

I tried on a few dresses from the selection William sent, and decided on my final two, but ended up staying in the black spangly one as being pregnant I was a bit conscious of the way I looked and felt. This one looked a million dollars and made me feel comfortable, so the costume changes went out of the window that night.

I really felt like I'd been working my way up to this and I was totally ready for it. I now had enough experience behind me to do it and although I'd already done the Royal Albert Hall to kick off the *Anthems* tour, we'd fired the songs out bang, bang, bang, and there wasn't much room for chat. This was my show and personal to me. I had put it together, chatted to the audience and basically controlled the whole thing, which was a massive game changer. I remember just sitting there on the stage one day when there was no one else around thinking, *"Oh my god this is massive; I mean Liza Minnelli has played here!"* I had played at the Palladium before in various concerts but this was my own show, this was my moment and it was a massive deal. The timing was right bar the pregnancy, which hadn't been the case at the time of booking! That always seems to be the way, I do something massive in my career but then there is something else going on just to make it that extra bit challenging for me, to test my resolve!

I like to think I passed the test because by the end of the show, the packed audience were on their feet cheering for all they were worth and I did make a little bit of money from it.

CHAPTER 37

James and I never really made a conscious decision to start a family. We'd always talked about kids, and knew we wanted them, but had never actually sat down and said, right, now is the right time, let's try. It just happened naturally. I remember the day I took the pregnancy test and coming downstairs into the kitchen to tell James. *"Oh"* was all I could say as I showed him the positive result. *"Oh my god"* was his reply as we both just stared at each other taking it all in. Of course, we were delighted.

That actually happened both times, as we weren't really trying for either of them, which is brilliant, as I know how difficult it is for some people and how lucky we are. To have had two easy pregnancies, and healthy boys, touch wood, has been a blessing. We have friends who have struggled to have one child, and then are still struggling for a second. It is so hard and we are really grateful. As testing as they can be at times, they are an amazing part of my life.

When I found out I was pregnant we took James' parents and Dad and Sal out for lunch. Coincidentally, it just happened to be Mother's Day as well because I remember giving them cards with a little message inside, which must have been really cryptic, because they didn't have a clue what we were going on about until the penny finally dropped! We took my Mum and grandparents out separately for lunch and did the same thing. Everyone was so happy and my Dad was beside himself. He'd desperately wanted a grandchild for years and was destined to be a brilliant grandad. I sometimes think my kids would happily give up James and I to go and live with Dad and Sal, such is the love! Although it might be to do with the Oreos for breakfast!

I was keen to keep working throughout both pregnancies and didn't take a break even when they were born. I've always worked and have always earned money and never really had any time out in my life. I think it would frighten me to have too much time out. I'd achieved some really good things by this time, so I wasn't so much scared of being forgotten, I'm just happiest when I'm working, I love it and it's who I am. I'm just not me if I'm not working.

It's tough for new mums. I think for anyone returning to work, you have to make that choice quite soon, because you can get quite consumed with staying at home and being with your babies. Having made that decision myself, it gave me a focus and I needed to get back out there. I also knew they were going to be with me so it wasn't like I had to make a decision to go back to work and not see my kids for the majority of the day. I was lucky as I didn't have to part with them, and I knew they'd be around, which I think really helped. It's never easy in this business, and always a challenge for the next job. Even in lockdown I've had to do something and I've found other ways. I believe if you want to find a way then you do.

I was keen to stay fit and healthy during my pregnancies. I've always been relatively active, and I've always loved classes, which I think stems back to my dance training. For me it's all about being active without realising I'm being active. I've always had a gym membership of some sort or gone to exercise classes and I can't remember a time when I didn't, although when I'm in a show that kind of takes over, and can be a workout in itself, so it's usually when I'm not in a show.

I first found yoga around the time of *Wicked* in New York. I had done the odd class before but while I was there I found a class I could go to between shows, where I just fell in love with the teacher. Something clicked with me and I really enjoyed it. It was like a meditation but physical at the same time. I dabbled a bit during that time, and also found Hot Yoga which I loved. When I came back to London I would find little odd classes in Soho. There was a particular studio called Yotopia that I would drop into sometimes, although even then it wasn't a regular thing. It's only been since just before I had Alfie that I've taken it seriously, and on a more regular basis.

There was a great teacher, Nicky, at my local gym who had been dance captain in *Miss Saigon* in Drury Lane, so had a strong dance background and we really hit it off and connected straightaway. It's funny, I just knew immediately that she was an ex-performer because of the way her body moved. I can spot anyone who goes into any form of exercise from a dance background. It's like a club.

Once we had this understanding that we were both from the theatre world, we clicked on another level, and she would push me in a certain direction because she knew I'd had that training. She was fantastic and became like a yoga guru for me. She did just the best classes and ignited my love for it. Practising yoga helped me through both my pregnancies and its kind of stuck ever since then and I've become a little bit obsessive about it. A lot of it is about the meditation, and the fact I can really switch off. It's an hour when I can't think of anything else, and I have to concentrate on the breathing and what I'm doing. I'm not a big meditator as such, so yoga has become my meditation. It keeps me calm and without sounding too 'hippyish,' I've found a kind of spirituality, and it is something I can buy into, and invest myself in. It's my little mecca and keeps me level-headed, especially nowadays when everything is so stressful and life goes at a hundred miles an hour. I can have my own little hour of space and calm and meditation.

I think yoga generally is more accessible, and there are more classes out there. Mental health is a big topic at the moment so it has become much more popular as it is so good for your overall mental wellbeing. It's good for the body and the brain, it gets people off their screens and just allows you to centre yourself a little bit and be grateful for who you are and what you are and to take a moment to take things back to basics. There is a real community in yoga of like-minded people. It changes me and calms everything whilst making my body feel good and helping me to keep active and moving.

Exercise is slightly different and requires more effort. I will sometimes drag my heels in going if I'm not feeling it, but when I get there I love it and I love the after feeling. I still do all my HIT and exercises but that is more so I can eat and drink! I like to change it up a bit but I always do something. During lockdown I managed to keep going with it, doing some of my own, some online classes and a few outdoor ones. Like nearly everyone else I was also obsessed with Joe Wicks at one point. I always feel better if I exercise. I grew up being active and if I don't have it in my life then I don't feel right. I need to get rid of that excess energy. I also hired a Personal Trainer just before lockdown to try and step up my fitness a bit, after which we continued online, and that worked out really well as it kept me going and motivated although it's not something I would normally do as I prefer being able to get out and do my own thing.

Doing yoga online proved more difficult as I don't often get the opportunity with the kids around. For me it's all about the escapism and not thinking about anything else at all for that hour, which I just can't do at home.

Both my pregnancies were straightforward but the births were horrific, and I was in labour for three days with Alfie. I had an epidural which didn't quite work as I could still feel my legs, and I was so sick afterwards. I'm sure James remembers far more than I do about the births but I do remember talking about Harry Redknapp to the anaesthetist when I was having Alfie. He had just given me the epidural so I felt a bit woozy and was just chatting away to him about Harry Redknapp and driving down to Devon which sounds bonkers now. Freddie's birth was even worse as it all happened too quickly so I couldn't have an epidural, and thinking about it now still fills me with anxiety, although I was lucky I had no interventions. James was present at both births and I remember there were moments when he was in the bed, and I wasn't, because he was so exhausted. I think I threw a few choice words his way, especially when I was in labour with Fred, because I was in more pain. I kept looking at the clock and saying: "*This has been too long...*" However, the main thing is that I have two healthy children at the end of it, but oh my goodness, as any mother will understand, it was quite an experience, and I was broken when I came out of the hospital.

Everyone likes to tell you about pregnancy and the birth itself, but no one talks about the bit when you get home, or what to expect. I was so lucky as I didn't suffer with post-natal depression like my Mum did after having my brother. In my mind, I knew I was going on tour in a couple of months and I had to get it together for that. I think that was quite good for me as it gave me a bit of a goal and, as my whole career has been, something to look to, plan for and focus on. It was really hard and I was shattered initially, and I remember having a few down days as I was so sleep deprived plus I wasn't the best at breastfeeding and I couldn't get on with the pump. I honestly don't know how single parents do it, as James and I worked together as a team. When you first come home from hospital you are quite literally broken and exhausted and your body is so done, so to then not have that practical and emotional support must be really tough. Although the pressure is mainly on the woman because babies just want their mum, it's also really difficult for a new Dad to do the right thing whilst the mum and baby are busy bonding. I consider myself so lucky that I had James as he is brilliant. He has always been really hands-on with the boys and is an amazing husband and Dad.

Having my kids has just changed my life completely. They're the hardest job I have ever had, but also by far the best I've ever had, which I am sure every parent can relate to. Being a parent is challenging and exhausting, but so rewarding. You love like you've never loved before and they give me a purpose and confidence plus a meaning to my life that I've never had. Being a mum also makes me value being a performer so much more. I am so much more appreciative of all the jobs I get to do now. Before, because I was rattling through all these big shows, I was taking it all in my stride and yes, I was grateful that I was doing all this work, but I never stopped to just take a moment and appreciate the scale of it. Anything I get to do now I think, "*Wow this is brilliant. How amazing that I get to be a parent and still do the job that I love.*"

I'm much more grateful and don't take any of it for granted.

Once they were born the boys came everywhere with me. I remember taking them to gigs in car seats and then taking them into dressing rooms. I remember certain concerts, which I think were the Christmas ones, where I would ask our company manager to keep an eye on the dressing room door while I literally ran on stage to sing a song, then ran off again to relieve him of his babysitting duties. On the *Rent* tour my Dad or Sally would sit in the dressing room and James would always come along whenever he could. It was tough taking the boys away from James but we just made it work and I was, and still am lucky to have such a strong support network around me. I didn't want to stop working and I didn't want to be out for too long. There was no reason for me to be out, plus it gave me that focus, to get back and get moving and get back into the swing of it.

Physically, after pregnancy your body changes, so for me, going back into *Wicked* after having Alfie was like going back into a fitness programme, because suddenly I became incredibly active again, and was putting my body through this intense daily regime which actually was really good. Mentally it changed things for me and I was a lot easier on myself on stage. I wasn't too hung up on little things. I was how I was on the day and I was okay with that. I wasn't stressing about the fact I didn't sing a note as well as I could do. I was okay to let that go a little bit, whereas before I would stress for ages and really beat myself up over it. Now, the intention was more important to me.

I suffer more guilt when I go away now that the boys are older and at school. I try and choose jobs that are short enough so I don't have to be away for long but at the same time balancing that with working enough. I've turned job offers and castings down for that reason. I don't feel the need to say yes to everything at the moment. I can be at home and maybe go away for a week and do some concerts here and there in the UK or perhaps do the odd voiceover or a recording. That's not to say that if the right show came up, or something massive that I would love to do, that I would dismiss it. It would be really difficult and we'd have to work it out to see if we could find a way. I haven't had to face that yet, partly because I make myself so busy that I am not open to it. I fill my diary up so that doesn't happen. There's always a sacrifice to make, but I am so supported that I know if I'm away and James has to work, my parents, or his, will step in with no hesitation and the boys are so comfortable with them that I know they are ok and that is priceless. I couldn't do it without them.

Taking the boys on tour with me is great for me, but it's hard for them to be away from their Dad. Me being away has also had its challenges. I can be thrown together with a company of people and we become like a dysfunctional family for a certain length of time, and then once the show has finished we don't see each other again. It can be really hard but it's something I have become used to over the years.

I always say that the difficulty with James and I is that we are both very dominant. We both think we are in charge and top dog, so in that respect we are kind of equal and it is probably why we butt horns. We both think we are the alpha male although the truth is we probably move around at various points and the shift can change. James knows that I will do what I want to do. He will always offer advice whether I want it or not, and his advice is always quite good because he puts a different perspective on it. With certain things now it has to be a joint decision because of the boys, but we always say when a job comes in it has to be either worth it financially, or to advance my career, or something I desperately want to do.   If it's something that has no meaning I can't do it. James and I will often discuss this and he will offer his opinion. We are definitely a yin to a yang, without doubt. I am the optimist and he's more of a realist.

Apart from the fact we really liked the name, I have a Great-Grandad Alfie and we also loved the musical connection with the song *Alfie*. However the main reason we chose that name for our first son was that James was super-close to his Grandad Alfie. James got a little tattoo saying '*What's It All About Alfie*' after he was born. We love that it is traditional name with a bit of showbiz in it and a family connection. When I was pregnant we were always of the opinion that whatever comes is meant to be, but for some reason we were convinced that Freddie was a girl and he was going to be a Molly, we didn't even think about boys names although Freddie was thrown about in the background, but not seriously.

He wasn't named after Freddie Mercury as such, but at the same time he wasn't 'not' named after him. In fact, once we knew he was a boy, we even discussed if it was perhaps a bit close, because of my connection with Brian, but we loved the name and Alfie and Freddie seemed to go really nicely together. We definitely wanted the 'eee' sound at the end but at the same time we loved the shortened version to Fred, plus I have an Uncle Fred.   It's just a nice connection to my 'Queen' family too, and a nod to Freddie Mercury.   I always used to say I wanted two boys and I love having them.   We are very boy heavy in my family, so it's all about football, and it can be very boisterous, but it suits me and I love it.

CHAPTER 38

Back in February 2012, Brian and I had performed at the San Remo Music Festival, an annual televised Italian song contest a little bit like Eurovision, where they end up with about ten finalists who have already been through previous rounds, and they then get to sing on this massive show, which is broadcast all over Europe. I think it is the final five who go on to perform with an international artist and get to suggest who they want to sing with. We were chosen by Zucchero Fornaciari's daughter Irene, possibly because Brian knew her Dad, and Irene and I duetted '*I Who Have Nothing*' with Brian playing. The Italians love Queen, and it was quite a big deal for us, because that performance had given us a stepping stone for the forthcoming European leg of the *Born Free* tour in July where we did four dates in Italy.

We performed more UK dates on the second leg of the tour with a week's break before we then embarked on the third leg, which was the European dates. Both combined were only about three weeks and we would stay no longer than two or three nights in any one place. Travelling round Europe was just mental, and so were the fans. It felt like Brian was the Pope, such was the adulation and I've never seen paparazzi like it before in my life. We were treated so incredibly well for the whole of the tour, the food was unbelievable and the hotels were just out of this world, for which I was grateful being five months pregnant! The people were warm and welcoming and the audiences were just the best.

We played Paris for one night at La Cigale, a tiny little venue which was so unbelievably hot, and being pregnant I really felt it. We had these massive fans on the side of the stage and we were both just sat there in silence, the sweat literally dripping off us, it was so uncomfortable. I remember Brian saying to me before we went on, "*I speak a little bit of French but not a lot, so I'll do what I can*" He then went on and practically did the whole show in French and I had no idea what he was saying, but the packed audience loved it and were on their feet cheering.

When we came off I said, "*What do you mean you only speak a little French? I was expecting Bonjour.*" I must have looked so bemused watching him as I didn't have a clue what he was on about and I was so taken aback, and we really laugh about that now.

Our date at The Montreux Jazz Festival 2013 came at the end of the tour, and oh my god I absolutely loved it. It was incredible not only to be at the heart of where Queen did a lot of their recording, at what was then Mountain Studios, but to be part of such an amazing festival and unique atmosphere, in the most picturesque of settings. It was definitely another career highlight. Brian's Manager lives in Montreux so he'd been over quite a bit previously, especially as Queen's studio was being turned into a museum and he was due to open it in December of that year. We visited Freddie's statue, which was poignant, and we stayed in the same hotel where Queen used to stay. My room had a balcony overlooking Lake Geneva with the Alps as a backdrop and it was stunningly gorgeous.

We played at the Auditorium Stravinski, which had incredible acoustics. The venue was pretty big and was a very grungey, sticky floor type of place which felt more like a rock venue. It was a massive standing only area, holding about 4000 people, which was weird for us acoustically but they stood, and they listened, and then when we rocked out at the end they were already on their feet and rocked with us. It was amazing.

CHAPTER 39

Everything was happening so quickly and I seemed to be busier than ever. I started 2014 by joining the cast of the 20th anniversary concert UK tour of *Rent*, playing Mimi. Brian and I then toured for three weeks around Eastern Europe with our *Acoustic by Candlelight* tour which was a similar set up to the *Born Free* Tour the previous year as in, still acoustic, but with different songs and videos. We later toured again in 2016 with our *One Voice* acoustic tour and even now I get a bit muddled remembering them as they were similar shows and it was all a bit of a whirlwind. What I do know is, it was the most incredible and crazy time ever. We were selling out three thousand seater venues. Obviously they knew who Brian was, but for me this was just mind-blowing, to be in a different country and selling out these huge venues.

We travelled everywhere by tour bus, which was like a home from home with bunk beds, a kitchen area, tables, toilet and a lounge area at the back where we could relax and watch television. It was really social and just great fun. From Romania to Russia, it was amazing being able to see the diversity of all these different countries that we travelled through from the tour bus perspective. I seem to remember us turning up in Krakow one day and just thinking to myself how bizarre it was that I was there. My memories do blur a little and it almost seems surreal now looking back. I clearly remember going into coffee shops in Russia and finding it odd that everyone was smoking inside. It was like stepping back in time with some of the places, and experiencing their traditions and cultures, which of course were very different, was fascinating.

At one point we had a bit of a crisis somewhere en-route between Romania and Bulgaria. I think the driver must have gone the wrong way and as a result we realised the quickest way to get back on track was via this little ferry which we really shouldn't have attempted, as the bus was far too big. Apart from being very old and probably only just sea worthy, it was barely big enough to take a car, let alone a tour bus. We had no choice though, it was a risk we had to take as we were literally in the middle of nowhere and we would have been late for the gig, or even not made it at all. Not surprisingly, our bus got stuck whilst trying to drive onto it. We were stuck tight with a concert to do in a couple of hours and we didn't know what we were going to do. Everybody got off the boat and panic was beginning to set in as we desperately tried to think what to do. It was then we randomly saw a fork lift truck parked up in the port, and this little old boy who could barely speak a word of English was standing by it. He could see our dilemma and walked over to us. As he approached us he saw Brian and became really animated shouting out, "*Ohhh we will rock you, we will rock you...*" he exclaimed excitedly, and started the famous signature hand clapping.

After a bit more of his animated hand clapping and a few signals from us, he soon understood the seriousness of our problem and ended up driving his fork lift truck up behind the bus and literally pushed us onto the boat, staying with us for the crossing. Next came the problem of if we would make it across and I think I held my breath for the entire crossing. When we got there I remember just saying to Brian, "*Thank god you wrote We Will Rock You.*"

I think we offered that chap a ticket for the show but he didn't take up on it. I'm not sure he had ever been to a theatre in his life. We did have our photos taken with him though.

Another memorable occasion where we had to be rescued was a bit closer to home when we played the Pavilion Theatre in Bournemouth. We were actually staying in Christchurch in a hotel right by a river, and as it was a lovely day, Brian and I thought it would be fun to hire a little motor boat. We were chugging along down the river, but encountered a bit of a steering problem, and ended up stuck tight in some bushes on the riverbank for what seemed quite a long time until we eventually managed to push ourselves out! It was very funny!

The venues in Europe were mostly huge and more spaced out than here where they generally have a more intimate feel, which creates a great atmosphere. These were more like conference centres really, with endless corridors and long walks to the stage. Our theatres or concert halls are usually in the middle of cities, whereas these were mainly on the outskirts of the cities or towns.

The audiences would also react very differently. We never quite knew in each city, how different crowds would react to us. I think it may have been Romania, where at the end of each song, people would come and lay roses and various other flowers on the stage. Because of this each song took forever and the whole show took about four hours! Our accommodation was quite mixed on that tour as most hotels were stuck in a time warp, and one particular hotel could have been straight out of The Shining. The different traditions around Eastern Europe were both fascinating and bizarre but the people were lovely and we went to some great places.

We did lots of meet and greets before the shows whilst we were there and got to meet loads of fans. Even though we couldn't speak the languages, we felt a real connection to those people through their love and warm welcome. We were inundated with so many gifts, letters and cards. I actually felt quite regal as we were so doted on and revered. Brian has a brilliant PA, Sara, and she would pack up all our gifts in a box, or a big touring trunk, and would arrange for them to be shipped back with all the touring equipment, for us to look at when we got home, to save us taking it round with us whilst gathering even more. If I was given toys for the kids, of course they would get them there and then, but most of my local offerings and traditional trinkets and such like I have kept.

Anita would occasionally join us for a few days, although she was usually super busy herself, and often Brian's youngest daughter Emily would fly out and spend a couple of days with us as it was before she had kids. My family would also pop in and out. Brian has known my boys for all their lives and they just think of him as Uncle Brian. James also thinks of him as part of the family like we all do, as Brian has been around since way before we met, and came to our wedding.

Mine and Brian's working relationship has evolved so greatly over the years. In the early days of performing and touring I was still learning and Brian would offer suggestions and ideas. As I've matured and become more experienced, the whole collaboration is much more balanced and equal. We bounce off each other are more of a team.

He has seen me grow up in my career and helped shape who I am today as an artist.

Ironically Brian and I didn't get to chat to each other very much on these tours. Touring is really tiring and leaves little energy or time to really see or do anything else, and I'm sure for Brian when he does his arena tours it's even worse. Obviously, we would be on the bus together but usually we were knackered, plus I had the boys to look after which was chaotic. Once at the venue it's a case of sound check, maybe a bit of dinner with everyone to come together, do the gig, after which we were straight back to the hotel, then up the next morning and moving on to the next venue. As glamorous as it sounds, most of the time you just see the hotel and the venue and that's it. In fact quite often I had to really think where I was which is why I struggle to remember now.

All the towns and cities blurred into one, and it was sometimes difficult to know where we were at any point, let alone see any sights, given our tight schedule. Before I knew it I'd seen twenty hotels, twenty venues and a tour bus. Three or four weeks of our lives had gone and we hadn't seen anything else. Brian came up with the idea that if we could go to the highest point in every city, we could then literally see where we were. I thought it was a great idea, as the time flew by so quickly and we would at least have a bit of awareness of where we were playing. That way it was not only cultural, but it would make us feel like we'd done something. We started this a little bit on the European leg of the *Born Free* tour but not too much as I was pregnant. We really went for it on both Eastern European tours and on some of our UK dates too, such as Brighton where we not only went up the British Airways i360 observation Tower on the seafront, but also played in what was probably one of the smallest venues on the tour. We'd played quite a few churches in the UK but this was particularly tiny. It was packed out with people and the audience was queuing out of the door, unable to get in!

We ended up doing our own 'highest tower tour', so in every venue we went to, if we had a morning free, or a day off, we would get Brian's PA, Sara, to research the tallest tower in that town or city and we would go along, climb up it, look at the whole city, take a picture and come back down. We did that all over Europe and the UK, and it was a great way to see the city and see where we were, plus it gave us a focus. We climbed the Szkieletor tower in Krakow, the Z Towers in Riga, the Duomo in Florence, and the Bolt Tower in Ostrava in the Czech Republic, complete with hard hats, as I think it is in an old industrial area and was built on top of a blast furnace. It was brilliant and anyone who was up for it would join us including family and touring crew.

I remember in Milan the year before, we'd had some lunch during which Brian mentioned that we must visit the Duomo Milan Cathedral, as the architecture and ceiling were amazing. James and the boys were with us and we all went along, but there was a massive queue of people outside, all waiting to go in.   We thought it would take forever and we had to get back for the gig so we started to leave. With that Sara toddled up to this guy on the door, had a quick word in his ear, I could see him looking over at Brian, and with that we were all ushered into another entrance, and within seconds were being shown around this amazing cathedral.

CHAPTER 40

Wicked's original Broadway Glinda, Kristin Chenoweth, was over here doing a tour and was performing at the Royal Albert Hall as part of that. I had a call asking if I would like to join her on stage and sing '*For Good*' as a surprise guest appearance for the audience. Would I?

There was no rehearsal at all, I just turned up before the show and briefly met her. We'd never met before, although I'd seen her perform on Broadway, but I can honestly say she is the nicest woman ever, and so incredibly tiny, like a little doll! I'm not that tall, but I felt like a giant next to her. What was particularly good about this was the timing. Not only was the performance a magical one, but the announcement that I was going back into *Wicked* happened a day or two later which of course I knew, but nobody else did. It was a perfect precursor for me returning to the show.

When Alfie was six months old, I'd received a last-minute call to ask if I'd go back into the show for a short stint as Willemijn Verkaik, who by then had played Elphaba all over the world and was the only actor to have played the role in more than one language, was currently over here but had hurt her back quite dramatically and they needed someone to step in for her in two weeks' time. The idea was that because Willemijn was injured, they wanted to make a positive out of something which was quite tragic. They didn't want her to go out having damaged her back and with the very real possibility of not returning to the show with the standby taking over. They wanted to make something exciting come out of the situation and I guess they saw that as asking the original Elphaba to return for a limited run.

My first thought was "*I don't think I am capable of doing this anymore*". I'd got married, had a baby, and done other jobs since leaving, and I really didn't think I would have the physical or mental power required for that role again, let alone be able to sing it. Plus I had left on such a high, and had such good memories, that I had kind of closed that door, and didn't want to taint the memory, so it was a really big decision. Alfie was only six months; how would I cope juggling both demanding roles? The answer was I went for it, and somehow managed. In fact, I probably enjoyed it more than the first time, because I was a bit more mature, understood the role a lot more and understood the commitment of the show even more. I had done a load of other stuff, and I felt more comfortable being there.

I had a short rehearsal period and needed every second as far as the script was concerned. The dialogue which I thought would be easy to remember, wasn't, and I had to relearn it which was really weird. For some reason, I'd just expected I would walk in and know it all. However, as soon as I got in the rehearsal room and started moving around, my body just went in the right direction. It was so strange, my body was moving, I knew what was happening, but I was really having to think about what I was saying. Talk about muscle memory. I never expected that after five years. I wasn't too bad as far as the songs were concerned because I'd been singing a few of them along the way. A few of the lyrics were gone and I didn't have a clue about '*No Good Deed*', especially the spell. I think that happens naturally though. You have to get rid of some stuff to make space in your brain for new material!!

The audiences were as responsive as ever and went nuts every time I came on the stage which was amazing. Michael McCabe called me soon after and said, "*Kerry I shouldn't really tell you this but when you came back we called it 'the Kerry effect', as suddenly the tickets sold out.*"

I wasn't one of these household names that was brought in purely to sell tickets, so to have that effect when I am not a well-known name felt so good. I had worked hard and earned this privilege and it was what I wanted – people to come and see me for doing the job well is what it is all about for me, and the reason why I do it.

Now, having done everything that I have, I really feel like I've paid my dues and earned my stripes. Doing all that crazy stuff I gained loads of experience, and more importantly I learned how to deal with all that was thrown at me. The business is so different now. When I go into a company, there is a distinctively different feel, and young students and aspiring performers are just so much more confident. I did '*Wonderland*' relatively recently, and the young ensemble were so confident in their own talent, and so ready for any role that came their way, even those who I perhaps doubted were ready. They just oozed this self-confidence, which is much more the norm now.

219

CHAPTER 41

The downside of owning dogs is losing them, and amidst my chaotic work schedule came the saddest of times, when I lost my dog Jack. He had become such a big part of the family and when he died, I can honestly say I've never known loss like it, it was horrific and it traumatised me. Since I'd got him when I was first in *Wicked*, he'd literally been my baby and had been through everything with me. In 2014 he somehow randomly escaped from the house and was hit by a car just down the road. He'd never got out before so I've no idea how it happened. He must have gone out through our cat flap, and maybe had just dug a hole somewhere into the neighbour's garden as Jack Russell's do and escaped that way. I remember getting the call early one morning to tell me the news, and I just fell on the floor sobbing. It was a small consolation that whoever had knocked him over had picked him up and taken him to a vet. I felt completely lost for about three or four days, wandering around in shock, unable to come to terms with what had happened. In a way it was even harder to deal with than when I lost my grandparents more recently, maybe because it was so sudden and unexpected. I threw myself into looking after Alfie and continuing to work hard.

Brian was really busy now, and away a lot touring, and I didn't want to just sit around waiting for the next thing to come along. I decided to use the time constructively, so got busy and recorded my first solo album, '*Kerry Ellis*' which I did through Pledge, a crowdfunding platform. It was great for me at the time though, and recording this album was brilliant fun and meant I could take everything I had learned from Brian and the previous albums and try it all out myself to see if I could do it. It was a real learning curve. It felt right to me to do this and didn't feel like a massive project. It was an ideal moment in time for reflection, and I came to the realisation that I could do this on my own, which was quite empowering.

The plan was to try it out and see how it went, but I was so proud of the end result and I subsequently toured it on my own in small intimate 500 seater venues. It felt very special touring an album that I had made, and which came from my choices. I was also quite hands-on with arranging the tour as well. Fane Productions, who are massive now, but were just starting out at the time, supported us and I was suddenly aware of ticket sales, promotion and the production side in general. I would walk into a venue and suddenly everyone was looking to me for direction and answers, from the musicians, to the production company, to the box office. Silly little things like where does the merchandise go? Where does everything need to be set up? I was suddenly the boss. My eyes were being opened to new responsibilities. If the show failed it would be on me. If it didn't sell it would be on me. It was just me and the band. Of course Daniel was on board as well and supported me all the way.

The fact it proved successful and I could pay the band plus come out with a bit of money for myself, was an added bonus. Again, it was a step in the right direction for me, I liked putting it all together and the challenge of finding out what worked and what didn't, and we evolved with it along the way. Also if I got tired I could change things around a bit or if I felt particularly good we would throw in an extra song. I tried to change it up in each venue too, so it was a little bit different. That's the beauty of being the boss and I really enjoyed the whole experience.

It stood me in good stead for my *Golden Days* album tour which came in 2017. Doing it a second time round was great and this time I knew what to do and how it worked, so I was confident that I'd got this. It was great to get back into the studio after the Queen world had been ignited again with the release of the *Bohemian Rhapsody* film and their subsequent tour. Brian had been pretty busy, so for us to get *Golden Days* out was quite an achievement.

We were at a different stage by now as we had done a few albums and a lot of touring and we'd honed our craft a bit, meaning we were a bit quicker and knew our direction a bit more. I was really proud of the album and Sony records took it on, which was a bonus. Ordinarily we both would have toured it but Brian had another massive world tour with Queen lined up which just kept growing and growing, and we didn't have an opportunity.

I made the decision to tour the music but didn't call it the Golden days tour as it didn't feel right without Brian there. I was due to tour anyway as I hadn't done a solo tour for a little while, so asked him if he minded me playing some of the songs.

"Absolutely not..." he replied, "This is why I do it, so you have your own material."

Craig was busy teaching and couldn't commit to a tour, so I used a new band and we played pretty much all of the *Golden Days* album, which was really exciting

We did a couple of weeks, and it was really successful. It just felt good to be doing my own stuff as there was a good mix of originals and covers on the album. However, it was also quite scary, because when you're singing completely new material to an audience, you can never be sure of what the reaction will be. It turned out most people who came to see me already had the album and appeared to know the songs, which I wasn't expecting, and was really lovely. I felt like I had really achieved something by the end of that tour. Me and my band on the road was great, although Brian did turn up at one of the venues and sing, which was a brilliant surprise.

CHAPTER 42

I would love to go and see loads more shows and live entertainment generally, but I'm usually too busy working myself. If I do take time out to go see a show, I just feel dreadfully guilty as I'm away from home such a lot anyway, and it is too much of an ask for the family. It's a rare treat if the situation does present itself where I can go and see something, and I do love it. It is also a bit of a risk because I then want to be blown away by what I am seeing. It is such an important and precious couple of hours in my life.

I like to be excited and inspired from the moment the overture begins, and for it to make me feel like I want to be up there on that stage doing it myself. I remember going to see Billie Piper in *Yerma*. I went on a whim, as I was doing *Murder Ballad* at the time and our Director Sam Yates, who incidentally was brilliant, had already been to see it, and recommended I go. It was completely sold out but I managed to get a return, and I went on my own after rehearsals one day. I was completely and totally blown away by Billie's performance. She was so absolutely brilliant and that is what I want. I want to be deeply affected by theatre or moved in some way. To me that is the whole point of live theatre, to make you feel something and provide a memorable experience.

In the Autumn of 2014 I had a phone call and availability check for *CATS*, which was coming back to the West End, asking if I would be interested in the role of Grizabella, which I was thrilled about. I really thought my chance for that role had long gone and that I wouldn't be right for it anymore, so of course I was available, absolutely. I was so excited, and on tenterhooks awaiting confirmation that they wanted me, but it all went very quiet and we didn't hear anything further for ages. The next thing I heard was that CATS was coming to London with Nicole Scherzinger opening in the role. "*Damn it,*" I thought, "*That's it then,*" and I quickly resigned myself to the fact it wasn't to be.

A couple of weeks later, we then got a phone call saying that they would love for me to come in and take over from Nicole at the London Palladium. She was only doing the first three months and would I do the next few months.

After all my touring it was lovely to be back in a musical once more, plus I got to work with Trevor Nunn again, who I hadn't worked with for years, since the Eva Cassidy workshop. Trevor has always been a massive supporter of mine throughout my career, and always makes time to come and see my concerts and shows, and if he can't come backstage he will always drop a note round. To do another show with him was really lovely, even though I only spent a day with him. Most of my dance rehearsals were with Chrissy Cartwright, who was Gillian Lynne's right hand woman; I only had about two weeks rehearsal time as the show was established and I was going in on my own. The whole process took me right back to my roots doing that kind of dancing, and I just immersed myself in it. Grizabella's costume had been completely transformed and I had a new sassy beautiful costume.

I got a couple of hours with Gillian Lynne too, which I was terrified about as I knew I could dance but I wasn't a dancer. She was such a proper dance legend and she had choreographed the original productions in London and Broadway. Going through the Grizabella dance with her was such a special almost surreal moment for which I am forever grateful. To work with somebody so iconic blew my mind and I could instantly see why she had reached the pinnacle of her career.

I never thought I would ever play the role, so when I did, singing that song, working with Gillian and back at the Palladium was the stuff of dreams for me. Unbeknown to the audiences, Grizabella joins in with the big opening eight-minute dance routine with the rest of the company, but dressed as another character called Baby Griz, where I could mix in with the rest of the cast anonymously. That was almost my favourite part, because I got to be part of the company doing those amazing routines with those incredible dancers, but without the spotlight on me. I loved it.

Baby Griz gets to sing a line in this opening routine; The costume is completely different and you're not meant to be recognised. On my first night, I went on for the opening routine, and it got to the part where I sang my line, "*When you're walking alone...*" and with that the crowd immediately erupted!

It was hilarious, I'd been well and truly spotted! I couldn't believe it, but it was really cool. It only really happened on the opening night which might have been down to the excitement of me going into the show, but it was brilliant, and totally caught me off-guard as I just wasn't expecting it. Then of course later in the show, I got to come on and sing the big song that people are waiting for. It was a magical time.

I had originally met Andrew Lloyd Webber when Brian and I did the Don Black concert at the Royal Festival Hall. We met him very briefly in the corridor and he just said to me, "*Wow, you can certainly sing.*" Whilst I was in *CATS* he came backstage one night with the Producer, David Ian, and again said, "*You're fantastic, wow, you really are something special.*"

Who does my make-up depends on what I am doing. Sometimes I will do my own but I don't have any real interest in it. I'm not one of those girls who enjoys going out and buying up all the latest stuff. I'm a bit lazy really, and don't even follow a skin care regime. As I don't often wear make-up at home, I quite enjoy getting all zhuzhed up for my gigs. I'm all or nothing really. Show mode or nothing. Make-up for me feels like a tool, and a means, so more like a necessity than a pleasure.

In *CATS* they initially had someone in who did my make-up for the first week or so, where I got trained up until it got to the point where they made up half my face and I did the other half. Because I'd done loads of stage and theatrical make up by then, I was quite quick off the mark learning how to do it. All the make-up was provided, which included a lot of pansticks and a lot of oil. *CATS* make-up was a lot heavier and more oil-based than the *Wicked* make-up and as such felt so much thicker. MAC created the green Chromacake make up for Elphaba in *Wicked*, and I didn't even feel like I had any on, as it was so light and weightless, whereas in *CATS* the make-up felt so greasy, oily and heavy in comparison.

As I'm getting older I'm becoming more aware of myself, my body, and how I'm ageing, particularly regarding my level of fitness and how active I am, and I desperately try to hold on to that and try to look as good as I can within my own limitations. I'm not a slave to it though and I certainly don't care enough to stop eating or for it to become a problem, but I am conditioned to think about it, and it is important to me. I like to stay fit and enjoy it, but behind it is always the motivation of wanting to lose a couple of pounds and look a bit younger.

When I was younger I could eat anything, at any time, when I was working, and didn't really have to think much about it, but now I find it so much harder. It's a balance between eating enough before a show to sustain my energy levels, but not too much so that my body is digesting food and my brain is focused on that. I would never for example drink a pint of milk before going on stage. *Wicked* was the hardest one, because it was the first time I actually needed a certain amount of energy to get me through the show. It was the same with *CATS*, because of the dancing I needed to eat properly. With most of the other shows, I could be a bit more relaxed as I didn't have that ultimate responsibility.

CATS was a job I was so grateful to do as I just never thought I would get the opportunity, and I loved every second. I was only in it for about six months as the show was going to Blackpool for the summer and then returning to the Palladium. However, by then I was three months pregnant with Fred so it was time for me to leave and Beverley Knight took over. Pregnant Cat wouldn't have worked!

Sometime after leaving *CATS*, and before performing with Brian at the Verona Arena, that incredible concert which was one of the highlights of my career, I was invited to go along and sing '*Feed The Birds*' at Disneyland, Hong Kong, for a special awards ceremony for Disney Heads of Department all over the world, which was a huge event. This was another first for me as I hadn't had any dealings with Disney prior to that. I took my Dad along with me and found out whilst I was there that '*Feed The Birds*' had been Walt Disney's favourite song. If he was having a stressful day he would go into the office, play that song and it would just calm him down. I loved that story, and loved singing the song, and I subsequently included it on my most recent album, '*Feels Like Home*' which I funded myself and had mainly recorded to sell exclusively on my 2020 tour dates as merchandise. Of course, the tour was postponed so I ended up selling it through my website. Hong Kong was only a five-day trip but really memorable.

Another first for me came much later in 2019, when I had the chance to go to Japan, where Queen are massive. While Brian was out there years ago he'd written a couple of songs for a Japanese artist. He played one to me and I loved it, so we recorded it and it ended up as the title track on the *Golden Days* album. I was desperate to go to Japan and Brian had always said that we should go at some point. Like in Italy we knew they would accept us. I'd had a few offers to go in previous years but it just hadn't worked out timing-wise, so when I had a call offering me a few concerts out there, with Ben Forster, John Owen-Jones, Sophie Evans and Hadley Fraser, I was eager to go. We did four days of concerts with a big orchestra and tagged my two solo shows on to the end. It was like a completely different world of experience. Everybody had always told me that the audiences are so reluctant, they don't say anything and they don't applaud or react in any way and are generally just really quiet. That wasn't what we experienced at all. The only thing that we did find odd was that they don't make any noise when they go into the theatre. Backstage you can usually hear that buzz of an audience on the tannoy system with the crisp packets or sweets rustling, and the hum of conversation with a sense of anticipation, but in Japan there was nothing. I often doubted if there was anyone out there and would peek through the curtains to make sure. As soon as we got on stage and start the show they were incredible and so responsive. We did have to encourage them a bit, but they were so loud and engaging and warm.

I did my solo show in a slightly smaller venue, at the end of our run, where I played a lot of my *Golden Days* material and they all knew it, which left me gobsmacked. I took with me Andy Waterson, who had been my MD on my previous solo tour, and we used local musicians. To go half-way across the world and play new music to audiences you have never met before and for them to know your music is unbelievable and really quite flattering. I was only there for ten days but completely fell in love with the Japanese, their culture, their way of life and for their respect and love for the arts.

Dad and Sal were with me and we did a little bit of tourist stuff whilst we were out there, visited a few temples and saw some geisha girls, and went to a market. We also went on the tube, which was a great experience but very strange as they all queue up to go on it! They are so well mannered and polite in Japan. We visited a bar area and had sushi for dinner, which I love. In fact the food suited me really well, as I eat a lot of fish and loads of vegetables anyway.

I didn't have much spare time though as it was really intense. We basically flew out, had a day to get over the journey then did back-to-

227

back shows followed by my own two shows. I didn't even have time for shopping either, which is very unlike me. Next time hopefully!

It was when I was still in *CATS* that I realised I hadn't put on my own London show for a while, and it crossed my mind that although Louise Dearman and I had been good mates for twenty-odd years, we had never really performed together in a show. I wanted to do something about that and talked it through with Steven.

He suggested we book a theatre, he would direct the show, Craig would be the MD and Lou and I would perform. We booked the Prince Edward Theatre for September 2015 which meant by then I'd be seven months pregnant with Fred.

Our respective fans made for a wonderful audience, and a special and memorable evening for us both. Using all the people we have known and loved for years, including Caroline Deverill and Jennifer Tierney on backing vocals, and bringing them together to create a show and a vehicle for Lou and I to sing together was lovely.

Notes from…

I think it must have been 1995 when I first met Kerry. We both took part in a summer school for young performers at Laine Theatre Arts and it was clear even then that she had a very special gift. Her voice instantly stood out with its unique tone and crazy mega belt! We went on to train professionally at the same college, which I think for both of us became some of the best years of our lives. Kerry and I were always linked because of our voices and Betty Laine, the college principal, would put us together to sing duets at every opportunity. I think that's why our voices blend so well now, because we have sung together from such a young age. Since college, we have remained friends and what I find so inspiring about Kerry is how supportive she is of fellow performers, including myself. We are regularly on the phone trying to come up with ideas and ways to get to perform together. She has brought so much to the world of musical theatre and proves that the word DIVA can simply describe someone blowing away an audience and delivering a powerful and emotional performance without the backstage drama! A wonderful friend, brilliant mum and an inspiration to budding young performers and those who have been around for a while (like me!). Yep I'm indeed a friend and a fan.

Louise Dearman

CHAPTER 43

I have been so lucky in terms of my general health. I get the odd cold but I've never broken any bones, and I've never been in hospital apart from having my kids. I try to be sensible though and keep fit and eat well. Yes I have my vices, I do eat chocolate, and I do drink wine and eat junk food, but never enough to impact on me. When I am in a show I try and consciously look after myself even more, and if I feel I am becoming slightly run down, I will kick up my vitamin intake or eat more healthily, which I think helps massively. Being active is a massive factor to remaining fit and well, and I still love the great outdoors. We go on bike rides as a family whenever we can, and I love nothing more than walking the dog. I'm always doing something, and love to find new things to keep me active and my adrenalin pumping.

I'd always wanted to do a sky dive, but somehow the right time and right place had never materialised. If you are in a show you are actually not allowed, contractually, to do one. When I was in *Wicked*, I bought James a sky dive as a present for his 30th, and I was desperately jealous of him doing this as I knew I wasn't allowed to and hadn't been able to figure out a way round it. Last year James arranged to do another one with Luton Town football club. The club supports local charities, and someone had come up with this idea to raise money for Luton Foodbank.

James was the first to volunteer, and he and his colleague Jordan, put their names down to do it. I wasn't in a show this time and this was my chance, and I kept pressing James to see if I could join in. I was on the point of threatening to phone up and add myself to the list, when we found out Jordan was leaving the club to go to another, and I was able to take his place.

This worked out really well for me, but also the foodbank, as we did lots of press about it and as a result we were able to raise a bit more money. On our way to Northamptonshire I was feeling relaxed and really looking forward to it. Getting in a little Jump Plane didn't bother me at all and I was quite chilled at that point. However leaving the plane was a different matter, and as I sat on the edge and tipped forward it completely took my breath away. In fact I actually don't think I took a breath for about the first sixty seconds of free-falling. The guy I jumped with was brilliant, and calmly talked me through the whole thing, and we had a nice little chat on the way down. To see all over Hertfordshire was amazing, and I managed to take it all in. As soon as my feet touched the ground I wanted to go back up again. The adrenalin rush was incredible and even now I'd do it again in a heartbeat. James is an adrenalin junkie and a bit of a thrill-seeker like me, but of course it was the second time for him, and he's not fazed by anything, so he did enjoy it but maybe didn't get as excited as I did. The whole experience was amazing, and I absolutely loved it.

I turned 40 last year as did James and many of our friends, so there were lots of parties and travelling which was great fun. I think turning 40 has definitely made me slow down and appreciate time with family and friends. It's tough making time for everyone, but I think the older we get, the more important it is and like my dad always says, *"The most important thing you can give people Kerry is your time."*

Since having the boys I've learned to adapt my career to fit in with family life. They have been to a couple of my concerts and they just take it all in their stride and accept that is what Mummy does. If they perhaps hear a Disney song on the radio, or even a song that I have sung, one of them might comment that it sounds like me or that's what I sing but I think they are still too young to have an opinion. I'm sure that will change.

Quite recently the whole family came on a P&O Caribbean Cruise with me where I was doing my own show, and James brought the boys along to watch one of my early evening shows. It's a bit easier and more relaxed on a ship as everyone can just walk in and out casually. I was chatting to the audience about the boys in between songs and announced that they were sat out there watching. *"Are you there boys?"* I said, shielding my eyes from the spotlight whilst searching for them amongst the crowd. All I could hear was, *"Hi Mummy..."* as they chorused in unison, and with that they both ran down to the stage looking very excited. I brought them onto the stage to say hello to everyone, which got lots of oohs and ahhs from the audience. I sat Alfie on my stool, which swivelled round, and thought it would be a lovely idea to sing my next song, '*Can't Help Falling In Love*', whilst they were there, which turned out to be a big mistake. I started the song and Freddie was fine, he was looking up at me and smiling, and couldn't believe his luck. Alfie meanwhile, was fine for the first couple of minutes, during which time I began to relax, until he discovered that the stool moved round, which of course proved irresistible, and he began slowly swivelling himself round whilst I calmly tried to stop him. Next thing was he slowly began to stand up on this stool which was still moving and I was pulling him down to sit whilst still trying to sing this song. The audience by then were howling with laughter and I got to the end of the song to huge applause. What was very interesting to me was that neither of them was fazed in the slightest by being on the stage and under the lights, in front of a huge room filled with people. They weren't daunted at all. I think they were just so used to that type of environment and it was normal to them.

They have also been to loads of sound checks with me, and I let them run around the auditoriums when I'm sound checking because everyone knows they're there so they can have that freedom. They love doing all that stuff and running around the backstage areas of big theatres. That way they're around me singing, but don't have to sit still and watch me. They can be involved and get up on stage.

When I was in *Wonderland*, at the end of Act One I used to run through the big looking glass with all the smoke effects. When James brought Alfie to see me in it he just sobbed his heart out when he saw me doing this, and I had to facetime him in the interval to tell him it was alright and Mummy was fine. He was okay then and watched the second half.

To step onto a stage and for everyone to not only know who you are, but to be there because of you, is quite something. This happened when I was asked to appear in *West End Live* in my own right, and not just under the umbrella of a musical, and felt like quite an important step. *West End Live* is an annual weekend event of free musical theatre live in Trafalgar Square. The audience is huge and it has that festival feeling. I'd taken part in West End Live with *Wicked, Murder Ballad* and a few other shows before but to then get my own slot as me was quite an achievement, and all those musical theatre people and fans gathering outside in one place is my ideal audience.

At around the same time I was also presenting my own radio show every Sunday, for a couple of hours, which I did for about two years. I loved it so much and I must admit I would love to do a bit more radio, it was so much fun. I originally went on as a guest spot for Jamie Crick, a radio presenter who worked on Classic FM, Jazz FM and all sorts of channels. He was starting up the station, along with another company UKRD, and as content director it was him that brought me in. The whole concept was based on musical theatre, and he thought I would be a good presenter so gave me my own slot which I would record in a little studio in the Jazz FM studios in London. Jamie would help me put the show together and assist me with the links and history of the songs and that side of it. I would record a couple of weeks at a time, predominantly playing show tunes and talk all things musical theatre, a bit like Elaine Paige's Radio 2 show. Sadly, after a couple of years the station was acquired by a bigger company who then decided to close it as it was too similar to one of its own offerings. It was such a shame, as it was gaining in popularity and people seemed to love it. We got so much back from it. Jamie and I went on to do a podcast together for a while called Acting Up, where we would invite guests in to chat about the business. It was this steady progression that gave me the confidence to do my own podcast which I recorded all over zoom in lockdown,

I was busy rehearsing for a show called *Heaven on Earth* which was meant to be a classic re-telling of the story of Adam and Eve and their fall from Paradise. This big extravaganza of singing, dancing, and acrobats had completely new music and was due to tour arenas in late 2017 and the beginning of 2018. We rehearsed it for nine weeks in London, the costumes were unbelievable and it promised to be a huge spectacle.

We were literally just about to go into an arena, and do the technical rehearsal, when out of the blue we were all just suddenly told that was it, to stop everything, no more rehearsals and the show was cancelled. It was something to do with the investment and the funding but it was all very sad for everyone involved who had worked so hard.

That sort of news travels very fast and in no time at all it was all over the internet, on WhatsOnStage and all over theatre district. Subsequently, I was approached by Alastair Whatley who was directing *The Importance of Being Earnest* for The Original Theatre Company. He called Daniel saying he understood that I was suddenly available for work, and would I be interested in doing a play. I'd been waiting for this opportunity for a long, long, time, as I'd never done a play before. The Eva Cassidy workshop, Way Beyond Blue, which I'd done with Trevor Nunn all those years previously was the nearest I'd got but it never got staged and was just presented as a workshop. Twenty years later and I was desperate to give it a go. It was definitely a box to be ticked. The fact that it was a classic play was perfect.

We met in London over a cup of tea and before long, I was in rehearsals. It was tricky as I had a couple of my own tour dates in the middle of it, so I had to have a couple of days out, which they agreed to.

Plays have a very different 'aura' and I know a lot of my musical theatre contemporaries believe they are never going to get seen properly for a play as they won't be taken seriously. As a result, I was a little bit nervous going into the rehearsal room, probably the most nervous I have been in my career and I felt out of my comfort zone. I suppose because of the way I was thrown into various shows previously, like with *My Fair Lady*, I almost didn't have time to be nervous as I had too much to think about. The same with *Wicked*, although it had a massive build-up, I was just thrown on that very first time and didn't have time for nerves as I had to focus on what I was doing. I must have had those moments of fear, but it wasn't uncontrollable, and nothing really stands out in my mind. I certainly haven't experienced major stage fright or a debilitating moment in my career like some people have, which I'm thankful for. I've had moments of not remembering my lines in long runs, but that's quite normal, and everyone goes through those waves and those ups and downs, and then I re-educate myself and it all comes back to me.

It was a traditional play that everyone knew and I felt the pressure. I was working alongside Gwen Taylor, who was just the most magical woman I've met, and to work with her and Susan Penhaligon, and indeed the whole company, was a great privilege and they were so supportive.

One of the strange things about the play was the fact we had no microphones. I'd worked with microphones my whole life and to suddenly have to project my lines out felt really strange. The other thing was walking on stage to the sound of my own footsteps because of course, in a musical there is always underscoring, or applause, whereas in a play there is literally nothing, and to walk on and off in virtual silence and no audience reaction I found weird and quite disconcerting. It was probably amplified to me as it was something I particularly noticed. I'll be honest

I did miss the music but at the same time enjoyed the intensity of the acting.

Plays are usually shorter, and this one ran for a couple of months, and I was just so grateful that they took a chance on me. We played a week in each venue so I could take the boys with me sometimes and commute each day at times.

I'd love to do more straight acting roles in the future. *The Importance of Being Earnest* was my first acting role and I loved it, and the people I was working with. There were lots of things that were strange about it, but to be honest it wasn't so far from what I do. It's so hard when you have a very big presence in musical theatre to then get seen for anything else. Television is something else I'd like to try, again because I've never really done it. I know a lot of my friends who do television say they miss theatre. TV is so quick and instant and you don't get that time to rehearse but I would certainly like to try it. I wouldn't say no to a role in EastEnders!

CHAPTER 44

It was when we were playing at the Belfast Grand Opera House in Ireland with *The Importance Of Being Earnest*, when my Mum phoned to tell me my Grandad had died. James and the boys had joined me and on that particular day we were trying to find things to do to keep them amused, and had found a random swimming pool, as you do when you're away touring, We were having such fun and a great family day and I'd just come out of the pool when I got the call. I was devastated. Nan and Grandad were both so self-sufficient and apparently had been out shopping in Stowmarket that morning and got the bus as usual, and everything was fine. At 94, Grandad would always walk a couple of miles in the morning and was super-active. When they got home from Stowmarket, he tripped over, and that was it, he was gone. It was so quick and a huge shock for all the family.

I had a show to do that night and James tried to persuade me to take the night off, but things are a bit different with a play as you don't really have understudies, plus I needed to do it, not only for myself, but I think Grandad would have wanted me to do it and not let everybody down. I was so thankful James and the boys were with me as it gave me something to deflect my sadness. I knew I could grieve afterwards, which is what I did, and I somehow managed to get through the play. I didn't tell anybody and just got on with it. It was the last show of the week and we were flying home the following day, so I just kind of powered on. It was a tough show but I was almost numbed to my feelings and I was able to blank it out and focus on what I had to do, which is what got me through and gave me strength. Looking back I'm kind of proud that I did that, as it would have been awful to let everyone else down.

The worst thing about Grandad's funeral was seeing my Nan so upset and thinking of her being on her own was horrific. Nan was so strong and didn't want to crumble in front of the rest of us. She stood at the front and I just held her hand throughout the whole service and it wasn't until his coffin went behind the curtain that she buckled a bit. Also, when we were walking out her legs gave way a little and I had to support her. Watching her go through that was one of the worst moments of my life, and then to know she was on her own after that was heart breaking. After losing Grandad, Nan still remained super-active and self-sufficient but her health got progressively worse quite quickly, which was hard to watch. She had cancer in her stomach and developed dementia but still insisted on staying in her own house, and going out on her own, then kept having these falls. It was so stressful for everybody because she just didn't want to be helped, as she thought that everything was okay. My brother and I were going back and forth during this time and my Mum was visiting her regularly. Not a few weeks would go by without her calling to say she'd had another fall and was in hospital. We would all traipse down to the hospital and make sure she was okay when she came out. It was an horrific time made worse by the fact that none of us were that near her. I was probably the closest at an hour and a half away, my Mum two and a half hours and my brother nearly three hours, so it was tricky getting to her. Luckily she had a great community in Bacton.

The day my mum called to say Nan had died, I wasn't working this time thank god, as it hit me really hard and I don't know if I could have gone on stage that night. I had been so incredibly close to her throughout my whole life. It's a shame she went through as much pain as she did, not that she ever complained or mentioned it, but it was obvious she was slowing down and suffering. They'd both been so active, always in the garden or going down to town, and to watch all that being taken away from her slowly was just awful. It was also hard to see her in that little house on her own. I'm just glad she wasn't around for the coronavirus pandemic though, at least they've been spared all this. They were such a team, he was 94 and she was 92 and they always kept each other going. I think once she lost Grandad her defences were lowered. Nan's funeral was just horrific and can still get to me and feels pretty raw even now. I dabble with gardening a little bit, but not very much, and a couple of years before she died, Nan gave me a beautiful rose plant which, after moving round the garden a bit, has now blossomed and all the flowers are coming out, which is such a lovely way of remembering her, although she will forever be in my heart.

When my Dad's parents died, although it was sad as I loved them both dearly, seeing my Dad get upset at his own father's funeral was particularly tough. He was only 70 when he died in February 1998 and it was the first funeral I had ever been to. At his Mum's funeral about five years later I remember laughing with my cousins saying how ridiculous it was that we only ever met up at funerals, which I think a lot of families do.

My mood absolutely affects my performance, but I really think that is the beauty of live theatre. You work with the person you are on that day. As performers, our moods change daily, so we are always going to give a slightly different performance. I think that's a positive thing because if people come to see you more than once in the same show, they are going to get something different. That performance can depend on a lot of things. One day I might be really up for it, everything is brilliant and my voice is in full health, but then another day I may feel really emotional and that will come through in the performance which is quite powerful. It's not only working with who you are on the day but being ok with that. I've had days where I have been poorly or run down and some of those shows have been the best I've given because I have been driven in a different way.

I think there's nothing worse than someone who just can't be bothered at all and gives a lacklustre performance. That infuriates me more than anything, especially if you are the lead in a show and you turn around and catch it or don't feel that support around you. I've been there, and have been that person, and I understand how important it is to create that support for the show. Many people would kill for these jobs, and it is important and a privilege which should be embraced. Every person on that stage has a duty to give one hundred percent of whoever they are on the day.

CHAPTER 45

If I had to sum myself up I would say I am level-headed, loyal, strong, passionate, ambitious and creative, which I think are all qualities that are needed for this business.

Workwise I am very headstrong. I wouldn't say I am a great networker and I'm not driven like that, but once I'm in a production or doing something, and I'm committed to it, I try and push as much as I can with it. I'm not a people pleaser or a yes person; however, when I was inexperienced and starting out in the business, I would bow down to anyone, and agree with whatever they were telling me, not wanting to voice my opinion, whereas now I will have my say and I will fight my corner, and hopefully find a compromise. I feel like I have the experience to question things. I might be wrong, but at least I will have that conversation. That said, I am not confrontational, as it makes me feel nervous and awkward which I don't like, and I will do anything to avoid it. The only time I would step up that way is for the boys. I will find my way of getting round something, or achieving what I want to, without all the arguing. I can get my point across in a nice way, and if I want something I will find a way to get it.

In my career it's important for me to be nice to people and put out a good persona, and as such, things can be frustrating and I have to move on, although sometimes poor James is on the receiving end of a lot of my frustrations, which I think happens in most relationships. I'm quietly confident but not outspoken and I'm certainly not the loudest person in the world. It's James who is loud, fiery and explosive but the most amazing human being I know and I wouldn't be me, or be able to do what I do without him. He is the love of my life.

I've been lucky to have had the privilege of meeting and working with some amazing people in this business, both on stage and behind the scenes, some famous and some not so, but equally talented. If I'm being honest, I still don't feel as if I am there yet. Yes, people know me in my world, and perhaps a little bit in the Queen world, but I still want to sell out arenas and millions of albums and that is what really keeps me driven, alongside the fact that I am a mother and have to support my family and pay the bills. I feel like there is still so much more for me to achieve, which is a good thing as you can't afford to sit back and be complacent in this business. It is changing and evolving all the time, and you have to keep up with it, stay in people's minds and remain relevant. I'd love to do one of the reality shows, especially Strictly, which I've been close to a couple of times. I enjoy exercising, and my roots are in dancing and I would just love the challenge and the physicality of it. I would also love to go in the jungle. Never say never!

Every so often imposter syndrome strikes me which I'm sure other people must get, and I look around wherever I am thinking "*Why am I here...?*" It's not that I doubt my talent or ability, but I am constantly surprised and delighted at being asked to do these epic concerts and productions. I can't help but think of that little country bumpkin with dirty knees who never doubted she would appear on some of the biggest stages in the world. It happened just last year when Mike Dixon, who I had worked with in *We Will Rock You* all those years ago and has been the MD and composer for *Miss World* since 2003, approached me. "*Kerry it's the finals of Miss World in a couple of weeks at the Excel Arena London. Would you come and sing 'Rise Like a Phoenix' in the opening ceremony?*" Of course, I didn't hesitate and it was a privilege to be at such an amazing event. Peter Andre and Megan Young were presenting the evening and Lulu was also going to be singing. There's nothing better to bring on imposter syndrome than turning up at one of these occasions to find you are on a line-up of superstars!

People are always asking me when I am going to do another show, and my main issue is that I'm reluctant to potentially commit myself to a year. I wouldn't be able to do any of my concerts, or have the freedom to be creative, but most importantly it would mean I'd be away from home almost every evening, although at the time of writing this in lockdown that sounds quite appealing! It's been so frustrating not being able to do anything during this weird time. So many performers have live streamed shows on their YouTube or Instagram channels and at first I was reluctant to do that as I didn't want to feel like I was cashing in on the terrible situation. However, I had such an influx of people requesting me to do something that I came to the conclusion it was the right thing for me to do too.

For me social media is great, because it allows me to interact with my supporters. If I've got a gig to sell that's not a massive event and is perhaps somewhere small and intimate, I can just tell my fans directly and then ask them what they want to hear and get their input. My podcast definitely wouldn't have sold if I didn't have my Instagram account as I did all the promo myself on there. What I do find frustrating nowadays, is that casting can often depend on the number of followers or interactions you have on social media channels and can be a factor in whether or not you get the job, which I think is really sad. I don't think that is a true reflection of your talent, or how you're going to behave on a stage. Producers still think that followers relate to ticket sales, and we all know it doesn't. It's a shame, but at the same time I get it from their point of view. If you're putting on a show and you cast somebody who's really popular, then just maybe that will translate into ticket sales.

I do think the internet has its place in bringing some people to the fore although you still have to have the knowledge, talent, and that likeability factor to become a YouTube sensation, or vlogger, or influencer, whatever it is they do now, and to create a following. The same goes for reality shows which are such a massive part of our television viewing now, which is one of the reasons I put myself up for *The Voice*. I still maintain you have to have that talent to make it on those platforms, because the viewing public aren't stupid and should never be underestimated; they don't watch or follow people for no good reason. I like that I can control what I put out on social media. It's like having my own little TV station, which is a good thing when used in the right way. There's such a massive celebrity culture now and I'm friends with a lot of them and I find it really interesting to hear their views on some of it. Some of them are acutely aware that they are there purely because of a certain television show, and a certain following, but some of them don't seem to realise. Yes, it's frustrating when you are overlooked for something that you know you could do well and have the experience for, in favour of someone who has a social media following, but that is the business we are in. I get it now having produced my own shows. I understand the money and importantly I understand the risk so I can let it go when it happens to me and I will find my own way.

One of those ways is doing little Q&A sessions with various colleges during lockdown and joining in zoom chats. Colleges have been reaching out during this time as they wanted to keep their students inspired and were looking at other avenues and ways of doing that. I subsequently came up with the idea of doing some one-to-one as well as group acting sessions through song, again all on my Instagram, which went quite nuts. I didn't want to make it too official so didn't advertise it on my website or have a big campaign for it, because of the uncertainty at the time, and I didn't want it to become a full time job. I just wanted to offer a few sessions while we were in lockdown, not only to keep me occupied focused and creative, but also to offer something I don't usually have the time to do as I'm so busy. I wouldn't do one-to-one sessions usually because I'm working and just don't have the time. It's been really interesting to work with different people, finding out what they want to know, what they do and just seeing who's out there, and it's been lovely getting to know them, giving them some pointers and a bit of guidance. They're not all students either and are from all walks of life. For instance I had one guy who works in a nursing home and used to be a singer, who just wanted a bit of escapism and to find his love for music again. I have to say he was brilliant, and such a good singer and I really hope I helped ignite his love for music again. There was another slightly older lady who gigged in pubs and clubs and had such a powerful voice, and another lady who I remembered I had previously heard singing in Hitchin Town Square and stopped to sit and listen to her because she had such a lovely voice. I was so surprised when she booked a session with me some time later.

Prior to lockdown I had said that I would love to run my own studio one day, to work in myself, and also have other artists in, but I really don't see myself on the other side behind the scenes. I just don't have that drive to visualise and bring something else to fruition. Not at the moment anyway.

When I recorded my podcast, the last question I put to all my guests was, *"If you could go back in time and give your 20 year-old self, one piece of advice on how to Keep Calm and Kerry On, what would that be?"*

My own answer would be to just stop for a minute every so often and take in everything that is going on around you, because when you're younger everything happens so quickly. It doesn't necessarily feel like that at the time, but I was always moving on to the next thing and looking for what was happening next or looking at everyone else to see what was around. It's only now that I look back on everything and realise the extent of my achievements, but at the time I was so focused on what I was doing and what was coming next that I didn't give myself time to appreciate it. I would also say, be okay with who you are much earlier in your life as it's taken me so long to get to that point. I look back at myself and wonder what on earth I was worrying about back then as I was absolutely fine. I wanted to be thinner, change my shape and have better hair. I would say be okay with yourself Kerry and embrace the good stuff about YOU. It's so much more than how you look. It's about being kind and a good person that's important.

Lockdown has certainly given me this opportunity. The opportunity to stop, reflect on my career so far, write it all down, be grateful for all the wonderful opportunities I have been given over the years, enjoy precious time with my family, and the knowledge that, whatever the future holds, I will find my own way.

TOP TIPS FOR WORK LIFE BALANCE

- Do what is right for you. Being a parent tips your world upside down and changes your life completely. It's tricky at times; however, it can be the best thing and so worth it. It is a constant battle but take things day by day and do your best, which is all we can ever do. I get to have a career I love and I am passionate about, but I also have a family who mean the world to me. There are people who have been in the business for many years and get to the point where they want to have kids and don't want to go back working, and I totally understand that. I also know people who don't want to have kids because they are loving what they are doing so much and want that career which is also great. It's all about personal choice, doing what is right for you and how you make it work.

- Keep fit and healthy. For me, the older I get the more important it becomes to stay healthy. Obviously our bodies change and it becomes harder so cutting down calories for a weekend or doing an extra class to lose that excess weight doesn't work any more. As I have said before, I think fitness has a huge impact on your mental health and even now I think it is underestimated how by doing a bit of exercise, whatever it is, improves your mental health and wellbeing. I also want to be physically fit for my kids, run around with them and join in with all their activities. I don't want to be restricted just because my body lets me down. I know not everyone has that choice but if you do, start investing in your health as soon as you can.

- Consider all offers of work but choose wisely. As performers it is in our blood to automatically say yes to everything. Now I have other responsibilities and James and I agree that any job offer that comes in has to tick a box. Either it's something I desperately want to do creatively, someone I really want to work with, it will further my career, or is financially rewarding. I can't drop everything for no money anymore, which I would have done before. It has to be worth it now and we always discuss it as a family. They have to be involved. It's tough but no one said it would be easy.

244

- Understand that your priorities will change over time. For example, it was important for me to be around when Fred started school, no question. It's hard but it's about considering all of us as a family unit now and not just myself.

- Stop every so often to reflect and appreciate everything you have achieved in your life, and always be grateful.

"If you could give one piece of advice to your 20-year-old self for when things get tough – how would you Keep Calm and Kerry On?"

Arlene Phillips

I wanted to be a skinny five foot six blonde more than anything else in the world. I was a short stocky dancer who never felt pretty or good enough. I would say believe in yourself, believe in who you are so strongly. I wish I could have done.

Beverley Knight

I'd say don't be so bloody serious. Lighten up Bev! Enjoy it. ENJOY it. We are the joy givers and we need to receive a little bit of that joy back for ourselves. Just stop and sit in the moment sometimes, and think wow, this is incredible, and then keep moving on.

Kimberley Walsh

I wish I could have had the perspective that I have now. I gave myself such a hard time about everything and cared so much because I wanted to be the best. I'd say give yourself a break and chill out a little bit.

Shoshana Bean

I'd say who you are is enough. You are enough. Yes, take inspiration from others but, you are enough. You cannot rank art. Stop comparing. There is no 'better than', there is just different. Keep your eyes on your own page. I am still learning that lesson.

Alfie Boe

If I met my 20-year-old self I'd probably walk in the other direction! I'd say trust, believe, visualise your goals. Life has a plan. Sometimes it might not go to your plan. Mistakes that we make are planned learning exercises. Enjoy your successes but, as my mother used to say, 'don't let it go to your head'. Be real.

Marisha Wallace

I'd say be patient and keep doing what you are doing 'cos it's all going to work out even better than you planned it. It's the ones who stick around and fight and the ones who don't give up who make it. Remember though that success looks different to everyone. When I was on Broadway I didn't feel as successful as I wanted to be. Oh, I'd also say get voice and dance lessons!

Alice Liveing
I'd say don't worry if the market you want to enter is really saturated as it doesn't mean that there isn't room for you, plus you might bring something to it that is special and that people are looking for. See yourself as unique and own that space.

Samantha Barks
My 20-year-old self would not believe I would be sat having a chat with Kerry Ellis! I cried and cried when I first saw you in *Wicked*. I was obsessed with it and still am! I would say don't be afraid to dream but be okay with the fact that it won't always happen in the way you think it's going to happen. Be open to that.

Shaun Escoffery
I'd have to sit down and have a real lecture with my 20-year-old self! I'd say really study your craft and get deep into it not just on a technical level, but on a spiritual level as well. Learn how to lose yourself in the moment and don't be afraid of it or to embrace it. That is the essence of performing. Be in it for the right reasons. If you just want to be famous you won't last. Love the people you are working with and be kind and respectful. Oh, and plenty of water and 8 hours sleep!

Emma Barton
You can never cast yourself in anything, that's not your responsibility. If people don't like you it's none of YOUR business. Don't take it personally. Keep the belief that the part, film or television show will come your way. Sometimes it's okay to say no. I went to so many auditions that I didn't want to do so if it stresses you out that much, just say no.

Matt Flint
Don't just aim to be a choreographer or a singer. I feel I have been successful because I have learned various skills. Make it as broad as possible in what you do and you'll have more chance of working.